THOU SHALL CALL HIS NAME

JESUS

THOU SHALL CALL HIS NAME

JESUS

For He Shall Save His People From Their Sins

MARSHA MATTOX-LEDWIG

TATE PUBLISHING
AND ENTERPRISES, LLC

Published by Tate Publishing & Enterprises, LLC
127 E. Trade Center Terrace | Mustang, Oklahoma 73064 USA
1.888.361.9473 | www.tatepublishing.com

Tate Publishing is committed to excellence in the publishing industry. The company reflects the philosophy established by the founders, based on Psalm 68:11,
"The Lord gave the word and great was the company of those who published it."

Book design copyright © 2014 by Tate Publishing, LLC. All rights reserved.
Cover design by Junriel Boquecosa
Interior design by Jimmy Sevilleno

Published in the United States of America

ISBN: 978-1-63185-998-4
1. Religion / Biblical Studies / Jesus, the Gospels & Acts
2. Religion / Christianity / General
14.05.27

CONTENTS

FOREWORD

Jesus is the Word of God. We know that the Bible is the written word of God. The Bible is the sacred word of God written by men who were inspired by the Holy Spirit of God. The Bible is the anointed word of God. Therefore, the books of the Bible are able to reach the hearts and souls of men and women as no other words can.

The written word of God proves to us that God exists and that he is a living spirit who communicates with mankind through his written word. The written word of God is the basis for this book. The Old Testament and the New Testament are not separate and exclusive of each other. Together they explain the communications of God to mankind.

The Bible belongs to God alone. He alone has the authority to declare what any part or all of it means. Like God himself, the Bible can never be completely understood by any man. God is so vast and incomprehensible that no one human being can see or understand all of him. No created human person can declare what the total truth of God's word is. Therefore, as God's children, we are expected to be nonjudgmental of other Christians. We don't need to share their beliefs, but we do not have the right to judge others. We all see through the glass darkly. We should pray to God individually that he will reveal his truth to us.

The intent of this book is to use the holy scriptures of God to understand other scriptures. God never changes. His words in the Old Testament prepared mankind for the coming of the living Word of God. All of the Old Testament is a foreshadowing to prepare mankind to understand and receive Jesus, the only begotten Son of God when He was sent to redeem us.

Because the scriptures carry a powerful anointing, they are the most important words included in this book. If you are a child of God, you should never accept the words of another person unless the Holy Spirit gives you confirmation of the truth in your heart. If someone tells you something about God, there should be proof that the words are true in the Holy Bible. Therefore, please, read every scripture reference given in this book from a Bible. Some of the verses will be given in the text of the book; other references were too long to print. Please read every one of the references given in the book and look them up for yourself if they are not printed in the book.

THE BOOK OF MATTHEW

The book of the generation of Jesus Christ, the son of David, the son of Abraham.

Abraham begat Isaac, and Isaac begat Jacob; and Jacob begat Judas and his brethren;

And Judas begat Phares and Zara of Thamar; and Phares begat Esrom; and Esrom begat Aram;

And Aaram begat Aminadab; and Aminadab begat Naasson; and Naasson begat Salmon;

And Salmon begat Booz of Rachab; and Booz begat Obed of Ruth; and Obed begat Jesse;

And Jesse begat David the king; and David the king begat Solomon of her that had been the wife of Urias;

And Solomon begat Roboam; and Roboam begat Abia; and Abia begat Asa;

And Asa begat Josaphat; and Josaphat begat Joram; and Joram begat Ozias;

And Ozias begat Joatham; and Joatham begat Achaz; and Achaz begat Ezekias;

And Ezekias begat Manasses; and Manasses begat Amon; and Amon begat Josias;

And Josias begat Jechonias and his brethren, about the time they were carried away to Babylon;

And after they were brought to Babylon, Jechomias begat Salathiel; and Salathiel begat Zorobabel;

And Zorobabel begat Abiud; and Abiud begat Eliakim; and Eliakim begat Azor;

And Azor begat Sadoc; and Sadoc begat Achim, and Achim begat Eliud;

And Eliud begat Eleazar; and Eleazar begat Matthan; and Matthan begat Jacob;

And Jacob begat Joseph the husband of Mary, of whom was born Jesus, who is called Christ.

So all the generations from Abraham to David are fourteen generations; and from David until the carrying away into Babylon are fourteen generations; and from the carrying away into Babylon unto Christ are fourteen generations.

Matthew 1:1–17 (KJV)

W HEN MATTHEW SET out to write about Jesus, his first intent was to prove that Jesus was a fulfillment of God's words and promises throughout the Old Testament. He wanted to prove that Jesus did not introduce a new religion or a new God; Jesus came to bring a message from God that explained and fulfilled every communication that God had sent to his people before. Jesus came to bring us the ultimate proof of God's love and God's salvation from our sins.

Jesus was a fulfillment of the promise from God explained in Genesis 17:7–8.

> And I will establish my covenant between me and thee and thy seed after thee in their generations for an everlasting covenant, to be a God unto thee, and to thy seed after thee.
>
> And I will give unto thee, and to thy seed after thee, the land wherein thou art a stranger, all the land of Canaan, for an everlasting possession; and I will be their God.
>
> Genesis 17:7–8 (KJV)

Matthew used the genealogy of Joseph to prove that Jesus was the rightful descendent of Adam, Abraham, and David.

Matthew was one of the twelve apostles chosen by Jesus. As a tax collector, Matthew would have been more widely known than most of the other followers of Jesus because of his political position. He would have been disdained by most of the Jews because they felt that he was a traitor to his own people; he collected money from the Jews to give to the Roman conquers.

As a Jew and a tax collector, Matthew recorded Joseph's genealogy for legal purposes. As the man in his family, Joseph would be the person whose genealogy would be traced. Joseph had to journey to Jerusalem to pay taxes because he was a descendent of David; the legal identity of Jesus's family would have been established by Joseph's identity as a descendent of David. Matthew wanted to prove that Jesus was the fulfillment of God's promise to Abraham.

There is another revelation when we look at the genealogy of Joseph. Joseph's lineage proves that Joseph was not Jesus's real biological father. Joseph's lineage proves that Jesus was born to a virgin mother. God had placed a curse upon King Jechonias and his descendants; even though they were descendants of King David, not one of their lines would be able to reign as a king on David's throne.

Please read Jeremiah 22:17–29.

> Thus saith the LORD WRITE ye this man childless, a man that shall not prosper in his days: for no man of his seed shall prosper, sitting upon the throne of David, and ruling any more in Judah.
>
> Jeremiah 22:30 (KJV)

By applying this knowledge to the question of Jesus's lineage, we see that the lineage given in Luke is for Mary's descent from King David. Mary had no brothers, so Mary inherited her father's possessions and rights. Joseph became Heli's heir when he married Mary.

Please read Numbers 27:1–7

> And thou shalt speak unto the children of Israel, saying, If a man die, and have no son, then ye shall cause his inheritance to pass unto his daughter.
>
> Numbers 27:8 (KJV)

> This is the thing which the Lord doth command concerning the daughter of Zelophehad, saying, Let them marry to whom they think best; only to the family of the tribe of their father shall they marry.
>
> So shall not the inheritance of the children of Israel remove from tribe to tribe: for every one of the children of Israel shall keep himself to the inheritance of the tribe of his fathers.
>
> And every daughter, that posesseth an inheritance in any tribe of the children of Israel, shall be wife unto one of the family of the tribe of her father, that the children of Israel may enjoy every man the inheritance of his fathers.
>
> Numbers 36:6–8 (KJV)

Marriage to Mary made Joseph Heli's son-in-law. Jesus was not Joseph's biological son. Jesus was Mary's son by the Holy Spirit. Because Jesus was not of Joseph's lineage, he was not affected by the curse. As Mary's son, Jesus was descended from Nathan. From Mary, Jesus would inherit his maternal grandfather's rights. The lineage listed in Matthew proves that Jesus was born of a virgin and that he was not under the curse.

The lineage in Matthew connected Jesus to the promises made to Joseph's and Mary's ancestors. Abraham received a promise for his descendants.

> And said, By myself have I sworn, saith the Lord, for because thou hast done this thing, and hast not withheld thy son, thine only son:
>
> That in blessing I will bless thee, and in multiplying I will multiply thy seed as the stars of the heaven, and as the sand which is upon the sea shore; and thy seed shall possess the gate of his enemies;
>
> And in thy seed shall all the nations of the earth be blessed; because thou hast obeyed my voice.
>
> Genesis 22:16–18 (KJV)

The lineage in Matthew recorded the promise made to King David and his son Solomon. Please read 2 Samuel 11:14, 2 Samuel 11:26, and 2 Samuel 12:22–24.

JESUS'S BIRTH IS ANNOUNCED TO MARY AND JOSEPH

Now the birth of Jesus Christ was on this wise: When as his mother Mary was espoused to Joseph, before they came together, she was found with child of the Holy Ghost.

Then Joseph her husband, being a just man, and not willing to make her a publick example, was minded to put her away privily.

But while he thought on these things, behold, the angel of the Lord appeared unto him in a dream, saying, Joseph, thou son of David, fear not to take unto thee Mary thy wife: for that which is conceived in her is of the Holy Ghost.

And she shall bring forth a son, and thou shalt call his name Jesus: for he shall save his people from their sins.

Now all this was done, that it might be fulfilled which was spoken of the Lord by the prophet saying,

Behold, a virgin shall be with child, and shall bring forth a son, and they shall call his name Emmanuel, which being interpreted is, God with us.

Then Joseph being raised from sleep did as the angel of the Lord had bidden him, and took unto him his wife:

And knew her not till she had brought forth her first-born son: and he called his name Jesus.

Matthew 1:18–25 (KJV)

THERE IS GREATEST importance in the fact that God's messengers specifically told Joseph and Mary that the son was to be given the name Jesus. By looking back to Genesis, we can see that the name of a person shows significant information about the person who is being named. Adam's name meant of the earth or a human being; Adam actually is for male or female gender. Adam named Eve; Eve means to have life or mother of life. It is written in Genesis 3:20 that Adam and Eve's third son was named Seth. God gave them the third son to replace Able after Cain killed him. The name Seth meant appointed or substitute. (Genesis 4:25)

God changed Abraham's name from Abram (exalted father) to Abraham (father of a multitude). God also changed Sarai's name to Sarah (princess). Isaac was named Isaac because Abraham laughed when God told Abraham that he and Sarai would have a son when Abraham was ninety-nine years old and Sarah was ninety years old. (Genesis 17:5 & 15) (Genesis 21:3)

When Isaac and Rebekah's twins were born, they were named Esau, because he was covered with hair, and Jacob who tricked Esau and Isaac so that he could have Esau's birthright. Jacob means one who supplants. (Genesis 25:25). Jacob's name was later changed to Israel when he wrestled with an angel all through the night. (Genesis 32:28) Israel means fought with God or God will prevail. Moses was given his name by Pharaoh's daughter after she found him in the river. (Exodus 2:10) Moses meant drawn out of the water.

Jesus changed Peter's name from Simon to Peter. (John 1:42) Thomas, one of the disciples, was called Didymus because he was a twin. (John 21:2) Those who tried to discredit Jesus called him a carpenter's son. Jesus called James and John the sons of Thunder. Levi, the tax collector, became Matthew. In Greek, Matthew means Gift of God. So we can see that some of the names in the Bible are given to give an identity or tell something significant about that person.

Many of the names we use in modern times can be traced back to something that identified one of our ancestors. Some of those are Ford (a river crossing), Farmer, Fisher, or Adamson (the son of Adam).

Hence it was greatly significant that God chose the names that he wanted his son to be given.

> And she shall bring forth a son, and thou shalt call his name Jesus: for he shall save his people from their sins.
>
> Now all this was done, that it might be fulfilled which was spoken of the Lord by the prophet, saying,
>
> Behold a virgin shall be with Child, and shall forth a Son, and they shall call his name Emmanuel, which being interpreted is God with us. (Isaiah 7:14)
>
> Matthew 1:21–23 (KJV)

Jesus (and Joshua) is interpreted as Savior or God is Salvation; Emmanuel is interpreted as God with us.

Mary was a virgin descended from King David; she was espoused to Joseph who was also a descendent of King David. By Jewish custom there were two steps to be accomplished before a man and woman were married. The first step was the espoused period. The man and woman were formally promised to one another; during the next period of time, the husband prepared a place for them to live building a dwelling within the complex of homes under his father's authority. The groom's father decided when the preparations were completed and called together the wedding feast guests; at the wedding feast the groom and bride drank from a cup of wine provided by the groom's father and became husband and wife.

Mary and Joseph were living during the period of time when they were espoused to one another (promised). In the Book of Luke we are given the story of Mary's agreement with God to become the mother of the Messiah.

> And in the sixth month the angel Gabriel was sent from God unto a city of Galilee named Nazareth,
>
> To a virgin espoused to a man whose name was Joseph, of the house of David; the virgin's name was Mary.
>
> And the angel came in unto her, and said, Hail, thou that art highly favoured, the Lord is with thee; blessed art thou among women.
>
> And when she saw him, she was troubled at his saying, and cast in her mind what manner of salutation this should be.
>
> And the angel said unto her, Fear not, Mary: for thou hast found favour with God.
>
> And, behold, thou shalt conceive in thy womb, and bring forth a son, and shalt call his name Jesus.
>
> And he shall be great, and shall be called the Son of the Highest: and the Lord God shall give unto him the throne of his father David:
>
> And he shall reign over the house of Jacob for ever; and of his kingdom there shall be no end.
>
> Then said Mary unto the angel, How shall this be, seeing I know not a man?
>
> And the angel answered and said unto her, The Holy Ghost shall come upon thee, and the power of the Highest shall overshadow thee; therefore also that holy thing which shall be born of thee shall be called the Son of God.

And, behold, thy cousin Elisbeth, she hath also conceived a son in her old age: and this is the sixth month
with her, who was called barren.

For with God nothing shall be impossible.

And Mary said, Behold the handmaid of the Lord; be
it unto me according to thy word. And the angel departed
from her.

Luke 1:26–38 (KJV)

The angel Gabriel was sent by God to speak to Mary while
she lived in Nazareth. The angel greeted Mary and said that she
was highly favored (approved by God), and God was with her.
He said that Mary was most blessed of all women. When Mary
saw the angel and heard what message he brought from God, she
was very confused and fearful. Gabriel told her not to be afraid
because she was to be honored greatly by God.

Gabriel told Mary that she would conceive a son whose name
would be Jesus (Saviour). Her son would be great, and he would
be called the Son of God. Her son, Jesus, would be given the
throne of his ancestor David. Her son would rule over the house
of Jacob (God's chosen people) forever; his rule would never end.

Mary was still confused. She asked how she could become
pregnant if she had never had intercourse with a man. The angel
answered her telling Mary that the Holy Ghost (third person of
the Trinity of God) would overshadow her so that the baby she
would give birth to would truly be the son of God.

Gabriel told Mary that Mary's cousin, Elizabeth, was carrying a child even though she was elderly and had always been
barren (unable to have children) because nothing is impossible
with God.

Mary responded by agreeing that she was God's servant. She
agreed to become the mother of God's Son just as Gabriel had
said. We should remember who Mary was. She was descended
from a race of people who had been taught that God spoke to
people sending angels and messengers to deliver his words to

members of his chosen people, the Jews. She knew that she was part of a special family descended from King David who had been proclaimed to be God's chosen king. Mary was very young, but she believed in God absolutely. She never questioned what God wanted her to do or what would happen to her when other people learned that she was pregnant. She would be shamed and shunned. Her only question was about how she could be pregnant if she was a virgin. Mary believed God; that was a very significant point. Man's sin had been that man did not believe what God said.

Joseph was a very devout man adhering to the will of God as he had been taught. When he learned that Mary was pregnant, and he knew that the child was not his, he knew that he should not marry her. He was a very fair and kind man. He did not know how Mary became pregnant. Had she been raped? Was she responsible? He decided to set aside their betrothal and not marry her. He would not embarrass her publicly. He would refuse to marry her quietly.

While Joseph was thinking about what he should do, God sent an angel to speak to Joseph. The angel appeared to Joseph in a dream. The angel instructed Joseph to go ahead and marry Mary. He was not to be afraid because the child that she carried was not another man's baby. The baby that Mary was carrying was conceived by the Holy Ghost. The angel said that Mary would have a son, and Joseph was to name the baby Jesus. The name Jesus means salvation, and Jesus would save his people. The angel reminded Joseph about the prophecy which said that a virgin would have a son, and he would be called Emmanuel which means God with us.

When Joseph woke from the dream, he did what God's angel had told him to do. He took Mary into his home as his wife, but he did not have intercourse with her until after the baby was born. When Mary's first son (child) was born, Joseph named him Jesus.

We should look at the traits that Joseph possessed that made him qualified to be the adopted (earthly) father of God's own son. Joseph devoutly believed in God and followed the rules given by God to the Jews. He was a gentle, kind person. Joseph was a responsible man who worked to support and protect his family even when he knew that he himself was in danger and that his task would be very difficult. But greatest of all, Joseph believed God. He never questioned what the angel told him to do. He was obedient to God. He believed God's words to be the total truth. From this point on as we read the gospels, God will not speak directly to Mary. God honored Joseph as Mary's husband. When God gave them instructions from this point forward, he always sent the message to Joseph.

HEROD TRIES TO KILL
THE NEW KING

Now when Jesus was born in Bethlehem of Judaea in the days of Herod the king, behold, there came wise men (astrologers, priests) from the east to Jerusalem,

Saying, Where is he that is born King of the Jews? For we have seen his star in the east, and are come to worship him.

When Herod the king had heard these things, he was troubled, and all Jerusalem with him.

And when he had gathered all the chief priests and scribes of the people together, he demanded of them where Christ should be born.

And they said unto him, In Bethlehem of Judaea: for thus it is written by the prophet,

AND THOU BETHLEHEM, IN THE LAND OF JUDA, ART NOT THE LEAST AMONG THE PRINCES OF JUDA; FOR OUT OF THEE SHALL

COME A GOVERNOR, THAT SHALL RULE MY
PEOPLE ISRAEL.

Then Herod, when he had privily called the wise men,
enquired of them diligently what time the star appeared.

And he sent them to Bethlehem, and said, Go and
search diligently for the young child; and when ye have
found him, bring me word again, that I may come and
worship him also.

When they had heard the king, they departed; and, lo,
the star, which they saw in the east, went before them, till
it came and stood over where the young child was.

When they saw the star, they rejoiced with exceeding
great joy.

And when they were come into the house, they saw the
young child with Mary his mother, and fell down and worshipped him: and when they had opened their treasures, they
presented unto him gifts; gold, and frankincense, and myrrh.

And being warned of God in a dream that they should
not return to Herod, they departed into their own country
another way.

And when they were departed, behold, the angel of the
Lord appeareth to Joseph in a dream, saying, Arise, and
take the young child and his mother, and flee into Egypt,
and be thou there until I bring thee word: for Herod will
seek the young child to destroy him.

When he arose, he took the young child and his mother
by night, and departed into Egypt:

And was there until the death of Herod: that it might
be fulfilled which was spoken of the Lord by the prophet,
saying, OUT OF EGYPT HAVE I CALLED MY SON.

Then Herod when he saw that he was mocked of the
wise men, was exceeding wroth, and sent forth, and slew all
the children that were in Bethlehem, and in all the coasts
thereof, from two years old and under, according to the
time which he had diligently enquired of the wise men.

Then was fulfilled that which was spoken by Jeremy the
prophet, saying,

IN RAMA WAS THERE A VOICE HEARD,
LAMENTATION, AND WEEPING AND GREAT
MOURNING RACHEL WEEPING FOR HER
CHILDREN AND WOULD NOT BE COMFORTED
BECAUSE THEY ARE NOT.

Matthew 2:1–18 (KJV)

JESUS WAS BORN in Bethlehem in Judaea while Herod was king. After Jesus's birth wise men (Astrologers or priests who came from a nation far away.) came from the east to Jerusalem.

The wise men began to ask people in Jerusalem questions. They wanted to know where the new King of the Jews who had just been born was staying. The wise men had followed a star from the east so that they could worship (pay homage) to the new King.

When King Herod heard about the wise men, he was worried. Everyone in Jerusalem was worried too. No one not even the Jews wanted a war to break out between different rulers; if war began, everyone in Jerusalem would suffer.

King Herod gathered all the Jewish chief priests and scribes (teachers) together. He demanded that they tell him where the Old Testament scriptures said that the Messiah would be born.

The Jewish leaders told him that the scriptures said that the new king would be born in Bethlehem. They even quoted scripture from Micah 5:2 to prove that they were right. " But thou, Bethleham Ephratah, though thou be little among the thousands of Judah, yet out of thee shall he come forth unto me that is to be ruler in Israel, whose goings forth have been from of old, from everlasting" (Micah 5: 2 KJV).

Note that the Jewish leaders did not try to protect the child who might be God's chosen Messiah. They didn't really want things to change in Jerusalem taking away some of their power.

King Herod called the wise men to talk with him privately. He asked them very specific questions about the time the star appeared in the sky. He sent them on to Bethlehem so that they would find the young child. Herod told the wise men to definitely come back to him after they located the child so that he could go and worship the baby too.

After the wise men talked with Herod, they left, and the star which they had followed from their homes in the east led them to the place where Jesus was living. They were very happy that the star had appeared again, and that it led them to Jesus.

When they came to the house where Jesus was living, they saw Jesus and his mother Mary. They fell down on their knees and worshiped him. The wise men gave gifts to Jesus of gold, frankincense, and myrrh.

When God told Moses to make the Sanctuary where the people would come to worship Him, he described the things to be made for the Sanctuary; the items for the Sanctuary were to be made of gold or overlaid with gold. The gold was to be provided from a free will offering given by the children of Israel.

Please read Exodus 25:1–40

Frankincense was sweet-smelling incense used by the priests in preparing offerings to present to God. In Exodus God told Moses that the sweet smelling holy anointing oil made with frankincense was not to be used for anyone but God.

> And the Lord said unto Moses, Take unto thee sweet spices, stacte, and onycha, and galbanum; these sweet spices with pure frankincense of each shall there be a like weight:
>
> And thou shalt make a perfume, a confection after the art of the apothecary, tempered together, pure and holy.
>
> And thou shalt beat some of it very small, and put of it before the testimony in the tabernacle of the congregation, where I will meet with thee: it shall be unto you most holy. And as for the perfume which thou shalt make, ye

shall not make to yourselves according to the composition thereof: it shall be unto thee holy for the Lord.

Exodus 30:34–37 (KJV)

Moreover the Lord spake unto Moses.

Take thou also unto thee principal spices, of pure myrrh five hundred shekels, and of sweet cinnamon half so much, even two hundred and fifty shekels, and of sweet calamus two hundred and fifty shekels.

And of cassia five hundred shekels, after the shekel of the sanctuary, and of oil olive an hin:

And thou shall make it an oil of holy ointment, and ointment compound after the art of the apothecary: it shall be an holy anointing oil.

And thou shalt anoint the tabernacle of the congregation therewith, and the ark of the testimony,

And the table and all his vessels, and the candlestick and his vessels, and the altar of incense,

And the altar of burnt offering with all his vessels, and the laver and his foot.

And thou shalt sanctify them, that they may be most holy: whatsoever toucheth them shall be holy.

And thou shalt anoint Aaron and his sons, and consecrate them, that they may minister unto me in the priest's office.

And thou shalt speak unto the children of Israel, saying, This shall be an holy anointing oil unto me throughout your generations.

Exodus 30:22–31(KJV)

We can see from the passage in Exodus 30 that myrrh was the principal ingredient in the anointing oil used on people and things to be consecrated (set aside, devoted) for use in the Sanctuary.

The gifts given by the wise men to Jesus become very significant. Gold for the vessels and other items in the Sanctuary, frankincense for the perfume for the Sanctuary, and myrrh for the holy anointing oil to be used in the Sanctuary for consecration (dedication) were the gifts given to Jesus. The gifts given were those which were designated by God himself to honor God. Jesus was being recognized as God's Son.

God warned the wise men in a dream not to return to Herod; they left Jerusalem to return to their homes by another route.

After the wise men had left, an angel of God appeared to Joseph in a dream. Joseph was told to take Jesus and Mary and flee to Egypt immediately. Joseph followed directions without question; he took the baby and his wife and left to flee to Egypt during that night.

Again we must stand in awe of Joseph and his faith in God. Joseph had come to Jerusalem to pay his taxes and return to Nazareth. He had only what he could carry himself or on the small donkey. He was a carpenter; he needed tools to support himself and his family. He did not know anyone in Egypt to go to for help.

Joseph never questioned the angel's directive. He acted immediately. He risked his own life and his own ability to support and to protect his family. Joseph and Mary went to Egypt alone with a baby with almost no material resources. They believed God without question.

Joseph kept Mary and Jesus in Egypt until God told him it was safe to go back home. This action fulfilled the prophecy in Hosea that God would call his son out of Egypt. "When Israel was a child, then I loved him, and called my son out of Egypt" (Hosea 11:1, KJV).

When Herod learned that he had been mocked (tricked) by the wise men, he was furious. Herod sent his men to kill every baby two years old and younger in Bethlehem. Herod's action fulfilled another prophecy from the Old Testament. "Thus saith the Lord; A voice heard in Ramah, lamentation, and bitter weeping; Rehel (Rachel) weeping for her children refused to be comforted for her children, because they were not" (Jeremiah 31:15, KJV).

And they journeyed from Bethel, and there was but a little
way to come to Ephrath: and Rachel travailed, and she had
hard labour.

And it came to pass when she was in hard labour, that
the midwife said unto her, Fear not; thou shalt have this
son also.

And it came to pass, as her soul was in departing, (for
she died) that she called his name Benoni: but his father
called him Benjamin.

And Rachel died, and was buried in the way to Ephrath
which is Bethlehem.

Genesis 35:16–19 (KJV)

Rachel was Jacob's favorite wife. He worked seven years for
her father so that he could marry her. Her father tricked Jacob
into marrying his other daughter, Leah, instead. Jacob had to
work another seven years so that he could marry Rachel.

Jacob became Israel, and was the father of twelve sons. Only
two of the sons were Rachel's. After being away from his home
and family for twenty-one years, Israel was returning to his home
with his wives, his children, his servants, and his flocks. Rachel
was pregnant, and it was a long journey.

Just after they had passed Bethel, Rachel went into a very
difficult labor. The midwife assured Rachel that her second son
would be delivered safely. But Rachel knew that she was going
to die. Before Rachel died, she named her new baby Benoni,
but Israel changed the name to Benjamin. Rachel was buried at
that location.

Bethlehem, where all the babies were killed, was the same
location where Rachel had cried for her baby and had died.

JESUS IS TAKEN TO NAZARETH

And when Herod was dead, behold, an angel of the Lord appeareth in a dream to Joseph in Egypt.

Saying, Arise, and take the young child and his mother, and go into the land of Israel: for they are dead which sought the young child's life.

And he arose, and took the young child and his mother, and came into the land of Israel.

But when he heard that Archelaus did reign in Judaea in the room of his father Herod, he was afraid to go thither: notwithstanding, being warned of God in a dream, he turned aside into the parts of Galilee:

And he came and dwelt in a city called Nazareth: that it might be fulfilled which was spoken by the prophets, He shall be called a Nazarene.

Matthew 2:19–23 (KJV)

WHEN KING HEROD was dead, God sent an angel to speak to Joseph in a dream again. The angel told Joseph to leave that place, and take Jesus and Mary into the land of Israel. Joseph was told that King Herod and his advisors were dead so Jesus would be safe.

When Joseph had reached Israel, he was warned again that it would not be safe to take Jesus into Judaea (where Jerusalem was located) because Herod's son, Archelaus, had become king there after Herod died. (Archelaus ruled as king of Judaea from 4 BC to AD 6.) After Joseph had been warned in a dream, he took Jesus and Mary into the region of Galilee to the town of Nazareth. This is the area where Joseph and Mary had come from before they went to Egypt. Jesus was to live in Nazareth so that God's word through the prophet would be fulfilled.

In Isaiah 9:1–2 God specified that Galilee was the place from which the Messiah, Jesus, would come.

> Nevertheless the dimness shall not be such as was in her vexation, when at the first he lightly afflicted the land of Zebulun and the land of Naphtali, and afterward did more grievously afflict her by the way of the sea, beyond Jordan in Galilee of the nations.
> The people that walked in darkness have seen a great light: they that dwell in the land of the shadow of death, upon them hath the light shined.
>
> Isaiah 9:1–2 (KJV)

God gave Moses specific steps and procedures a person had to fulfill so that they could be a person consecrated to the Lord for a specific purpose (a Nazarite). Jesus was consecrated to the Lord to fulfill God's plan for him to become our savior from birth. "And the Lord spake unto Moses, saying, Speak unto the children of Israel, and say unto them, When either man or woman shall separate themselves to vow a vow of a Nazarite, to separate themselves unto the Lord" (Numbers 6: 1–2, KJV).

"For, lo, thou shalt conceive, and bear a son; and no razor shall come on his head: for the child shall be a Nazarite unto God from the womb: and he shall begin to deliver Israel out of the hand of the Philistines" (Judges 13:5, KJV). "But he said unto me, Behold, thou shalt conceive, and bear a son; and now drink no wine nor strong drink, neither eat any unclean thing: for the child shall be a Nazarite to God from the wonb to the day of his death" (Judges 13:7, KJV). The life of Samson, who was the Nazarite talked about in Judges, was a foreshadowing of the consecration of Jesus and the fact that Jesus died destroying the power of death that Satan held over God's people.

Samson was a man consecrated by his parents to be a Nazarite devoted to destroying the Philistines who ruled over God's people. He was deceived by Delilah, and she shaved the hair of his head which robbed him of the power that God had given him. Without his great strength, he was seized and blinded by the Philistines. The Philistines gathered together to offer a sacrifice to their God, Dagon. The Philistines brought Samson into the temple where they were celebrating and praising Dagon so that they could make fun of Samson. There were about three thousand people in the temple. They tied Samson between two pillars, and he asked a boy to fix the bonds so that he could lean on the pillars. Samson prayed to God and asked him to restore his strength one more time.

> And Samson took hold of the two middle pillars upon which the house stood, and on which it was borne up, of the one with his right hand, and of the other with his left.
>
> And Samson said, Let me die with the Philistines, And he bowed himself with all his might; and the house fell upon the lords, and upon all the people that were therein. So the dead which he slew at his death were more than they which he slew in his life.
>
> Judges 16:29–30 (KJV)

JOHN THE BAPTIST PREACHES

In those days came John the Baptist, preaching in the wilderness of Judaea.

And saying, Repent ye: for the kingdom of heaven is at hand.

For this is he that was spoken of by the prophet Esaias, saying, "The voice of one crying in the wilderness, prepare ye the way of the Lord, make his paths straight."

And the same John had his raiment of camel's hair, and a leathern girdle about his loins; and his meat was locusts and wild honey.

Then went out to him Jerusalem, and all Judaea and all the region round about Jordan.

And were baptized of him in Jordan, confessing their sins.

But when he saw many of the Pharisees and Sadducees come to his baptism, he said unto them, O generation of vipers, who hath warned you to flee from the wrath to come?

Bring worth therefore fruits meet (suitable) for repentance:

And think not to say within yourselves, We have Abraham to our father: for I say unto you, that God is able of these stones to raise up children unto Abraham.

And now also the ax is laid unto the root of the trees: therefore every tree which bringeth not forth good fruit is hewn down, and cast into the fire.

I indeed baptize you with water unto repentance: but he that cometh after me is mightier than I, whose shoes I am not worthy to bear: he shall baptize you with the Holy Ghost, and with fire.

Whose fan is in his hand, and he will thoroughly purge his floor, and gather his wheat into the garner; but he will burn up the chaff with unquenchable fire.

Matthew 3:1–12 (KJV)

I N LATER DAYS John the Baptist began preaching in the wilderness (desert) of Judaea. He preached repentance. John told the people to repent for their sins seeking God's forgiveness and turning away from doing sinful things. He warned the people that they should repent (confess and turn away from sin) now to prepare themselves because God's kingdom was about to begin. John did not preach about salvation. He was sent by God to tell the people to repent cleansing themselves for what was to come soon. The Jews had been taught to cleanse themselves with water before they met God.

The prophet Isaiah had spoken of John and his message. "The voice of him that crieth in the wilderness, Prepare ye the way of the Lord, make straight in the desert a highway for our God" (Isaiah 40:3, KJV).

John's life had been consecrated for service to God. He wore clothing made of camel's hair (very course) and a leather girdle.

His food was locusts (bugs) and wild honey. He ate only what God provided.

Many of the Jews in Jerusalem and Judaea and the area around the Jordan River went out to see and hear John. The people who went to hear John's message confessed their sins and were baptized in the Jordan River by him.

When John saw that the Pharisees and the Sadducees came to be baptized, he told them that they were vipers (snakes). Satan took the form of a snake when he tempted Adam and Eve with his lies to sin against God. The Pharisees were a sect of Jews who had their own doctrines and believed that they were more holy and acceptable to God. Their hypocrisy is preached against in the gospels and the New Testament because they forced others to live by their severe teachings; they only kept the letter of the law of Moses but did not follow the meaning of the law. Jesus preached about their practices of making a big show of their religious practices instead of praying and giving to the poor quietly.

> Therefore when thou doest thine alms, do not sound a trumpet before thee, as the hypocrites do in the synagogues and in the streets, that they may have glory of men. Verily I say unto you, They have their reward.
>
> But when thou doest alms, let not thy left hand know what thy right hand doeth:
>
> That thine alms may be in secret: and thy Father which seeth in secret himself shall reqard thee openly.
>
> And when thou prayest, thou shalt not be as the hypocrites are: for they love to pray standing in the synagogues and in the corners of the streets, that they may be seen of men. Verily I say unto you, They have their reward.
>
> But thou, when thou prayest, enter into thy closet, and when thou hast shut thy door, pray to thy Father which is in secret; and thy Father which seeth in secret shall reward thee openly.

But when ye pray, use not vain repetitions, as the heathen do: for they think that they shall be heard for their
much speaking.

Be not ye therefore like unto them: for your Father
knoweth what things ye have need of, before ye ask him.

(Matthew 6:2–8, KJV)

Moreover when ye fast, be not, as the hypocrites, of a sad
countenance: for they disfigure their faces that they may
appear unto men to fast. Verily I say unto you, They have
their reward.

But thou, when thou fastest, anoint thine head, and
wash thy face;

That thou appear not unto men to fast, but unto thy
Father which is in secret; and thy Father, which seeth in
secret, shall reward thee openly.

(Matthew 6:16–18, KJV)

There are other passages about the Pharisees in the book
of Matthew which will be discussed in other parts of the text.
(Matthew 15:1–9; Matthew 16:1–12; Matthew 21:33–46;
Matthew 23:2–33)

The Sadducees were another sect of Jewish people made up
primarily of ruling priests. Jesus warned his disciples about the
Sadducees (Matt. 16:6–12). This sect rejected doctrines that were
not stated in the Mosaic Law such as resurrection from death,
retribution in a future life, and the existence of angels.

John the Baptist told the Pharisees and Sadducees to act with
true repentance. He warned them not to depend upon their her-
itage of being descendants of Abraham to save them. John told
them that God is able to change rocks into Abraham's descendants.

When John said that the ax was about to chop down the tree
at the roots, he meant that the Pharisees and Sadducees could be
cut off from God's people if they did not change their attitudes
and behavior. He said that a tree that gives no edible fruit will be
destroyed. Their lives were not evidencing the fruit of the spirit

so they could find themselves cut off from God's chosen people. "But the fruit of the Spirit is love, joy, peace, longsuffering, gentleness, goodness, faith, Meekness, temperance: against such there is not law" (Galatians 5: 22–23, KJV).

John preached that he baptized with water to cause the Jews to become repentant (sorry for their sins, asking forgiveness and turning away to live better lives). John said that someone who was much more powerful than himself was coming to baptize with the Holy Ghost and with fire. The one who was coming was so much greater than John that John was not even good enough to carry his shoes.

God's hand was holding the fan that he would use to clean the floor where he separated the chaff from the grain. John said that God would gather the souls of his chosen people to himself, but God would burn up the chaff (trash – those who refused to believe and obey) in a fire that never ends.

JESUS COMES TO BE BAPTIZED

And then cometh Jesus from Galilee to Jordan unto John, to be baptized of him.

But John forbad him, saying, I have need to be baptized of thee, and comest thou to me?

And Jesus answering said unto him, Suffer it to be so now: for thus it becometh us to fulfill all righteousness. Then he suffered him.

And Jesus, when he was baptized, went up straightway out of the water: and, lo, the heavens were opened unto him, and he saw the Spirit of God descending like a dove, and lighting upon him:

And lo a voice from heaven, saying, this is my beloved Son, in whom I am well pleased.

Matthew 3:13–17 (KJV)

And the spirit of the Lord shall rest upon him, the spirit of wisdom and understanding, the spirit of counsel and might, the spirit of knowledge and of the fear of the Lord.

Isaiah 11:2 (KJV)

Behold my servant, whom I uphold; mine elect, in whom my soul delighteth; I have put my spirit upon him: he shall bring forth judgment to the Gentiles.

Isaiah 42:1 (KJV)

JESUS CAME FROM Galilee to meet John the Baptist at the Jordan River where John was baptizing and preaching. Jesus came to be baptized by John, but John refused to baptize Jesus. John said that he needed to be baptized by Jesus instead.

Jesus responded telling John that the will of God must be done, and the prophesies from the book of Isaiah must be fulfilled. So John baptized Jesus. When Jesus came up out of the water, John saw the clouds go apart, and the Holy Spirit came down from heaven in the form of a dove. The dove lit upon Jesus. A voice came from heaven that identified Jesus as God's Son. The voice said that God was very pleased with Jesus. It was important that God the Father himself testified as the first one identifying Jesus as God's Son. Later Jesus would be challenged by the Pharisees that he did not have two witnesses who said that Jesus was God's Son.

THE HOLY SPIRIT LEADS JESUS INTO THE WILDERNESS

Then was Jesus led up of the spirit into the wilderness to be tempted of the devil.

And when he had fasted forty days and forty nights, he was afterward an hungred.

And when the tempter came to him, he said, If thou be the Son of God, command that these stones be made bread.

But he answered and said, It is written, MAN SHALL NOT LIVE BY BREAD ALONE, BUT BY EVERY WORD THAT PROCEEDETH OUT OF THE MOUTH OF GOD.

Then the devil taketh him up into the holy city, and setteth him on a pinnacle of the temple.

And saith unto him, If thou be the Son of God, cast thyself down: for it is written, he shall give his angels charge concerning thee, and in their hands shall bear thee up, lest at any time thou dash thy foot against a stone.

Jesus said unto him, IT IS WRITTEN AGAIN, THOU SHALT NOT TEMPT THE LORD THY GOD.

Again, the devil taketh him up into an exceeding high mountain, and sheweth him all the kingdoms of the world, and the glory of them;

And saith unto him, All these things will I give thee, if thou wilt fall down and worship me.

Then saith Jesus unto him, Get thee hence, Satan: FOR IT IS WRITTEN, THOU SHALT WORSHIP THE LORD THY GOD, AND HIM ONLY SHALT THOU SERVE.

Then the devil leaveth him, and, behold, angels came and ministered unto him.

Matthew 4:1–11 (KJV)

WHEN THE HOLY Spirit had come to indwell (be one with Jesus), the Spirit lead Jesus out to the wilderness (desert) to be tempted (tested) by the devil. Jesus was God's own son, but he was also man; God willed that he share all of the temptations with which man lived.

When Jesus had fasted (done without food) for forty days and forty nights, he was very hungry. The significance of the forty days is to symbolize the forty years that the Children of Israel wandered in the wilderness.

The first time that Satan tested Jesus, he reminded Jesus that Jesus had the power to turn the rocks into bread. Remember that man's first sin was suggested to him by Satan's challenge to Eve that she could provide food for herself just like she was a god. Jesus said over and over again that he only did and said the things that God the Father told him to do or say. Jesus never tried to compete with God the Father. Jesus always answered Satan with God's own words. God's words are God's truth.

And he humbled thee, and suffered thee to hunger, and fed thee with manna, which thou knewest not, neither did

THOU SHALL CALL HIS NAME JESUS

thy fathers know; that he might make thee know that man doth not live by bread only, but by every word that proceedeth out of the mouth of the Lord doth man live.

Deuteronomy 8:3 (KJV)

When the Children of Israel were in the desert for forty years, God taught them that they were totally dependent upon God for their food so that they would know that it was God who provided for their needs and gave them life. They had no bread (food) except the manna that God provided for them daily. The scripture tells us that in Jesus we live and move and have our being. We have no life except the life we receive from God himself.

When Satan tested Jesus the second time he used scripture (God's word) to challenge Jesus. "For he shall give his angels charge over thee, to keep thee in all thy ways. They shall bear thee up in their hands, lest thou dash thy foot against a stone" (Psalm 91:11–12, KJV)

Again Jesus answered the second temptation with God's own word. "Ye shall not tempt (provoke) the Lord your God, as ye tempted him in Massah. Ye shall diligently keep the commandments of the Lord your God, and his testimonies, and his statutes, which he hath commanded thee" (Deuteronomy 6: 16–17, KJV).

For Satan's third temptation he resorted to the same temptation that he used when he lied to Eve in the Garden of Eden. He told Jesus that he would make Jesus king over all the earth if Jesus would acknowledge Satan as his god. He tempted Jesus to believe Satan's lies instead of God's truth so that Jesus would have the power of a God himself. If Jesus had accepted Satan's promise as truth, he would have been under the power of Satan. Jesus answered the test with another scripture, God's word. Jesus ordered Satan to leave. "Thou shalt fear the Lord thy God, and serve him, and shalt swear by his name" (Deuteronomy 6:13, KJV). "Thou shalt have none other gods before me" (Deuteronomy 5:7, KJV).

When Satan had left, angels came and ministered to Jesus. (served him)

JESUS GOES BACK TO GALILEE AND CALLS THE DISCIPLES

Now when Jesus had heard that John was cast into prison, he departed into Galilee.

And leaving Nazareth, he came and dwelt in Capernaum, which is upon the sea coast, in the borders of Zabulon and Nephthalim.

That it might be fulfilled which was spoken by Esaias the prophet, saying,

the land of Zabulon, and the land of Nephthalim, by the way of the sea, beyond Jordan, Galilee of the gentiles;

The people which sat in darkness saw great light; and to them which sat in the region and shadow of death light is sprung up.

From that time Jesus began to preach, and to say, Repent: for the kingdom of heaven is at hand.

And Jesus, walking by the sea of Galilee, saw two brethren, Simon called Peter, and Andrew his brother, casting a net into the sea: for they were fishers.

And he saith unto them, Follow me, and I will make you fishers of men.

And thy straightway left their nets, and followed him.

And going on from thence, he saw other two brethren, James the son of Zebedee, and John his brother, in a ship with Zebedee their father, mending their nets; and he called them.

And they immediately left the ship and their father, and followed him.

Matthew 4:12–22 (KJV)

AFTER JESUS HEARD that John the Baptist had been put in prison, Jesus went down to Galilee. He went and stayed in Capernaum after he left Nazareth. By going to Galilee and staying there, Jesus fulfilled prophesy in Isaiah. Starting from that time, Jesus began to preach; he preached about the repentance of sin and about the fact that the kingdom of heaven was about to begin. " The people that walked in darkness have seen a great light: they that dwell in the land of the shadow of death, upon them hath the light shined" (Isaiah 9:2, KJV).

While Jesus was walking by the Sea of Galilee, he saw Simon whom Jesus called Peter and Peter's brother, Andrew, fishing. The brothers were professional fishermen. Jesus called to them to come with him, and he would make them fishers of men. We know from the Book of John that the brothers had talked with Jesus and heard him speak before that time. When he called them, they followed him immediately.

As Jesus walked on down the beach, Jesus saw the sons of Zebedee, James and John, sitting in their boat with their father. They were mending their fishing nets. Jesus called to them also, and they left their father and their nets to follow Jesus. All four of these men left their lives as they had known them without question and followed Jesus into his ministry.

JESUS BEGINS TO TEACH, PREACH, AND HEAL

And Jesus went about all Galilee, teaching in their synagogues, and preaching the gospel of the kingdom, and healing all manner of sickness and all manner of disease among the people.

And his fame went throughout all Syria: and they brought unto him all sick people that were taken with divers diseases and torments, and those which were possessed with devils, and those which were lunatick, and those that had the palsy; and he healed them. (Some were epileptics, and some were paralyzed.)

And there followed him great multitudes of people from Galilee, and from Decapolis, and from Jerusalem, and from Judaea, and from beyond Jordan.

Matthew 4:23–25 (KJV)

THEN JESUS BEGAN to travel in Galilee teaching in the synagogues (churches); he was preaching the good news that the kingdom of God was about to begin. As he traveled and preached, he was healing all different kinds of sickness and diseases.

His preaching and healing made him famous all over Syria. Many people began to come to him bringing people who needed all kinds of healing. They came for the healing, but they heard the preaching. The preaching was believed because the people saw the miracles. The illnesses and diseases that Jesus healed were widely varied; he also cast out devils (demons) and healed the lunaticks (insane, mentally ill). He healed those afflicted, those with palsy, epilepsy, and paralysis.

As he traveled from place to place, multitudes (hundreds, thousands) of people followed him. People from Galilee and Decapolis (ten cities east of the Sea of Galilee) and Jerusalem and Judaea and from the area beyond the Jordan River followed Jesus.

JESUS TEACHES THE MULTITUDES ON THE MOUNTAIN

And seeing the multitudes, he went up into a mountain: and when he was set, his disciples came unto him:

And he opened his mouth, and taught them, saying,

Blessed are the poor in spirit: for their's is the kingdom of heaven.

Blessed are they that mourn: for they shall be comforted.

Blessed are the meek: for they shall inherit the earth.

Blessed are they which do hunger and thirst after righteousness: for they shall be filled.

Blessed are the merciful: for they shall obtain mercy.

Blessed are the pure in heart: for they shall see God.

Blessed are the peacemakers: for they shall be called the children of God.

Blessed are they which are persecuted for righteousness" sake: for their's is the kingdom of heaven.

Blessed are ye, when men shall revile you, and persecute you, and shall say all manner of evil against you falsely, for my sake.

Rejoice, and be exceeding glad for great is your reward in heaven: for so persecuted they the prophets which were before you.

Ye are the salt of the earth: but if the salt have lost his savour, wherewith shall it be salted? It is thence forth good for nothing, but to be cast out, and to be trodden under foot of men.

Ye are the light of the world. A city that is set on an hill cannot be hid.

Neither do men light a candle, and put it under a bushel, but on a candlestick; and it giveth light unto all that are in the house.

Let your light so shine before men, that they may see your good works, and glorify your Father which is in heaven.

Matthew 5:1–16 (KJV)

W HEN JESUS SAW how many people had come to hear him, he went up on a mountain so he could be seen and heard. The disciples (followers) came to sit around him. He began to teach the people.

He said that those who were poor in spirit would have a place in the kingdom of heaven. Those who are poor in spirit realize that they live in spiritual poverty. They are not proud of how spiritual they are because they know that they have no spiritual worth of their own. They know that they are spiritually dependent on God. All have sinned and fallen short of the glory of God. None of us have spiritual power or life because of anything we have done or will do. We are totally dependent upon God. If we realize that we are spiritually dependent upon God and that all that we have is given to us by God's grace, then we can (will) live in God's kingdom where everything is done according to God's will. We will live in a state of thankfulness. "Thy kingdom come. Thy will be done in earth, as it is in heaven" (Matthew 5:10, KJV).

We should remember that Jesus was proclaiming that the kingdom of the God was coming. When he said that those who mourned would be comforted, he was referring to what the Father had sent Jesus to do. Part of what God the Father sent Jesus to do was to comfort all who mourned; a prophecy in Isaiah said that Jesus would give God's people comfort, the oil of joy, and garments of praise so that God the Father would be glorified. Jesus was to turn our mourning into dancing and gladness so that Jesus's glory would sing praises to God the Father forever. His people would give thanks to God forever.

Jesus would redeem God's people and his people would come to God the Father with singing and thanks. It would be God himself who comforts his people, and they would have no fear ever again. God would redeem his people. They would be provided for (fed) by God himself. They would be like a watered garden and never have sorrow again.

> The Spirit of the Lord God is upon me; because the Lord hath anointed me to preach good tidings unto the meek; he hath sent me to bind up the brokenhearted, to proclaim liberty to the captives, and the opening of the prison to them that are bound:
>
> To proclaim the acceptable year of the Lord, and the day of vengeance of our God; to comfort all that mourn;
>
> To appoint unto them that mourn in Zion, to give unto them beauty for ashes, the oil of joy for mourning, the garment of praise for the spirit of heaviness; that they might be called trees of righteousness, the planting of the Lord, that he might be glorified.
>
> Isaiah 61:1–3 (KJV)

> Hear, O Lord, and have mercy upon me: Lord, be thou my helper.

Thou hast turned for me my mourning into dancing: thou hast put off my sackcloth, and girded me with gladness;

To the end that my glory may sing praise to thee, and not be silent. O Lord my God, I will give thanks unto thee for ever.

Psalm 30:10–12 (KJV)

Therefore the redeemed of the Lord shall return, and come with singing unto Zion; And everlasting joy shall be upon their head: they shall obtain gladness and joy; and sorrow and mourning shall flee away.

I, even I, am he that comforteth you: who art thou, that thou shouldest be afraid of a man that shall die, and of the son of man which shall be made as grass.

Isaiah 51:11–12 (KJV)

For the LORD hath redeemed Jacob, and ransomed him from the hand of him that was stronger than he.

Therefore they shall come and sing in the height of Zion, and shall flow together to the goodness of the LORD for wheat, and for wine, and for oil, and for the young of the flock and of the herd and their soul shall be as a watered garden; and they shall not sorrow any more at all.

Then shall the virgin rejoice in the dance, both young men and old together: for I will turn their mourning into joy, and will comfort them, and make them rejoice from their sorrow.

Jeremiah 31:11–13 (KJV)

BLESSED ARE THE MEEK

WHEN JESUS SAID that the meek were blessed and would inherit the earth, he was quoting from one of David's psalms in the Old Testament. The psalm said that God's people should wait for God to make things right. To be meek does not mean to be spineless. To be meek means to depend upon God to defend you. A Christian should not be angry and worry because other people do evil things. A Christian should wait for the Lord. The people who do evil will be cut off from God. He will punish them. Those who wait for God to correct the evil, will live in peace forever. We can't tell if Jesus meant that the people of God would possess the earth, or if he meant that God's people would be provided for by God's bounty.

> Rest in the Lord, and wait patiently for him: fret not thy-self because of him who prospereth in his way, because of the man who bringeth wicked devices to pass.

Cease from anger, and forsake wrath: fret not thyself in any wise to do evil.

For evildoers shall be cut off: but those that wait upon the Lord, they shall inherit the earth.

For yet a little while, and the wicked shall not be: yea, thou shalt diligently consider his place, and it shall not be.

But the meek shall inherit the earth; and shall delight themselves in the abundance of peace.

Psalm 37:7–11 (KJV)

Jesus said that God's people who hungered and thirsted after righteousness would be filled. To be righteous is to be right with God; to be righteous a person must follow God's instructions and not sin against God. The righteous should remember God and live in the ways that God wills for us to live. The righteous should stay away from evil and do good. They should look for peace and try to increase it. No one can be righteous (without sin) but God. We have all failed to follow God's rules and directions. Therefore Jesus said that if we truly tried to live according to God's directions, that is if we tried to seek righteousness, we would be helped to become righteous. We cannot be righteous (right with God) by ourselves. Jesus is all righteousness. God knows the desires of our hearts; Jesus knows if we truly are trying to live righteous lives. If we live in union with him, Jesus will bring us into righteousness.

Thou meetest him that rejoiceth and worketh righteousness, those that remember thee in thy ways: behold, thou art wroth (angry); for we have sinned: in those is continuance, and we shall be saved.

But we are all as an unclean thing, and all our righteousnesses are as filthy rags; and we all do fade as a leaf; and our iniquities, like the wind, have taken us away.

And there is none that calleth upon thy name, that stirreth up himself to take hold of thee: for thou hast hid thy face from us, and hast consumed us, because of our iniquities.

Isaiah 64:5–7 (KJV)

Keep thy tongue from evil, and thy lips from speaking guile.

Depart from evil, and do good; seek peace, and pursue it.

The eyes of the Lord are upon the righteous, and his ears are open unto their cry.

The face of the Lord is against them that do evil, to cut off the remembrance of them from the earth.

The righteous cry, and the Lord heareth, and delivereth them out of all their troubles.

The Lord is nigh unto them that are of a broken heart; and saveth such as be of a contrite spirit.

Many are the afflictions of the righteous: but the Lord delivereth him out of them all.

Psalm 34:13–19 (KJV)

BLESSED ARE THE MERCIFUL

JESUS SAID THAT the people who are merciful to others would be shown mercy. This is a topic that Jesus returned to many times. We are commanded to forgive others. Most of the scripture that addresses mercy and forgiveness is in the New Testament. Our forgiveness of others is even given as a condition of God's forgiveness of us in the Lord's Prayer.

Pride is an abomination to God. God created all things; he created all things for his pleasure. God is before all things (more important), and all things exist in him. Sometimes the pride we feel about ourselves makes it very difficult to forgive others. If we recognize that as the creator God is entitled to all things, then it may become easier to recognize that God has the right to expect us to obey him and forgive others. If I acknowledge that God has a plan for my life, then I am more likely to accept that no one else is responsible for keeping me from having things that I think that I am entitled to have. The word says that all things work for good for those who love God and are called according to his purposes. I may be more able to forgive another human for taking something of mine or preventing me from having something I wanted if I remember that truth. If God allowed it to happen, then he is able to make that experience into something good. This does not make it acceptable to be resistant to forgiving others, but it may help us to comply with the commandment. Joseph's brothers sold him into slavery. They meant it for evil, but God allowed that circumstance to happen so that all of Israel's (Jacob's) family would be blessed.

> The Lord hath made all things for himself: yea, even the wicked for the day of evil.
>
> Everyone that is proud in heart is an abomination to the Lord: though hand join in hand, he shall not be unpunished.
>
> By mercy and truth iniquity is purged: and by the fear of the Lord men depart from evil.
>
> Proverbs 16:4–6 (KJV)

> For by him were all things created, that are in heaven, and that are in earth, visible and invisible, whether they be thrones, or dominions, or principalities, or powers: all things were created by him, and for him:
>
> And he is before all things, and by him all things consist.
>
> Colossians 1:16–17 (KJV)

God shows man what is good; God requires that we show mercy to others, that we seek justice for everyone, and that we are humble (not proud) with God. If we are humble, we acknowledge that God created everything for himself and we have no right to anything. If evil is done, we acknowledge that it is for God to judge and right the wrong. "He hath shewed thee, O man, what is good; and what doth the Lord require of thee, but to do justly, and to love mercy, and to walk humbly with thy God?" (Micah 6:8, KJV).

Humble yourself as God sees you. Then God will lift you up. Do not say evil things about others. If you speak evil and judge your fellow Christian, you are judging God's law. You are not doing what God says; you are setting yourself to judge the laws of God. There is only one who has the right to make laws; who are you to judge God?

> Humble yourselves in the sight of the Lord, and he shall lift you up.
>
> Speak not evil one of another, brethren, He that speaketh evil of his brother, and judgeth his brother, speaketh evil of the law, and judgeth the law: but if thou judge the law, thou art not a doer of the law, but a judge.
>
> There is one lawgiver, who is able to save and to destroy, who art thou that judgest another?
>
> James 4:10–12 (KJV)

Jesus said to forgive others seventy times seven if they continue to come and ask your forgiveness. God has forgiven us great sin punishable by death; it is a debt so great that nothing could pay back the debt but the life of his own son. The sins that we must forgive others are insignificant in comparison.

> Then came Peter to him, and said, Lord, how oft shall my brother sin against me, and I forgive him? Till seven times?
>
> Jesus saith unto him, I say not unto thee, Until seven times: but, Until seventy times seven.
>
> Therefore is the kingdom of heaven likened unto a certain king, which would take account of his servants.
>
> And when he had begun to reckon, one was brought unto him, which owed him ten thousand talents.
>
> But for as he had not to pay, his lord commanded him to be sold, and his wife, and children, and all that he had, and payment to be made.

The servant therefore fell down, and worshipped him, saying, Lord, have patience with me, and I will pay thee all.

Then the lord of that servant was moved with compassion, and loosed him, and forgave him the debt.

But the same servant went out, and found one of his fellowservants, which owed him an hundred pence: and he laid hands on him, and took him by the throat, saying, Pay me that thou owest.

And his fellowservant fell down at his feet, and besought him, saying, Have patience with me, and I will pay thee all.

And he would not: but went and cast him into prison, till he should pay the debt.

So when his fellowservants saw what was done, they were very sorry, and came and told unto their lord all that was done.

Then his lord, after that he had called him, said unto him, O thou wicked servant, I forgave thee all that debt, because thou desiredst me:

Shouldest not thou also have had compassion on thy fellowservant, even as I had pity on thee?

And his lord was wroth, and delivered him to the tormentors, till he should pay all that was due unto him.

Matthew 18:21–35 (KJV)

If another Christian (child of God) trespasses against you, tell him about his trespass; if he is sorry for the transgression, forgive him. As often as he is sorry for his trespass, forgive him. Your Heavenly Father forgives as often as you ask.

Take heed to yourselves: If thy brother trespass against thee, rebuke him: and if he repent, forgive him.

And if he trespass against thee seven times in a day, and seven times in a day turn again to thee, saying, I repent: thou shalt forgive him.

Luke 17:3–4 (KJV)

Ask God to deliver you from temptation; to deliver you from being controlled by evil. God will only forgive those who forgive others.

> And forgive us our debts, as we forgive our debtors.
> And lead us not into temptation, but deliver us from evil: For thine is the kingdom, and the power, and the glory, for ever. Amen
> For if ye forgive men their trespasses, your heavenly Father will also forgive you:
> But if ye do not forgive, neither will your Father which is in heaven forgive your trespasses.
>
> Matthew 6:12–15 (KJV)

If you want God to honor your prayers, forgive anyone that you have not forgiven. God honors the prayers of those who have obeyed him and forgiven others.

> Therefore I say unto you, What things soever ye desire, when ye pray, believe that ye receive them, and ye shall have them.
> And when ye stand praying, forgive, if ye have ought against any: that your Father also which is in heaven may forgive you your trespasses.
> But if ye do not forgive, neither will your Father which is in heaven forgive your trespasses.
>
> Mark 11:24–26 (KJV)

God wants you to love your enemies, do good to others, and lend to others not expecting a return or reward. God is kind to those who do not thank him and to those who choose to do evil. God wants us to emulate him and accept his values just as a child follows the example of its parent; God will be merciful (forgiving) to those who are merciful; God will not judge those who do not judge others; God will not condemn those who do not condemn others; God will forgive those who forgive others.

But love ye your enemies, and do good, and lend, hoping for nothing again; and your reward shall be great, and ye shall be the children of the Highest: for he is kind unto the unthankful and to the evil.

Be ye therefore merciful, as your Father also is merciful.

Judge not, and ye shall not be judged: condemn not, and ye shall not be condemned: forgive, and ye shall be forgiven.

Luke 6:35–37 (KJV)

God will give mercy to those who give mercy.

Psalm 18:25 (KJV)

God will forgive the humble when they ask for mercy. It is God who will chose those who will be given mercy and compassion. It is not for us to choose.

And the publican, standing afar off, would not lift up so much as his eyes unto heaven, but smote upon his breast, saying, God be merciful to me a sinner.

I tell you this man went down to his house justified rather than the other: for every one that exalteth himself shall be abased; and he that humbleth himself shall be exalted.

Luke 18:13–14 (KJV)

For he saith to Moses, "I will have mercy on whom I will have mercy, and I will have compassion on whom I will have compassion."

Romans 9:15 (KJV)

Because you were chosen by God to be His beloved child, you should please God. Obey God by being merciful, kind, humble, meek, and longsuffering because that is what pleases God who forgave us a much greater forgiveness. "Put on therefore, as the elect of God, holy and beloved, bowels of mercies, kindness, humbleness of mind, meekness, longsuffering; Forbearing one another, and forgiving one another, if any man have a quarrel against any: even as Christ forgave you, so also do ye" (Colossians 3: 12–13, KJV).

We have redemption (forgiveness) through God's grace (a free gift). Do not live with bitterness, anger, disputing, evil speaking (saying negative things about others) and thinking or doing evil things to others. "In whom we have redemption through his blood, the forgiveness of sins, according to the riches of his grace" (Ephesians 1:7, KJV).

> Let all bitterness, and wrath, and anger, and clamour, and evil speaking, be put away from you, with all malice.
> Be ye kind one to another, tenderhearted, forgiving one another, even as God for Christ's sake hath forgiven you.
>
> Ephesians 4:31–32 (KJV)

Why do you judge your brother? Why would you want to make your brother smaller in importance or guiltier? We will all stand before Jesus and be judged. Every one of us will be judged by God himself.

> But why dost thou judge thy brother? Or why dost thou set at nought (reduce to nothing) thy brother? For we shall all stand before the judgment seat of Christ.
> For it is written, as I live, saith the Lord, every knee shall bow to me, and every tongue shall confess to God."
> So then every one of us shall give account of himself to God.
> Let us not therefore judge one another any more: but judge this rather, that no man put a stumbling block or an occasion to fall in his brother's way.
>
> Romans 14:10–13 (KJV)

Don't judge now. Jesus will come to judge; he will reveal all things that are hidden to men and will know the desires of our hearts which we keep in secret. "Therefore judge nothing before the time, until the Lord come, who both will bring to light the hidden things of darkness, and will make manifest the counsels of the hearts: and then shall every man have praise of God" (1st Corinthians 4:5, KJV).

So we can see that being merciful and being willing to forgive others is supremely important to our Heavenly Father and Jesus. Our willingness to love, to be merciful, and to be willing to forgive are some of the greatest witnesses Christians can give to others about God the Father and Jesus, His Son.

BLESSED ARE THE PURE IN HEART

JESUS SAID THAT the people who are pure in heart would see God. A search through the scriptures will help us to better understand what he meant. The first scriptures about this concept are taken from the Old Testament. God's commandments are always right. If we hold his words in our heart, we will have joy. The commandments of God are pure; they enlighten our eyes so that we can see God. "The statutes of the Lord are right, rejoicing the heart: the commandment of the Lord is pure, enlightening the eyes" (Psalm 19:8, KJV).

God will destroy the proud, and he will build up the lowly. The thoughts of wicked people are an abomination to God. He welcomes hearing the words of the pure. A righteous person studies and thinks about the words of God; a wicked person pours out words that reveal the evil in his heart.

> The Lord will destroy the house of the proud: but he will establish the border of the widow. The thoughts of the

wicked are an abomination to the Lord: but the words of
the pure are pleasant words.

He that is greedy of gain troubleth his own house; but
he that hateth gifts (bribes) shall live.

The heart of the righteous studieth to answer: but the
mouth of the wicked poureth out evil things.

Proverbs 15:25–28 (KJV)

God told Samuel not to look at the man's outward appearance.
God looks at a person's heart (what he thinks and feels). "But the
Lord said unto Samuel, Look not on his countenance, or on the
height of his stature; because I have refused (rejected) him: for
the Lord seeth not as man seeth; for man looketh on the outward
appearance, but the Lord looketh on the heart." (1st Samuel 16:7,
KJV)

The Psalmist asked God to look at his thoughts, and see if
he was thinking about evil things. He wanted God to look at
his heart so that God could lead him to everlasting life. "Search
me, O God, and know my heart: try me, and know my thoughts:
And see if there be any wicked way in me, and lead me in the way
everlasting" (Psalms 139:23, KJV).

In Proverbs God wants the young man to listen to God's
words. He tells him to listen to God's sayings, to always look at
the scripture, and to keep God's words in his heart. God's words
give health and life to those who study them. Guard your heart
because out of your heart will come the ways you live your life.
Do not tell lies. Don't be distracted from thinking about God.
Think about what you are doing with your life; always move on
into righteousness.

My son, attend to my words; incline thine ear unto my
sayings.

Let them not depart from thine eyes; keep them in the
midst of thine heart.

For they are life unto those that find them, and health
to all their flesh.

Keep thy heart with all diligence; for out of it are the issues of life.

Put away from thee a forward (deceitful) mouth, and perverse lips put far from thee.

Let thine eyes look right on, and let thine eyelids look straight before thee.

Ponder the path of thy feet, and let all thy ways be established.

Turn not to the right hand nor to the left: remove thy foot from evil.

Proverbs 4:20–27 (KJV)

Whatever a person thinks in his heart (mind) is a reflection of the person that he/she really is. An evil person acts like he agrees with you and will help you, but he is really deceiving you. " For as he thinketh in his heart, so is he: Eat and drink, saith he to thee; but his heart is not with thee" (Proverbs 23:7, KJV).

The teachings about being pure of heart carry on into the New Testament. Jesus spoke about the temporary worth of wealth. Don't place your attention on becoming wealthy. Wealth can be stolen, and possessions can deteriorate. The word of God is eternal. "Lay not up for yourselves treasures upon earth, where moth and rust doth corrupt (ruin) and where thieves break through and steal. (Matthew 6: 19–21, KJV)

God is not deceived by those who pretend to be devoted Christians. If a person seems to be a devoted Christian but doesn't control what words come out of his/her mouth, he/she is deceiving herself/himself. That person's religion is worthless. God's idea of what is pure, undefiled (not soiled) religion is to help the widows and orphans (those who are helpless and in need). A Christian should not be influenced by what other people are doing.

If any man among you seem to be religious, and bridleth not his tongue, but deceiveth his own heart, this man's religion is vain (worthless).

Pure religion and undefiled before God and the Father is this, To visit the fatherless and widows in their affliction, and to keep himself unspotted from the world.

James 1:26–27 (KJV)

When Jesus told the Pharisees that they were snakes, he asked how they could say good things when their hearts were full of evil. He said that whatever was in a person's heart would come out in their speech. A good man draws good words out of his good heart, and an evil man draws evil words out of his evil heart. Every idle (unkind, judgmental, destructive) word someone says will have to be explained to God on Judgment Day.

O generation of vipers, how can ye, being evil, speak good things? For out of the abundance of the heart the mouth speaketh.

A good man out of the good treasure of the heart bringeth forth good things: and an evil man out of the evil treasure bringeth forth evil things.

But I say unto you, That every idle word that men shall speak, they shall give account thereof in the day of judgment.

Matthew 12:34–37 (KJV)

Jesus asked his followers if they did not understand that what they ate just went into their stomachs and then was thrown out with refuse. The things that come out of a person's mouth are coming from the person's heart; those are the things that make the man unclean. If a man holds evil thoughts, murders, adulteries, fornications (sexual sin), thefts, false witness (telling lies), or blasphemies (false thoughts, words, teachings about God) in his heart (mind), those things make the man unclean. Eating with unwashed hands does not make a man unclean spiritually.

Do not ye yet understand, that whatsoever entereth in at the mouth goeth into the belly, and is cast out into the draught?

THOU SHALL CALL HIS NAME JESUS

But those things that proceed out of the mouth come forth from the heart; and they defile the man.

For out of the heart proceed evil thoughts, murders, adulteries, fornications, thefts, false witness, blasphemies:

These are the things which defile a man: but to eat with unwashen hands defileth not a man.

Matthew 15:17–20 (KJV)

If you have bitterness, envy, and the desire to fight in your heart, don't be proud; don't deny the truth. Your view that you are a good Christian is not God's opinion. That view of yourself as a good Christian is given to you by the devil. God's wisdom says that a good Christian should be pure in their beliefs, peaceable, gentle, easily convinced, and merciful; a good Christian should do good things (deeds), should not show partiality, and not act like a hypocrite. To be judged righteous by God, a Christian should work to make peace between others.

But if ye have bitter envying and strife in your hearts, glory not, and lie not against the truth.

This wisdom descendeth not from above, but is earthly, sensual, devilish.

For where envying and strife is, there is confusion and every evil work.

But the wisdom that is from above is first pure, then peaceable, gentle, and easy to be entreated, full of mercy and good fruits, without partiality, and without hypocrisy.

And the fruit of righteousness is sown in peace of them that make peace.

James 3:14–18 (KJV)

Jesus was asked twice about which commandment in the Mosaic Law was the greatest. He said that the greatest commandment was that a man should love God with all his heart, with all his soul, and with all his mind. We usually think of a man as having a spirit, a soul, and a mind. The message is still clear;

we should love God with all that we are. " Master, which is the greatest commandment in the law? Jesus said unto him, "Thou shalt love the Lord thy God with all thy heart, and with all thy soul, and with all thy mind" (Matthew 22: 36–37, KJV).

Trying to test Jesus, a lawyer asked him what he should do to inherit eternal life. Jesus asked him what the Mosaic Law said. The lawyer responded, "Thou shalt love the Lord thy God with all thy heart, and with all thy soul, and with all thy strength, and with all thy mind; and thy neighbor as thyself. Jesus answered the lawyer saying that he had answered correctly; if the lawyer did that he would live eternally.

> And behold a certain lawyer stood up, and tempted him, saying, Master, what shall I do to inherit eternal life?
>
> He said unto him, "What is written in the law? How readest thou?"
>
> And he answering said, thou shalt love the Lord thy God all thy heart, and with all thy soul, and wih all thy strength, and with all thy mind; and thy neighbor as thyself.
>
> And he said unto him, "Thou hast answered right: this do, and thou shalt live."
>
> Luke 10:25–28 (KJV)

We should remember that Jesus is the Word of God. Jesus is therefore the discerner of all our thoughts and the intents of the heart. He is living and powerful and able to separate soul, spirit, and mind. Nothing is hidden from God. He is able to see and understand everything in our hearts. God knows what we think and feel. We are unable to deceive God no matter what we say or do with our outside appearance. "For the word of God is quick (living), powerful, and sharper than any twoedged sword, piercing even to the dividing asunder of soul and spirit, and the joints and marrow, and is a discerner of the thoughts and intents of the heart" (Hebrews 4:12–13, KJV).

We know that we are loved by God, and we know that we are God's sons and daughters. We don't know what we will be like (bodies, presence). We do know that we will be like Jesus when he comes. We will be able to see (perceive, know) him as he really exists. Everyone who hopes (believes in the future life) will work at making himself/herself pure just like Jesus is pure.

"Beloved, now are we the sons of God, and it doth not yet appear what we shall be; but we know that when he shall appear, we shall be like him, for we shall see him as he is. And every man that has this hope in him purifieth himself, even as he is pure" (1st John 3:2–3, KJV).

God's children should resist (don't obey) the devil. We should cleanse our hands by making sure that our lives are not soiled by sin. We should purify our hearts by making sure that we are not torn between God's will and the will of man. "Submit yourselves therefore to God. Resist the devil, and he will flee from you. Draw nigh to God, and he will draw nigh to you Cleanse your hands, ye sinners; and purify your hearts, ye doubleminded" (James 4: 7–8, KJV).

We can purify our hearts by singing to ourselves in scripture songs and hymns and spiritual songs. We can make melody in our hearts to God. "Speaking to yourselves in psalms and hymns and spiritual songs, singing and making melody in your heart to the Lord" (Ephesians 5:19, KJV).

We should serve God as the servants of Jesus Christ by doing the will of God from our hearts. We should not just obey God with surface actions and words appearing to other people that we serve God. We should gladly serve God and do His will. "Not with eyeservice, as menpleasers; but as the servants of Christ, doing the will of God from the heart: With good will doing service, as to the Lord, and not to men" (Ephesians 6: 6–8, KJV).

If we will serve God doing his will with willing hearts and filling our hearts with his truth and his words, we will be given freely from God so that our souls and spirits will be made stronger by the Holy Spirit in our hearts. Then Christ will live in our hearts, and we will be firmly grafted to Jesus with love. We will be able to understand how great Jesus's love for us is. We will be filled with the fullness of God. We will be able to see God. We will know Him as he truly is.

> That he would grant you according to the riches of his glory, to be strengthened with might by his Spirit in the inner man.
> That Christ may dwell in your hearts by faith; that ye, being rooted and grounded in love,
> May be able to comprehend with all saints what is the breadth, and length, and depth, and height;
> And to know the love of Christ, which passeth knowledge, that ye might be filled with all the fullness of God.
>
> Ephesians 3:16–19 (KJV)

And so we see that our hearts will be made pure. Our hearts will have been cleansed by the words of God. We will do God's will with eager hearts. We will sing and praise God in our hearts (our inter man). We will truly see (perceive) God as He is because our hearts will be filled with God's word, God's will, God's love, and our knowledge of who God is.

BLESSED ARE THE PEACEMAKERS

JESUS SAID THAT the peacemakers were blessed because they would be called the children of God. We see evidence in the Old Testament that God had begun to teach his chosen people that seeking after peace would benefit them. The psalms told them to avoid evil and try to make peace. "Depart from evil, and do good; seek peace and pursue it" (Psalm 34: 14, KJV).

The laws given to them by God through Moses told them not to give false witness meaning that they were not to lie. In Proverbs they were told that deceit (telling lies) is in the heart (thoughts and plans) of people who admire and seek after evil. People who try to influence others to make peace will have joy. "Deceit is in the heart of them that imagine evil: but to the counselors of peace is joy" (Proverbs 12: 20, KJV).

The Psalmist asked God to show them mercy (forgiveness) and to give them salvation. They were to listen to what God said because God would make peace with His people. God's people were not to go back to their foolish behavior. God's salvation was coming for those who respect God. When God's salvation (Jesus) had come, God's glory would be with them in their land. After they received salvation, forgiveness and God's truth would come. There would be righteousness and peace for God's people.

> Shew us thy mercy, O Lord, and grant us thy salvation. I will hear what God the Lord will speak: for he will speak peace unto his people, and to his saints: but let them not turn again to folly.
> Surely his salvation is nigh them that fear him; that glory may dwell in our land.
> Mercy and truth are met together; righteousness and peace have kissed each other.
>
> Psalm 85:7–10 (KJV)

God spoke through his prophet. Isaiah said that God would give perfect peace to the person who concentrates on God and trusts that God will take care of him. This was very close to the teachings that are to be found in the New Testament. "Thou wilt keep him in perfect peace, whose mind is stayed on thee because he trusteth in thee" (Isaiah 26:3, KJV).

Isaiah went on to say that God would create peace for them. He acknowledged that it was God who created all of our existence. God did make peace for His chosen people when he sent Jesus to atone for our sins. "Lord, thou wilt ordain peace for us: for thou also hast wrought all our works in us" (Isaiah 26:12, KJV).

Isaiah said that God wills that all people everywhere know that he is the only god. There are no other gods. God creates light and darkness. God makes peace, and he created evil (the devil). It is God alone who has all the power to do all those things. "That they may know from the rising of the sun, and from the west, that there is none beside me. I am the Lord, and there is none else. I form the light, and create darkness: I make peace, and create evil: I the Lord do all these things" (Isaiah 45:6–7, KJV).

At another time, Isaiah said that all God's children will be taught by God. God would give all his children great, unending peace. "And all thy children shall be taught of the Lord; and great shall be the peace of thy children" (Isaiah 54:13, KJV).

Isaiah also prophesized that the Messiah would come. He said a child would be born; a son would be given to them. He would rule over us. He would be a wonderful person, a counselor, the mighty God, the eternal Father, and the prince who brings peace. He would rule over all things. There would be no end to peace. He would rule on the throne of David to establish and maintain his kingdom. He will judge fairly and make sure that everyone has justice eternally. God would bring this kingdom into existence.

> For unto us a child is born, unto us a son is given: and the government shall be upon his shoulder: and his name shall be called Wonderful, Counsellor, The mighty God, The everlasting Father, The Prince of Peace.
>
> Of the increase of his government and peace there shall be no end, upon the throne of David, and upon his kingdom, to order it, and to establish it with judgment and with justice from henceforth even for ever. The zeal of the Lord of hosts will perform this.
>
> Isaiah 9:6–7 (KJV)

When Jesus, the Messiah, was born the angels appeared to the shepherds to announce that God had made peace between God and men. There had been no peace between God and man because man sinned against God. "And suddenly there was with the angel a multitude of the heavenly host praising God, and saying, Glory to God in the highest, and on earth peace, good will toward men" (Luke 2:13–14, KJV).

We are justified, made acceptable to God because we trust and depend upon Jesus to redeem us. We have peace with God because of Jesus's sacrifice for us; we are no longer separated from God. "Therefore being justified by faith, we have peace with God through our Lord Jesus Christ" (Romans 5: 1, KJV).

Jesus said that we must become like little children to enter the kingdom of heaven. We must put aside pride and become humble. We must become dependent on God and believe God without question. We must be obedient to God's will. We must be kind and loving without deception and hatred so that we can become part of God's kingdom.

Jesus also gave a warning to adults concerning their treatment of children. If any person takes care of a child, it is the same as if that person served Jesus himself. If anyone hurts a child who believes (trusts) in Jesus, it would be better for that person to be tied to an anchor and dropped in the deepest part of the ocean. God always gives attention to children. They are under his care.

> And verily I say unto you, Except ye be converted, and become as little children, ye shall not enter into the kingdom of heaven.
>
> Whosoever therefore shall humble himself as this little child, the same is greatest in the kingdom of heaven.
>
> And whoso shall receive one such little child in my name receiveth me.
>
> But whoso shall offend (hurt) one of these little ones which believe in me, it were better for him that a millstone were hanged about his neck, and that he were drowned in the depth of the sea.
>
> Matthew 18:3–4 (KJV)

Jesus said that he did not come to make peace for all people all over the world. He came to defeat evil not to make peace with evil. Each person must choose if he/she will believe God and obey Him. Each will choose if he/she will accept Jesus as their salvation or if they will follow the leadership of other people. A man cannot depend on his father's opinions. A woman cannot follow her mother's example without question. A daughter-in-law will need to choose between her mother-in-law's beliefs and God's words and will. "Think not that I am come to send peace on earth: I came not to send peace, but a sword. For I am come to SET A MAN AT VARIANCE AGAINST HIS FATHER, AND THE DAUGHTER AGAINST HER MOTHER, AND THE DAUGHTER-IN-LAW AGAINST HER MOTHER-IN-LAW" (Matthew 10:34–35).

Jesus said that salt was good to flavor. If the salt lost its properties and no longer tasted good, it was worthless. Each person must carry the word and truth of God in his/her own heart. Each person must live his/her own life according to God's will. Then the children of God will be at peace with one another if they chose to let God rule over all of them. "Salt is good: but if the salt have lost his saltness, wherewith will ye season it? Have salt in yourselves, and have peace one with another" (Mark 9:50, KJV).

When Jesus was preparing the disciples to live in the world without his physical presence, he told them that he was leaving his peace with them. He specifically said that his peace was not the same as the world's peace. "Peace I leave with you, my peace I give unto you: not as the world giveth, give I unto you. Let not your heart be troubled, neither let it be afraid" (John 14:27, KJV).

Jesus warned the disciples about the things that would happen in the future so that they would not be afraid. He wanted them to feel his peace as they trusted in God. The world would abuse and hurt them. They were to remember that he had overcome Satan and death. They would be cheered and have peace if they remembered that God knew what was going to happen and that the world had no power over their eternal lives with God. "These things I have spoken unto you, that in me ye might have peace. In the world ye shall have tribulation: but be of good cheer: I have overcome the world" (John 16: 33 KJV).

Scripture proclaimed that those Christians who brought the message of peace to others were made beautiful in God's eyes. The message of peace was the message that God had made peace with men, and salvation was given freely by God because Jesus had paid for our sins. "And how shall they preach, except they be sent? As it is written: How beautiful are the feet of them that preach the gospel of peace, and bring glad tidings of good things" (Romans 10: 15, KJV).

Christians are admonished to gather up their strength and move steadily forward to bring others the good news about salvation through Jesus Christ. If the Christians are faltering (growing tired and weak), they should ask God for strength to proceed. Christians are to carry the message of peace in Jesus and lead other people into God's holiness because no one can see (understand, perceive) God without being given the spiritual rebirth we receive from Jesus.

> Wherefore lift up (strengthen) the hands which hang down, and the feeble knees;
> And make straight paths for your feet, lest that which is lame be turned out of the way; but let it rather be healed.
> Follow peace with all men, and holiness, without which no man shall see the Lord.
>
> Hebrews 12:12–14 (KJV)

Paul wrote that the Gentiles were drawn into the family of God when Jesus Christ died as a sacrifice for all men's sins. Jesus brought peace not only between God and men; he brought peace between the Jews (God's chosen people) and the Gentiles who now became part of God's family of chosen people. Jesus had destroyed the hatred between Jews and Gentiles by fulfilling the commandments of the Mosaic Law in himself. By dying on the cross, Jesus had removed the hatred and division between the Jews and the Gentiles who trusted in Jesus. Through Jesus's sacrifice, both Jews and Gentiles now have access (are free to go) to God the Father believing that they will be accepted by God the Father.

> But now in Christ Jesus ye who sometimes were far off are made nigh by the blood of Christ.
> For he is our peace, who hath made both one, and hath broken down the middle wall of partition between us;

Having abolished in his flesh the enmity, even the law of commandments contained ordinances; for to make in himself of twain one new man, so making peace;

And that he may reconcile both unto God in one body by the cross, having slain the enmity thereby.

And came and preached peace to you which were afar off, and to them that were nigh.

For through him we both have access by one Spirit unto the Father.

Now therefore ye are no more strangers and foreigners, but fellow citizens with the saints, and of the household of God.

Ephesians 2:13–19 (kjv)

Paul told the Romans that the kingdom of God wasn't based upon physical existence like obtaining food. The kingdom of God requires people to seek after righteousness (right standing with God), peace, and joy obtained through the Holy Spirit. If a person serves Jesus Christ, he/she strives to have righteousness, peace, and joy. Then that person's life will be acceptable to God and admired by other people. Therefore it is necessary that all Christians become peacemakers and do things which will help to strengthen the faith of other Christians.

For the kingdom of God is not meat and drink; but righteousness, and peace, and joy in the Holy Ghost.

For he that in these things serveth Christ is acceptable to God, and approved of men.

Let us therefore follow after the things which make for peace, and things wherewith one may edify (build up) another.

Romans 14:17–19 (kjv)

If people are envious and argumentative, there is confusion, and people do not do God's will. Truth that comes from God is pure, peaceable, gentle, easy to accommodate, forgiving, and

MARSHA MATTOX-LEDWIG

diligent in doing good works. God's truth does not inspire people to show favoritism and be hypocrites. Actions that come from a person who is righteous create peace (peacemakers) for the peacemaker and others.

> For where envying and strife is, there is confusion and every evil work.
> But the wisdom that is from above is first pure, then peaceable, gentle, and easy to be entreated, full of mercy and good fruits, without partiality, and without hypocrisy.
> And the fruit of righteousness is sown in peace of them that make peace.
>
> James 3:18–18 (KJV)

Early Christians were admonished to not worry about anything. They were to pray for what they needed and give thanks to God for what they received. Then God's peace, the peace which they could not understand completely, would be in their hearts and minds to comfort them. If Christians trust God to take care of them, then their hearts and minds are not troubled; they have peace. "Be careful for nothing; but in everything by prayer and supplication with thanksgiving let your requests be made known unto God. And the peace of God, which passeth all understanding, shall keep your hearts and minds through Christ Jesus." (Philipians 4:6–7, KJV).

God chose us before the world was created so that we would be made holy and without blame for sin in Jesus Christ His Son. God predestinated (decided and created us specifically before he gave us life) to become his adopted spiritual children. Because God can see everything in the past and future he would have known who would accept Jesus as their savior. God caused us to become his children by giving us salvation through Jesus Christ. God willed that we would become his adopted children.

84

According as he hath chosen us in him before the foundation of the world, that we should be holy and without blame before him in love:

Having predestinated us unto the adoption of children by Jesus Christ to himself, according to the good pleasure of his will.

Ephesians 1:4–5 (KJV)

All Christians who are led by the Holy Spirit of God become the children of God. No Christian led by the Holy Spirit will accept enslavement to the fear of death from the devil. All Christians have been taught personally and individually by God's Holy Spirit that they are God the Father's children. The Holy Spirit tells us that we are God's spiritual children.

For as many as are led by the Spirit of God, they are the sons of God.

For ye have not received the spirit of bondage again to fear; but ye have received the Spirit of adoption, whereby we cry, Abba, Father.

The Spirit itself beareth witness with our spirit, that we are the children of God.

Romans 8:14–16 (KJV)

Jesus said, "Blessed are the peacemakers: for they will be called the children of God." It was always God's plan that we would be his spiritual children. It was always God's plan that his children would live in perfect peace. We have to choose to receive salvation through Jesus Christ so that we can become God's spiritual children. He wants us to choose to obey his word and believe his truth. He wants us to choose to do his will; he will not take away our free will.

God's words in the Old Testament prepared us to receive salvation from our sins through God's own son, Jesus Christ. We receive eternal life because we share his only begotten son's eternal life. Jesus was and is God's first peacemaker. He was and is

God's only begotten child. Jesus made peace between God and men. Jesus made peace between the Jews and the Gentiles. Jesus enables all Christians to live in peace with one another if we are all one with Jesus.

When Jesus said that the peacemakers would be God's children, he meant that all Christians will become peacemakers as we share Jesus's life. God wants us to make peace between God and men. God wants us to bring peace between all of his children. Jesus meant that all Christians will become God's children as we share the life of his only begotten son. We share Jesus's peace when we learn to believe and trust God completely.

BLESSED ARE THEY WHICH ARE PERSECUTED FOR RIGHTEOUSNESS SAKE

Blessed are they which are persecuted for righteousness'
sake: for their's is the kingdom of heaven.

Blessed are ye, when men shall revile you, and persecute you, and shall say all manner of evil against you
falsely, for my sake.

Rejoice, and be exceeding glad for great is your reward
in heaven: for so persecuted they the prophets which were
before you.

Matthew 5:10–12 (KJV)

W E MUST REMEMBER that we have no righteousness of our
own. Only God is truly righteous. In Matthew 5:10, Jesus is

speaking about those will be persecuted for righteousness sake. In Matthew 5:11, he is speaking about those who are persecuted for His sake. Both verses are meant to teach us about the same concept. That means that those who suffer persecution for Jesus's sake (He is our righteousness.) will be blessed and rewarded in heaven. When we testify about Jesus and his salvation and God's redeeming love, we will be persecuted because we will be revealing Jesus's message to the world. As we live out our lives in union with him obeying his directives, Jesus will be revealed to others through us. This does not mean that we can do whatever we want to do. When we reveal Christ to the world through words or actions, we will be rewarded in heaven. When people tell lies about us, we will be rewarded in heaven if we are serving Christ and the words that they speak about us are false. This does not say that every Christian who is having a disagreement with someone else is going to be rewarded. We will be rewarded if we are revealing Jesus and God's love.

Those who will be rewarded in heaven are those who will give God's message to those who are not saved by belief in Jesus Christ. The prophets of the Old Testament delivered God's words to God's people. They were rewarded for their service to God. Those who carry Jesus's message to others will be rewarded because they have obediently obeyed God.

Jesus admonished us to love our enemies. We are to bless (invoke divine care) people who curse us. Do good things for people who hate you. Pray for people who despitefully (with mean, cruel intentions) use (do things to injure, hurt) you. Pray for people who persecute (harass to injure or grieve, cause to suffer for a religious belief, annoy with persistent attacks) you.

Do these things (bless, serve, pray) for people who try to hurt you because God, your Heavenly Father, blesses and provides for them. He makes the sun rise for the evil and the righteous. He sends rain for the evil man and the righteous man. What good is it if you love people who love you? Publicans do that. What good is it if you salute (respect) only your family and friends? People who are not Christians do that. You are to be perfect because your Heavenly Father is perfect. You should treat everyone the same. Your actions should be determined by your Heavenly Father; you should not live and make choices because other people have controlled you with their actions.

> But I say unto you, Love your enemies, bless them that curse you, do good to them that hate you, and pray for them which despitefully use you, and persecute you.
>
> That ye may be the children of your Father which is in heaven: for he maketh his sun to rise on the evil and on the good, and sendeth rain on the just, and on the unjust.
>
> For if ye love them which love you, what reward have ye? Do not even the publicans the same?
>
> And if ye salute your brethren only, what do ye more than others? Do not even the publicans so?
>
> Be ye therefore perfect, even as your Father which is in heaven is perfect.
>
> Matthew 5:44–48 (KJV)

When Jesus taught us to pray, he acknowledged that God the Father will deliver us from evil. It is God whose will is supreme and unchallenged in heaven. It is God who has all power and glory. Jesus did not pray that God the Father would help us to wage war against and punish those who trespass against us. "And lead us not into temptation, but deliver us from evil: For thine is the kingdom, and the power, and the glory, forever, Amen" (Matthew 6: 13 KJV).

Jesus warned you to be careful to take care of yourselves. He said people will take you to make charges against you in front of councils. You will be beaten in the synagogues (churches). You will be taken to stand and speak to rulers and kings to proclaim my name and salvation. This must happen so that they have a chance to accept me as their savior and believe God about who I am. The good news about salvation through Jesus Christ must be made known (taught) in every nation (country).

When they lead you before councils, and kings, and rulers, don't worry before it happens about what you will say. Don't try to plan a speech. The Holy Spirit will give you the words to speak so that it will be Him who is speaking.

Brothers will accuse their brothers so that they will be sentenced to death. Fathers will accuse their sons. And children will betray (accuse to authorities) their parents so that the parents are killed. You will be hated by all men because you go in my name. But the ones of you who refuse to deny that I am God's Son and that I give salvation to all people, will be saved and given eternal life.

> But take heed to yourselves: for they shall deliver you up to councils; and in the synagogues ye shall be beaten: and ye shall be brought before rulers and kings for my sake, for a testimony against them.
>
> And the gospel must first be published among all nations.
>
> But when they shall lead you, and deliver you up, take no thought beforehand what ye shall speak, neither do ye premeditate: but whatsoever shall be given you in that hour, that speak ye: for it is not ye that speak, but the Holy Ghost.
>
> Now the brother will betray the brother to death, and the father the son; and children shall rise up against their parents, and shall cause them to be put to death.
>
> And ye shall be hated of all men for my name's sake: but he that shall endure unto the end, the same shall be saved.
>
> Mark 13:9–13 (KJV)

You are blessed by God when men hate you because you proclaim my word. You are blessed when they no longer allow you to associate with them. People will reproach (blame) you and say that you are evil because you speak for Jesus and declare the good news about salvation in Jesus. You should be joyous (filled with happiness) when those things happen to you. You will have a great reward in heaven for your faithfulness to Jesus. The people will persecute you as their forefathers persecuted God's prophets in the Old Testament.

> Blessed are ye, when men shall hate you, and when they shall separate you from their company, and shall reproach you, and cast out your name as evil, for the Son of man's sake.
>
> Rejoice ye in that day, and leap for joy: for, behold, your reward is great in heaven: for in the like manner did their fathers unto the prophets.
>
> Luke 6:22–23 (KJV)

You are in trouble when everyone speaks well of you and likes you. In the past the ancestors of those people praised and followed the false prophets (those people who gave false teachings about God). You should love your enemies, and you should do good deeds for people who hate you. If you love your enemies, do good (help people who try to hurt you), and lend money to people who will not pay you back, you will have a great reward. You will be the children of God the Father because He is kind to those people who are unthankful and to those who do evil things. "Woe unto you, when all men shall speak well of you! For so did their fathers to the false prophets. But I say unto you which hear, Love your enemies, do good to them which hate you." (Luke 6: 26—27 KJV) "But love ye your enemies, and do good, and lend, hoping for nothing again; and your reward shall be great, and ye shall be the children of the Highest: for he is kind unto the unthankful and to the evil" (Luke 6:35, KJV).

Before the end of the world and before Jesus returns, people will take you prisoner, and persecute you. They will take you before the leaders of the synagogues (churches). They will take you into prisons before they take you in front of rulers and kings because you speak God's truth and proclaim that I am God's Son. These occasions will be a testimony (witness) that you are my faithful servants, and they will be a testimony (witness) to the truth of who I am.

Settle it in your hearts that I will give you the words that I want you to say when you are arrested and brought to speak. I will give you the words and the wisdom to speak so that the accusers will not be able to argue against you or prove that you are wrong. You will be accused so that you can be arrested by your family members and friends. Some of you will be killed. Everyone will hate you because you speak in my name (Christians) and proclaim that I am God's Son. They will hate you because you teach the good news that I will give eternal life to everyone who trusts in me. They can in no way injure your spirit; by patiently and obediently refusing to say that Jesus is not God's Son, you will insure that you have eternal life in heaven as a living soul.

> But before all these, they shall lay their hands on you, and persecute you, delivering you up to the synagogues, and into prisons, being brought before kings and rulers for my name's sake.
>
> And it shall turn to you for a testimony.
>
> Settle it therefore in your hearts, not to meditate before what ye shall answer:
>
> For I will give you a mouth and wisdom, which all your adversaries shall not be able to gainsay nor resist.
>
> And ye shall be betrayed both by parents, and brethren, and kinsfolks, and friends; and some of you shall they cause to be put to death.
>
> And ye shall be hated of all men for my name's sake.
>
> But there shall not an hair of your head perish.
>
> In your patience possess ye your souls.
>
> Luke 21:12–19 (KJV)

When Paul and Barnabus had preached the good news of salvation through Jesus Christ in that city, they went back to Lystra, Iconium, and Antioch. In each place they taught the new Christians to continue to guard their souls from evil and to continue believing in Jesus and his salvation. They taught the followers that Jesus's disciples must endure tribulation so that they can enter into the kingdom of God. We enter heaven by passing through tribulation.

> And when they had preached the gospel to that city, and had taught many, they returned again to Lystra, and to Iconium, and Antioch.
> Confirming the souls of the disciples, and exhorting them to continue in the faith, and that we must through much tribulation enter into the kingdom of God.
>
> Acts 14:21–22 (KJV)

If we are God's children (heirs) with Christ who is God's only begotten son, we should suffer with Jesus so that we can be glorified with Jesus. "And if children, then heirs; heirs of God, and joint-heirs with Christ; if so be that we suffer with him, that we may be also glorified together" (Romans 8:17, KJV).

Who can separate us from Jesus Christ's love? What can take Jesus's love away from us? Can tribulation (hardship) or distress (fear, concern) or persecution or famine (hunger) or nakedness (poverty and want) or danger or war take Jesus's love from us? No, no matter what happens to us, we will not be defeated because we will survive in union with Jesus. Paul was sure that not death, not life, not angels, not spiritual beings, not power held by others, not things happening in the present, or things that would happen in the future could take away or lessen Jesus's love for us. Height or depth or any other created animal or being can not separate us from the love of God which is expressed to us through Jesus Christ.

Who shall separate us from the love of Christ? Shall tribulation, or distress, or persecution, or famine, or nakedness, or peril, or sword?

Nay, in all things we are more than conquerors through him that loved us.

For I am persuaded, that neither death, nor life, nor angels, nor principalities, nor powers, nor things present, nor things to come,

Nor height, nor depth, nor any other creature, shall be able to separate us from the love of God, which is in Christ Jesus of Lord.

Romans 8:35–39 (KJV)

Paul taught that as Christians we are attacked from various groups, but we are not distressed because we know that Jesus is with us. We are puzzled because we do not always understand what God is doing, but we are not filled with despair because he has warned us that these things will happen. We are persecuted by other people, but we are not abandoned by God because He gives us the wisdom and words to speak in Jesus's defense. As Christians we are knocked down from the attacks, but we are never defeated or destroyed. " We are troubled on every side, yet not distressed; we are perplexed (puzzled) but not in despair; Persecuted, but not forsaken; cast down, but not destroyed" (2nd Corinthians 4:8–9, KJV).

Paul said that he asked Jesus three times for his eyes to be healed. Jesus told Paul that Jesus's grace was sufficient (enough) for Paul. Jesus's strength is made more perfect (apparent, intensified), in weaker Christians. Even though Paul had prayed for many other people to be healed, Jesus refused to heal Paul. Jesus wanted Paul to depend upon Jesus for strength rather than upon Paul's own abilities.

Paul was then pleased with his weakness, so that Jesus's strength would be shown in Paul. Paul rejoiced that he endured illness, discredit and blame, poverty, persecution, and distress (anxiety, anxiousness) because he did it for Jesus. Paul felt that way because Paul knew that when he could not cope, go on in his own strength, he would be strengthened by Jesus's power.

> For this thing I besought the Lord thrice, that it might depart from me.
> And he said unto me, My grace is sufficient for thee: for my strength is made perfect in weakness, Most gladly therefore will I rather glory in my infirmities, that the power of Christ may rest upon me.
> Therefore I take pleasure in infirmities, in reproaches, in necessities, in persecutions, in distresses for Christ's sake: for when I am weak, then I am strong.
>
> 2 Corinthians 12:8–10 (KJV)

James spoke to his brothers in Christ's family asking them if God didn't choose the poor to be given strong faith. Weren't the poor chosen to be heirs of God's kingdom that God has promised to those people who love God? "Hearken, my beloved brethren, Hath not God chosen the poor of this world rich in faith, and heirs of the kingdom which he hath promised to them that love him?" (James 2:5, KJV).

Everyone who lives a life sharing in Christ Jesus's life as God wills for us to do will suffer persecution. "Yea, and all that live godly in Christ Jesus shall suffer persecution" (2nd Timothy 3:12, KJV).

God will protect us from every evil act that is aimed at us, and God will save us so that we will enter his heavenly kingdom. All glory is God's for ever and ever. "And the Lord shall deliver me from every evil work, and will preserve me unto his heavenly kingdom: to whom be glory for ever and ever, Amen" (2nd Timothy 4:18, KJV).

The reward that God has prepared for those who deliver the message about Jesus Christ's righteousness and salvation through Him will be incorruptible (It can never be destroyed.) The inheritance we will receive as God's children will be pure with no taint of sin. Our inheritance will not fade away and grow old. It is an inheritance reserved for each one of us in heaven. "To an inheritance incorruptible, and undefiled, and that fadeth not away, reserved in heaven for you." (1st Peter 1:4, KJV).

If you suffer because you reveal the righteousness of Jesus, you will be happy. Do not be afraid of the terror (fear) that will be inflicted on you by men of the world. Do not be troubled (worried). Honor God in your heart, and be ready to answer anyone who asks you why you have the hope of eternal life within your heart. If you hope, you believe God ; you believe (trust) that you have a future eternal life. If you are questioned, you are to proclaim your belief in Jesus and your hope (trust) that God has given you a future eternal life in Jesus Christ. You will answer with meekness trusting that God will protect you. You will answer with fear, respect for God, and not with fear of men or evil.

You will have a clean conscience knowing that no matter whatever evil of which they may accuse you, you are innocent. You will know that those who accuse you will be shamed when their false accusations are revealed. You will know that you spoke the truth about Jesus Christ. It is better, if it is God's will, for you to suffer for speaking the truth and doing good things than it would be to suffer for doing evil things. It is not God's will that you would suffer for doing evil things.

> But and if ye suffer for righteousness' sake happy are ye: and be not afraid of their terro neither be troubled (worried);
>
> But sanctify the Lord God in your hearts: and be ready always to give an answer to every man that asketh you a reason of the hope that is in you with meekness and fear:
>
> Having a good conscience; that, whereas they speak evil of you, as of evildoers, they may be ashamed that falsely accuse your good conversation in Christ.
>
> For it is better, if the will of God be so, that ye suffer for well doing, than for evil doing.
>
> 1st Peter 3:14–17 (KJV)

This is written to those who are loved by God. Don't think that it is strange that God would allow you to go through the terrible trial (experience) that will test your faith. Do not be afraid that a mistake has been made. God knew about the persecution that you will have to endure. You should be filled with joy because you are sharing Jesus Christ's suffering. If you are one with Jesus and share his suffering, you will be filled with joy when Jesus's glory if shown.

If you are scorned because you uphold the name of Jesus (You refuse to discredit Jesus.), you should be happy. This scorning is a sign that the Holy Spirit is with you. The people who persecute you speak evil (false statements) about God, but you glorify God.

None of you should suffer for being a murderer, or a thief, or someone who does evil things, or a meddler (Someone who stirs up problems for others). If someone suffers because they are a Christian, that person should not be ashamed. That person has glorified God.

It is time for God to judge His people. If God begins His judgment with his own people, then what will happen to those people who do not obey God's word when they are judged? If those who have been saved from eternal death by Jesus Christ's righteousness are judged, then what will the judgment be for those who do not obey God and sin against Him? So if it is God's will that you must suffer, commit (trust) your souls to his keeping by doing good works. He is eternally faithful to care for us; he created us out of love.

> Beloved, think it not strange concerning the fiery trial which is to try you, as though some strange thing happened unto you.
>
> But rejoice, inasmuch as ye are partakers of Christ's sufferings; that, when his glory shall be revealed, ye may be glad also with exceeding joy.
>
> If ye be reproached for the name of Christ, happy are ye; for the spirit of glory and of God resteth upon you:

on their part he is evil spoken of, but on your part he is glorified.

But let none of you suffer as a murderer, or as a thief, or as an evil-doer, or as a busybody (meddler) in other men's matters.

Yet if any man suffer as a Christian, let him not be ashamed; but let him glorify God on this behalf.

For the time is come that judgment must begin at the house of God: and if it first begin at us, what shall the end be of them that obey not the gospel of God?

And if the righteous scarcely be save where shall, the ungodly and the sinner appear?

Wherefore let them that suffer according to the will of God commit the keeping of their souls to him in well doing, as unto a faithful Creator.

1st Peter 4:12–19 (KJV)

The person who endures persecution because he lives and proclaims that Jesus is God's Son and that God has given eternal life to everyone who believes God's promise, will inherit the Kingdom of God. The person who overcomes suffering and fear of death because that person believes (trusts) God, will be given all of what God has promised us. The person who endures temptation and stays faithful to Jesus even though he or she is persecuted will live in the Kingdom of God where everything is done according to God's will. We have God's promise that if we hold fast to our faith in Jesus, God will be our God, and we will be His children. "He that overcometh shall inherit all things; and I will be his God, and he shall be my son" (Revelation 21:7, KJV).

YOU ARE THE SALT AND LIGHT OF THE WORLD

Ye are the salt of the earth: but if the salt have lost his savour, wherewith shall it be salted? It is thenceforth good for nothing, but to be cast out, and to be trodden under foot of men.

Ye are the light of the world. A city that is set on an hill cannot be hid.

Neither do men light a candle and put it under a bushel, but on a candlestick; and it giveth light unto all that are in the house.

Let your light so shine before men, that they may see your good works, and glorify your Father which is in heaven.

Matthew 5:13–16 (KJV)

As JESUS TAUGHT the multitude when he sat upon the mountain, he was giving them the instructions about how they should live their lives. Most of the followers he spoke to were Jews so they were familiar with the Old Testament. A Jewish person living in Jesus's time would have known what he meant in his references to salt.

When God gave Moses the instructions for the priests to use when they offered sacrifices in the tabernacle, God specified that every meat offering should be seasoned with salt. "And every oblation of thy meat offering shalt thou season with salt; neither shalt thou suffer the salt of the covenant of thy God to be lacking from thy meat offering: with all thine offerings thou shalt offer salt" (Leviticus 2:13, KJV).

After the Jews were taken captive, they were taken into Babylon. When Cyrus became king of Babylon, he commanded that a new temple dedicated to the God of Heaven and Earth was to be built in Jerusalem. The golden and silver vessels of the house of God which were taken by Nebuchadnezar to Babylon were to be returned to the temple in Jerusalem. Cyrus also ordered that the elders of the Jews were to be provided with all that they needed to offer sacrifices to their God. It was ordered that in addition to the animal sacrifices that the priests needed they were to be provided with wheat, salt, wine, and oil for use as sacrifices to the God of Heaven. "And that which they have need of, both young bullocks, and rams, and lambs, for the burnt offerings of the God of heaven, wheat, salt, wine, and oil, according to the appointment of the priests which are in Jerusalem, let it be given them day by day without fail" (Ezra 6:9, KJV).

Ezekiel was given instructions by God in a vision concerning the procedure that the priests of the Jews were to make in offerings to God. After the altar had been cleansed, they were to offer on the alter a young bullock without blemish, and a ram out of the flock without blemish. These were to be offered to God; the priests were to throw salt on the sacrifices as they burnt them on the altar. "And thou shalt offer them before the Lord, and the priests shall cast salt upon them, and they shall offer them up for a burnt offering unto the Lord" (Ezekiel 43:24, kjv).

God's chosen people, the Jews, would have been very much aware that any burnt meat offering prepared and dedicated to God must be seasoned with salt. Without the salt designated by God, the offering would not be pleasing to God.

Elisha, a prophet of the Lord, was begged by the men of Jericho to cleanse the water of that place. They wanted to stay in that location where their city was built, but they could not use the water. The land there was barren (would not grow crops). Elisha told them to bring him a new bowl and to fill the bowl with salt. He went to the spring of water and threw the salt into the water. The water was purified. From that time on the water no longer caused death, and the land would grow crops. It was the salt that God used to purify the water. After the salt purified the water, the land was fruitful. The new bowl was the new covenant that God made with men through Jesus Christ. After Jesus sent forth his message of salvation and eternal life, the people were purified (cleansed of their sins) and became eternally alive. The water in the New Testament came from the followers of Jesus who spread his word to the people of the world so that they were no longer dead in their sins. The water of life, Jesus, healed (cleansed) the people and gave them life as the water gave life to the barren land. The Spirit of God was the salt that was necessary to give life.

> And he said, Bring me a new cruse, and put salt therein. And they brought it to him.
>
> And he went forth unto the spring of the waters, and cast the salt in there, and said,
>
> Thus saith the Lord, I have healed these waters; there shall not be from them any more death or barren land.
>
> 2 Kings 2:20–21 (kjv)

In the ninth chapter of Mark, Jesus was talking to the people about obtaining entry into the kingdom of heaven. He taught that whatever there was in a follower's life that prevented him/her from pleasing God should be sacrificed. Every follower must be purified. Every Christian must give up the values and actions of the world. Our lives must be purified through the work of the Holy Spirit. All of the sacrifices we make to give up the world's influence upon us must be sacrificed with humility and obedience to God. Every sacrifice we make to giving up gratification of our selfish desires must be salted with the spiritual union (new life) we now share with Jesus. Our sacrifices must be purified with our repentance and the constant infusion of Jesus's life being manifested in us. If we are being taught by the Holy Spirit, and we are living in unison with Jesus, our lives will retain their saltiness. We will have salt in ourselves. If each one of us is being influenced by the Holy Spirit, and we are living our lives as branches to the vine that is Jesus, we will have peace with one another as we dwell in God's love.

WHERE THEIR WORM DIETH NOT, AND THE FIRE IS NOT QUENCHED.
For everyone shall be salted with fire, and every sacrifice shall be salted with salt.
Salt is good: but if the salt have lost his saltness, wherewith will ye season it? Have salt in yourselves, and have peace one with another.

Mark 9:48–50 (KJV)

Jesus did not depend upon his position in the world or his possessions. We cannot share the values and beliefs of the world (our culture). A true disciple of Jesus must give up his own plans for the future and the security of depending on worldly wealth and possessions. Many of Jesus's disciples have given up their physical lives. The true Christian must follow the leading of the Holy Spirit without question. So long as we try to be faithful to the wisdom and rules of mankind and to be obedient to God's will too, we will be torn between two value systems. God cannot and will not change. If we are to share our lives with him, we must change and adhere only to God's will. It is not likely that we as Christians will give all that we have to the church and live with only the elders' provision. That means that we must be even more constantly aware of setting God first in our lives. Jesus is revealed to the world through our lives and what other people can see of Jesus through our words and actions. If our lives do not bear fruit and enable others to see Jesus though us, we are of no use. We will have lost our saltiness. Our spiritual rebirth and our union with Jesus is what makes us acceptable to God the Father. We cannot serve two masters. We can listen to the world's invitations and serve the master of the world, Satan. Or we can listen to and obey our Heavenly Father, His Only Begotten Son, and the Holy Spirit. We can choose daily to serve the King of Heaven and Earth.

> So likewise, whosoever he be of you that forsaketh not all that he hath, he cannot be my disciple.
> Salt is good: but if the salt have lost his savour, wherewith shall it be seasoned?
> It is neither fit for the land, nor yet for the dunghill; but men cast it out. He that hath cars to hear, let him hear.
>
> Luke 14:33–35 (KJV)

Paul tells us to be constantly praying. This does not necessarily mean that we should ask God for the same thing over and over again. Paul means that we should be constantly conscious of God in our daily lives. We should be communicating with God as we need help in our daily lives and seeking His guidance as we make decisions. We should also be thankful for the blessings and peace and deliverance that God gives on a daily basis. Paul asked the members of the church to ask God to make opportunities for Paul to speak about the mystery of Christ who is our salvation and eternal life. He asked for prayers so that he would be led by the Holy Spirit to speak plainly to those who need Jesus in their lives. The Holy Spirit always knows what the other person will understand or needs to hear. If we let the Holy Spirit speak through us, we can truly serve Jesus as his messengers. Paul said to interact wisely with those who do not know Jesus; make yourself available to speak the words that Jesus and the Holy Spirit will for you to speak so that your opportunities to serve Jesus will not be wasted. We do not have grace in ourselves. God in His grace has given us salvation and spiritual life as a free gift. So if we are to speak to others with grace, we must speak freely of God's grace offering others the free gift of salvation that we have received. Our words, the things we say to others, should always be seasoned with salt. We must remember that our words are empty if they are not salted with the wisdom of the Holy Spirit.

> Continue in prayer, and watch in the same with thanksgiving. Withal praying also for us, that God would open unto us a door of utterance, to speak the mystery of Christ, for which I am also in bonds:
> That I may make it manifest (plain), as I ought to speak.
> Walk in wisdom toward them that are without, redeeming the time.
> Let your speech be always with grace, seasoned with salt, that ye may know how ye ought to answer every man.
>
> Colossians 4:2–6 (KJV)

In Matthew 5:13, Jesus told us a great deal about the Christian walk that will please God the Father. Any sacrifice that we might make in our lives must be seasoned with the salt of the Holy Spirit's guidance. Jesus was always guided by God the Father's will and the assistance of the Holy Spirit. We are what the world is able to see of Jesus Christ. Our words and our actions are the means that God has chosen to reveal God's salvation to the people of the world. If our words and actions are tainted by the world, then we will not reveal the true Word of God that is Jesus. Jesus is the Water of Life that will cleanse away sin and give life. Our words must be purified by the influence and wisdom of the Holy Spirit, the salt that purifies us. If the words and the actions that a Christian reveals to the world are not cleansed by the spiritual presence and influence of Jesus and the Holy Spirit, they have become salt that has lost its savor. Salt that has lost its savor is worthless.

Jesus told the disciples to wait until the Holy Spirit had come to lead them.

If our words to others are to be effective, they must be salted with spiritual confirmation in the listener's heart from the Holy Spirit.

Jesus goes on in Matthew 5:14 to admonish us to be the light of the world.

> Ye are the light of the world. A city that is set on a hill cannot be hid.
>
> Neither do men light a candle, and put it under a bushel, but on a candlestick; and it giveth light unto all that are in the house.
>
> Let your light so shine before men, that they may see your good works, and glorify your Father which is in heaven.
>
> Matthew 5:14–16 (KJV)

King David wrote that the Lord (God) was David's light and his salvation. David asked if God was his strength and salvation, of whom should he be afraid. Jesus lights our way (reveals) and leads us to God the Father's truth. The truth is that Jesus has paid for our sins and given us eternal life with Jesus. If God himself has provided us with salvation, is there anyone we should fear? "The Lord is my light and my salvation; whom shall I fear? The Lord is the strength of my life; of whom shall I be afraid?" (Psalm 27:1, KJV).

In Isaiah 49:6, God was speaking of Jesus as his servant. Jesus raised up the Jews (brought back the tribes of Jacob) and led them back to God; he restored those Jews who would believe on Jesus for their salvation as God's chosen people. God said that he had provided Jesus to reveal to the Gentiles God's plan of salvation so that all peoples could receive salvation through Jesus Christ. "And he said, It is a light thing that thou shouldest be my servant to raise up the tribes of Jacob, and to restore the preserved of Israel: I will also give thee for a light to the Gentiles, that thou mayest be my salvation unto the end of the earth" (Isaiah 49:6, KJV).

In the eternal kingdom of God, the sun and the moon will not provide our light. God will be our everlasting light. He will reveal His truth to us with his own eternal light.

> The sun shall be no more thy light by day; neither for brightness shall the moon give light unto thee: but the Lord shall be unto thee an everlasting light, and thy God thy glory.
>
> Thy sun shall no more go down; neither shall thy moon withdraw itself: for the Lord shall be thine everlasting light, and the days of thy mourning shall be ended.
>
> Isaiah 60:19–20 (KJV)

Jesus took Peter, James, and John up on a high mountain with him. On the mountain Jesus was changed in appearance so that they could see the true radiant light and life that he is. They were allowed to see physical evidence of Jesus's identity as the Light of Life, God's own Son. On the mountain Jesus spoke with Moses and Elias, the two servants of God. God spoke to the disciples telling them that Jesus was God's Son and that God was very pleased with Jesus. When Jesus and his three disciples came down from the mountain, he told them not to tell anyone of the vision they had seen until after Jesus had risen from the dead. "And after six days Jesus taketh Peter, James, and John his brother, and bringeth them up into an high mountain apart, And was transfigured (changed) before them: and his face did shine as the sun, and his rainment was white as the light" (Matthew 17:1–2, KJV).

John, Peter, and James had witnessed the transfiguration of Jesus on the mountain. They had witnessed the great light that is Jesus. Because they were with Jesus constantly, they knew more from personal knowledge about who Jesus truly was and why he came to live in a physical form. In the book of John, we see a better perspective of Jesus as a spiritual being. John realized that all life was created through the power of Jesus as God's Word. John knew that as God's Light Jesus was sent by God the Father to show mankind about who God the Father is and to reveal the plan of salvation that God the Father had created for mankind. John reminded the followers of Jesus that God the Father had sent John the Baptist to testify that Jesus was the true Light of God. The disciple John knew that Jesus was the only true Light of God; it is only through Jesus that any man or woman can see (understand) who God is.

> In him was life; and the life was the light of men.
> And the light shineth in darkness; and the darkness comprehended it not.
> There was a man sent from God, whose name was John.
> The same came for a witness, to bear witness of the Light, that all men through him might believe.
> He was not that Light, but was sent to bear witness of that Light,
> That was the true Light, which lighteth every man that cometh into the world.
>
> John 1:4–9 (KJV)

Jesus said that men were condemned (judged to be guilty of sin and sentenced to death) because God sent Jesus, God's Son and God's Light into the world to reveal God to mankind. Men were condemned because they did not want to see God's truth.

Men wanted to continue to disobey God and try to be gods themselves. Those men chose to believe the devil's lies instead of God's truth. Jesus had revealed God to mankind; Jesus is God's Light. Men chose to stay in darkness (ignorance about God) so that they could continue to sin. "And this is the condemnation that light is come into the world, and men loved darkness rather than light, because their deeds were evil" (John 3:19, KJV).

Jesus said that He was God's Light sent into the world so that men could see (accept) who God is. Even though God's truth had been revealed to men through Jesus, some men still walked in darkness (ignorance about God). All men could see (understand) God through Jesus; Jesus is the light that destroys the darkness (death) and reveals God to all men. Anyone who chooses to see God through the revelation (light) that Jesus is will have light (life with God) eternally. "Then spake Jesus again unto them, saying, I am the light of the world: he that followeth me shall not walk in darkness, but shall have the light of life" (John 8:12, KJV).

As long as Jesus remained in a physical body in the world, he was the light; he was the revelation of God. "As long as I am in the world, I am the light of the world" (John 9:5, KJV).

Jesus explained to the followers that he, the light, the revelation of God would not always be available for them to find God through him. The followers should use Jesus, who revealed God to them, as a means of finding God. When Jesus was gone, they would be left in darkness (ignorance of God), and would not know how to find a relationship with the true God. While Jesus was with them in a physical form, they needed to believe that Jesus was a revelation from God. If they believed that God sent Jesus to show them the way to God and trusted Jesus to save them from their sins, they would become the children of light. They could become God's children and share the eternal life and light of Jesus. After Jesus had warned the people to act quickly so that they could be saved, he went away, and they could not find him.

Then Jesus said unto them, Yet a little while is the light with you. Walk while ye have the light, lest darkness come upon you: for he that walketh in darkness knoweth not whither he goeth.

While ye have light, believe in the light, that ye may be the children of light. These things spake Jesus, and departed, and did hide himself from them.

John 12:35–36 (KJV)

After Jesus had risen from the dead and gone back to heaven to be with God the Father, he spoke to Paul on the road to Damascus. Paul came from a prominent Jewish family who also had Roman citizenship. He was a member of the group of Jewish leaders who wanted to destroy the teachings of Jesus and to destroy all those believers who taught about Jesus.

As a zealous leader of the Jewish elite who wanted to eliminate the Christians, Saul was traveling to Damascus to lead others in killing new Christians. Suddenly he was surrounded by a brilliant light, and Saul fell to the ground. Saul heard a voice calling his name and asking him why he was persecuting him. Saul asked the voice who he was. The voice replied that he was Jesus, the person that Saul persecuted. Note that Jesus said that anyone who persecuted the new Christians was persecuting Jesus himself because he was one with them. Saul was blinded by the great intense light. We should note that again Jesus identified himself as the Light of God. "And as he journeyed, he came near Damascus: and suddenly there shined round about him a light from heaven. And he fell to the earth, and heard a voice saying unto him, Saul, why persecutes thou me?" (Acts 9:3–4, KJV).

Paul teaches in Ephesians that before we were Christians we were darkness. He doesn't say we walked in darkness. Those who are not Christians are a part of the darkness. They are a part of the ignorance and rebellion against God. They are spiritually dead. When we accept Jesus as our Savior and are born again, we become part of the light. We have become one with Jesus; he is the light, the revelation of God the Father. In union with Jesus we become part of the revelation of God the Father. We are the children of God the Father. We are children of the Light.

" For ye were sometimes darkness, but now are ye light in the Lord: walk as children of light" (Ephesians 5:8, KJV).

As Christians we should lead blameless lives causing harm to no one. We are the children of God. We should live lives that no one can criticize even though we live surrounded by godlessness and evil. This evil being manifest in the world around us is the darkness. As Christians we should show the Light of Jesus. We are the lamps God has set in the darkness of a sinful world to reveal God in the world as the Light that is Jesus Christ lives within us. We are God's lanterns. We can only reveal the Light that is Jesus if our lives show that He is dwelling within us. Jesus is God's Holy Word; he is the Word of Life. Jesus lives through us to reveal God to the world. We are God's messengers: we carry God's message of salvation to the world around us.

> That ye may be blameless and harmless, the sons of God, without rebuke, in the midst of a crooked and perverse nation, among whom ye shine as lights in the world;
>
> Holding forth the word of life, that I may rejoice in the Day of Christ, that I have not run in vain, neither labored in vain.
>
> Philippians 2:15–16 (KJV)

The message we have received from Jesus is that God is Light. There is no darkness or death in God. There are no hidden sins in God. There is no evil in God. All that God is and will be is revealed openly. Nothing is hidden.

If we say that we are living our lives in union with Jesus, and then we embrace the evil in the world, we lie. We must obey all of God's rules and instructions. We must reject all the temptations of the world. We must resist the temptation of our carnal natures. We must live the truth of God in order to reveal it to the people of the world. We can't just talk about God's love and forgiveness;

we must live it. We cannot reveal Jesus unless we allow Him to manifest himself through us.

If we live our lives showing the light of who God is, we will share the eternal love and life of our Lord Jesus. We will live in peace with other Christians because we are all living as one in Jesus. We will all be cleansed of sin by the blood of Jesus Christ, God's Son.

> This then is the message which we have heard of him, and declare unto you, that God is light, and in him is no darkness at all.
>
> If we say that we have fellowship with him, and walk in darkness, we lie, and do not the truth.
>
> But if we walk in the light, as he is in the light, we have fellowship one with another, and the blood of Jesus Christ his Son cleanseth us from all sin.
>
> 1st John 1:5–7 (KJV)

> And a new commandment I write unto you, which thing is true in him and in you: because the darkness is past, and the true light now shineth. He that saith that he is in the light, and hateth his brother is in darkness even until now. He that loveth his brother abideth in the light, and there is none occasion of stumbling in him.
>
> But he that hateth his brother is in darkness, and walketh in darkness (ignorance about God and spiritual death) and knoweth (realizes) not whither he goeth, because that blindness hath blinded his eyes.
>
> 1st John 2:8–11 (KJV)

Jesus told the people that he was the Light of the world. He said that a person who followed him would never walk in darkness (death). They would have the light that gives life. Jesus is life. In God there is no darkness (death or the absence of life). When man lived in sin, he could not see life. Man could not see that God is love. Sinful man could not see the truth of who God is.

Jesus is the Word of God sent by God to reveal to man that God is truth and love.

A person cannot say that he is living in the light and hate his brother. A person who hates his/her brother is in darkness. The person who loves his/her brother lives in the light. The person who loves his/her brother will not cause another Christian to stumble spiritually. If a person hates his brother, the person is walking in darkness. That person does not realize where he/she is going because the darkness has blinded him/her.

Jesus is the Light of God that reveals God to man. Christians should be the light shining brightly in a dark world of death and denial of God. Christians should reveal Jesus and his love. The lives of Christians should glorify God.

JESUS CAME TO FULFILL THE WORD OF GOD AND TO EXPLAIN GOD'S LAW

Think not that I am come to destroy the law, or the prophets: I am not come to destroy, but to fulfill.

For verily I say unto you, Till heaven and earth pass, one jot or one tittle shall in no wise pass from the law, till all be fulfilled.

Whosoever therefore shall break one of these least commandments, and shall teach men so, he shall be called the least in the kingdom of heaven: but whosoever shall do and teach them, the same shall be called great in the kingdom of heaven.

For I say unto you, That except your righteousness shall exceed the righteousness of the scribes and Pharisees, ye shall in no case enter into the kingdom of heaven.

Ye have heard that it was said by them of old time, THOU SHALT NOT KILL; and whosoever shall kill shall be in danger of the judgment:

But I say unto you, That whosoever is angry with his brother without a cause shall be in danger of the judgment: and whosoever shall say to his brother, Raca, shall be in danger of the council: but whosoever shall say, Thou fool, shall be in danger of hell fire.

Therefore if thou bring thy gift to the altar, and there rememberest that thy brother hath ought against thee;

Leave there thy gift before the altar, and go thy way; first be reconciled to thy brother, and then come and offer thy gift.

Agree with thine adversary quickly, whiles thou art in the way with him; lest at any time the adversary deliver thee to the judge, and the judge deliver thee to the officer, and thou be cast into prison.

Verily I say unto thee, Thou shalt by no means come out thence,, till thou hast paid the uttermost farthing.

Ye have heard that it was said by them of old time, thou shalt not commit adultery;

But I say unto you, That whosoever looketh on a woman to lust after her hath committed adultery with her already in his heart.

And if thy right eye offend thee, pluck it out, and cast it from thee: for it is profitable for thee that one of thy members should perish, and not that thy whole body should be cast into hell.

And if thy right hand offend thee, cut it off, and cast it from thee: for it is profitable for thee that one of thy members should perish, and not that thy whole body should be cast into hell.

It hath been said, whosever shall put away his wife, let him give her a writing of divorcement.

But I say unto you, That whosoever shall put away his wife, saving for the cause of fornication, causeth her to commit adultery: and whosoever shall marry her that is divorced committeth adultery.

Again, ye have heard that it hath been said by them of old time, Thou shalt not forswear thyself, but shalt perform unto the Lord thine oaths:

But I say unto you, Swear not at all; neither by heaven; for it is God's throne:

Nor by the earth; for it is his footstool: neither by Jerusalem; for it is the city of the great King.

Neither shalt thou swear by thy head, because thou canst not make one hair white or black.

But let your communication be, Yea, yea; Nay, nay: for whatsoever is more than these cometh of evil.

Ye have heard that it hath been said, an eye for an eye, and tooth for a tooth.

But I say unto you, That ye resist evil: but whosoever shall smite thee on thy right cheek, turn to him the other also.

And if any man will sue thee at the law, and take away thy coat, let him have thy cloke also.

And whosoever shall compel thee to go a mile, go with him twain.

Give to him that would borrow of thee turn not thou away.

Matthew 5:17–42 (KJV)

JESUS ADMONISHED THE people listening to him on the mountain to believe that Jesus had not come to destroy God's previous commandments to them. He did not come to destroy the words and commandments in the Old Testament. He came to fulfill everything that been promised by God in the scriptures. In God's truth, Jesus said to them that as long as heaven and earth existed not one word of God's laws and commandments would be changed until God had fulfilled all that had been promised. Remember that Jesus is the Word of God; it was through Jesus that all of God's commandments and laws were given to the prophets. Jesus can truly explain what God means in his words and commandments.

Anyone who breaks even the smallest of God's commandments or teaches others to disregard God's commandments will be least (less important) in the kingdom of God's heaven. Anyone who obeys God's commandments and teaches others to obey them too will be elevated by God in the Kingdom of Heaven.

Because Jesus emphasized God's commandments and rules in the Old Testament were not to be replaced, we will explore the purposes and examples of God's commandments revealed to men.

God gave the Mosaic Law to Moses to present to the people of Israel. The following passage from Exodus contains the Ten Commandments, but these are not all of the Commandments given to Moses for Moses to give to the people. God was very specific about the relationship he willed to have with man. He was not willing to be one of a group of gods; He was to be the only God recognized by the people of Israel. He gave other commandments which were to be followed with no deviation. Six of the Ten Commandments dealt with the relationship people should have with other people.

> And God spake all these things saying,
> I am the Lord thy God, which have brought thee out of the land of Egypt, out of the house of bondage (slavery).
> Thou shalt have no other gods before (except) me.
> Thou shalt not make unto thee any graven image, or any likeness of anything that is in heaven above, or that is in the earth beneath, or that is in the water under the earth:
> Thou shalt not bow down thyself to them, nor serve them: for I the Lord thy God am a jealous God, visiting the iniquity of the fathers upon the children unto the third and fourth generation of them that hate me (punishing children and grandchildren);

And shewing mercy unto thousands of them that love me, and keep my commandments.

Thou shalt not take the name of the Lord thy God in vain (use God's name disrespectfully); for the Lord will not hold him guiltless that taketh (uses) his name in vain (foolishly).

Remember the Sabbath day, to keep it holy.

Six days shalt thou labour, and do all thy work:

But the seventh day is the Sabbath of the Lord thy God: in it thou shall not do any work, thou, nor thy son, nor thy daughter, thy manservant, nor thy maidservant, nor thy cattle, nor thy stranger that is within thy gates:

For in six days the Lord made heaven and earth, the sea, and all that in them is, and rested the seventh day: wherefore the Lord blessed the Sabbath day, and hallowed it.

Honour thy father and thy mother: that thy days may be long upon the land which the Lord thy God giveth thee.

Thou shalt not kill.

Thou shalt not commit adultery.

Thou shalt not steal.

Thou shalt not bear false witness against thy neighbor (tell lies about your neighbor).

Thou shalt not covet (want to take) thy neighbour's house, thou shalt not covet thy neighbour's wife, nor his manservant, nor his maidservant, nor his ox, nor his ass, nor any thing that is thy neighbour's.

Exodus 20:1–17 (KJV)

Moses spoke to the people in Deuteronomy reminding them that he taught them the rules and laws that God commanded him to give them. He told the people of Israel to keep those commandments because the people of other nations would believe that they were wise; other nations would respect the people of Israel when they saw that God's people lived by laws that honored God and respected the rights of others. The other nations would know that the people of Israel were protected by God;

they would know that they were a great nation because they lived with God.

> Behold, I have taught you statutes and judgments, even as the LORD my God commanded me, that ye should do so in the land whither ye go to possess it.
>
> Keep therefore and do them (commandments); for this is your wisdom and your understanding in the sight of the nations, which shall hear all these statutes, and say, Surely this great nation is a wise and understanding people.
>
> For what nation is there so great, who hath God so nigh unto them, as the LORD our God is in all things that we call upon him for?
>
> Deuteronomy 4:5–7 (KJV)

Moses reminded the people of Israel again that they must obey God's commandments. They must fear God (give God great respect). The people were responsible for teaching their children the commandments of God so that they would live long lives and prosper. The people of Israel were to love God with all their hearts. The parents were to teach their children the commandments while they were doing all their everyday activities.

> Now these are the commandments, the statures, and the judgments, which the Lord your God commanded to teach you, that ye might do them in the land whither ye go to possess it:
>
> That thou mightiest fear the LORD thy God, to keep all his statutes and his commandments, which I command thee, thou, and thy son, and thy son's son, all the days of thy life; and that thy days may be prolonged.
>
> Hear therefore, O Israel, and observe to do it; that it may be well with thee, and that ye may increase mightily, as the LORD God of thy fathers hath promised thee, in the land that floweth with milk and honey.
>
> Hear, O Israel: The LORD our God is one LORD.

And thou shalt love the LORD thy God with all thine heart, and with all thy soul, and with all thy might.

And these words, which I command thee this day, shall be in thine heart:

And thou shalt teach them diligently unto thy children, and shalt talk of them the when thou sittest in thine house, and when thou walkest by the way, and when thou liest down, and when thou risest up.

Deuteronomy 6:1–7 (KJV)

The people of Israel were to live their lives constantly thinking about the commandments of God. They should teach their children about the commandments during all of their everyday activities. They were to write the laws on their houses and their gates. If they obeyed the laws, their lives and their children's lives would be long and prosperous.

Therefore shall ye lay up these my words in your heart and in your soul, and bind them for a sign upon your hand, and they may be as frontlets between your eyes.

And ye shall teach them your children, speaking of them when thou sittest in thine house, and when thou walkest by the way, when thou liest down, and when thou risest up.

And thou shalt write them upon the door posts of thine house, and upon thy gates:

That your days may be multiplied, and the days of your children, in the land which the Lord sware unto your fathers to give them, as the days of heaven upon the earth.

Deuteronomy 11:18–21 (KJV)

King David described the commandments and the laws of God. He said that the teachings and instructions of God are perfect; they revive and strengthen the soul of a child of God. The testimonies (words) of God can be trusted. God's words make immature people wise. The commandments of God are always

119

right, and they make people happy. The laws of God are pure lighting our way to God.

The fear (respect) of God is clean, and it lasts forever. The judgments of God are true and always righteous. The words and commandments of God are to be desired (valued) more than precious, purest gold. God's words are sweeter than the finest honey. The words of God warn his servants; those who keep God's commandments will have a great reward.

> The law of the Lord is perfect converting the soul: the testimony of the Lord is sure, making wise the simple.
>
> The statutes of the Lord are right, rejoicing the Heart: the commandment of the Lord is pure enlightening the eyes..
>
> The fear of the Lord is clean, enduring for ever: the judgments of the Lord are true and righteous altogether.
>
> More to be desired are they than gold, yea, than much fine gold: sweeter also than honey and the honeycomb.
>
> Moreover by them is thy servant warned: and in keeping of them there is great reward.
>
> Psalm 19:7–11 (KJV)

In the King James translation of Psalm 119, we are told that those who are not soiled by sin, those who live their lives in obedience to God's laws, are blessed by God. A person who follows God's laws and who tries to please God with their whole heart will be blessed. God has ordered us to follow his laws explicitly. A Christian wishes to always follow God's laws. If a Christian respects all of God's laws he/she will never be ashamed of his/her actions. A Christian will praise God drawing from a pure heart after he/she has learned how righteous God's laws are. How will a young person live a life that has not been soiled by sin? A young person can live a life pleasing to God if he/she follows God's commandments. God's laws are held securely in a Christian's heart so that that person does not sin against God. We beg that God will teach us his laws. We will speak declaring the wisdom of God and His Word. We will be made joyful in valuing God's words for they are worth more than great wealth. We will think about God's commandments and respect God's rules. We will find joy in God's commandments; we will not forget God's rules. Our respect for God's Word and our constant obedience to God's commandments will bring blessing into our lives.

Blessed are the undefiled in the way, who walk in the law of the Lord.

Blessed are they that keep his testimonies, and seek him with the whole heart.

They also do no iniquity: they walk in his ways.

Thou hast commanded us to keep thy precepts diligently.

O that my ways were directed to keep thy statutes!

Then shall I not be ashamed, when I have respect unto all thy commandments.

I will praise thee with uprightness of heart, when I shall have learned thy righteous judgments.

I will keep thy statutes: O forsake me not utterly.

Where withal shall a young man cleanse his way? By taking heed thereto according to thy word.

With my whole heart have I sought thee: O let me not wander from thy commandments.

Thy word have I hid in mine heart, that I might not sin against thee.

Blessed art thou, O Lord: teach me thy statutes.

With my lips have I declared all the judgments of thy mouth.

I have rejoiced in the way of thy testimonies, as much as in all riches.

I will mediate in thy precepts, and have respect unto thy ways.

I will delight myself in thy statutes: I will not forget thy word.

Psalm 119:1–16 (kjv)

In Matthew 5:17 when Jesus said that he did not come to destroy the law, he was declaring that all of God's commandments given before Jesus was born are still to be valued above all else. Jesus did not change one word of God's previous words to man. He had come to obey and follow God's commandments perfectly. If any person teaches other people to break (disobey) one of God's commandments, that person will be the least of all people in God's kingdom.

Jesus continued telling the people that they must be more righteous than the scribes (teachers) and Pharisees if they want to be accepted into God's kingdom. The Pharisees were recognized by the Jews for making great public shows of how righteous (obedient to God) they were.

Jesus then went on to elaborate (explain the true meaning of God's commandments). The law given to the Jews by Moses said that they should not kill another person; (Exodus 20:13, Deut. 5:17) if they did murder, they were in danger of being judged for their actions. Jesus did not change God's law; he went on to amplify it so that it became a law which was more specific and binding. Jesus said that any man who was angry at his brother or sister (another person) without having a just cause was in danger of being judged. If a person calls others names like Fool, the person calling others names is in danger of being charged before the council (Sanhedrin). If a person calls someone an idiot or a moron, that person is in danger of being burned in the fires of hell (Gehenna was a valley outside of Jerusalem where pagans during the Old Testament times sacrificed (burned) children to worship pagan gods).

Jesus said that when a person brings a gift to offer in a sacrifice to God, and they remember that they have a disagreement with someone else, they should leave the gift at the alter and go and make peace (be reconciled to) with the other person. Then the one who wishes to honor God can come back and present his/her gift to God.

If your enemy (adversary, opponent) takes you to court, reach an agreement with that person quickly before you go to court. If you do not, your accuser might turn you over to the judge. Then you may be thrown in prison. Jesus said that he spoke truthfully, you may be held in prison until you have paid every penny you owed. Jesus indicated that God was never pleased with discord and fighting between the people of God. God expects his children to be forgiving as their heavenly father is forgiving.

Jesus expanded the law forbidding murder. He indicated that God is not willing that his children should try to destroy other Christians in any way. If a Christian wants to destroy another Christian in his heart, he is accountable to God for judgment. Christians are to forgive one another so that God will forgive them.

The Mosaic Law said, "Thou shalt not commit adultery." Jesus expanded that law to include what a person does in his/her heart or head. The law covered the physical behavior of the Jewish people. Jesus was magnifying the physical commandments to cover spiritual behavior. All three persons of the Trinity, God the Father; Jesus, God's Son; and the Holy Spirit are able to see (perceive) what is in a person's heart and mind.

> For the word of God is quick (living) and powerful and sharper than any twoedged sword, piercing even to the dividing asunder of soul and spirit, and of the joints and marrow, and is a discerner of the thoughts and intents of the heart.
>
> Neither is there any creature that is not manifest (hidden) in his sight: but all things are naked and opened unto the eyes of him with whom we have to do.
>
> Hebrews 4:12–13 (KJV)

> Thou hast set our iniquities before thee, our secret sins in the light of thy countenance.
>
> Psalm 90:8 (KJV)

God's commandments are directed not just to physical actions; the commandments are given to direct what we think and imagine in our minds. Therefore if a man looks at a woman who is not his wife and has sexual acts with her in his imagination he has committed adultery in his heart.

Jesus spoke of tearing out your own eye or cutting off your own hand if that part of your body prevented you from following God's commandments. He was speaking figuratively, but he wanted to stress how absolutely essential it is that Christians give up anything in their lives that keeps them from pleasing God. Again Jesus was using physical examples to teach spiritual truths. He meant that no matter how important something in your life is to you, you must give it up if it prevents you from having eternal life with God.

Paul further explained that concept in the letter to the Colossians. He said that if we are born again spiritually and live in union with Jesus Christ then we are dead to physical gratification. We should put our efforts into seeking spiritual treasures rather than those of the physical world. Our new lives are spiritual lives shared with Jesus. We should be dead to the pleasures of the physical life which would lead us to death.

We should kill (give up, reject) anything which is of the sinful world. We must give up fornication (any human sexual intercourse that is not between a man and a woman who are married), uncleanness (morally or spiritually impurity, infected with sin), inordinate affection (loving anything or anyone more than God), evil concupiscence (strong desire, sexual desire), and covetousness (great desire to have wealth or possessions that belong to someone else). These things are idolatry because they come before your desire to please God. If people seek after those things they will bring down upon themselves the anger of God.

You did those things before you became Christians. Now you should avoid anger (rage), wrath, malice (hatred), saying things to hurt others, slander, blasphemy (insulting or showing contempt for God), and filthy communication (abusive, filthy, obscene speaking). Do not lie to others. You have been reborn spiritually; you now live in the image of the God who created you.

> If ye then be risen with Christ, seek those things which are above, where Christ sitteth on the right hand of God.
>
> Set your affection on things above, not on things on the earth.
>
> For ye are dead, and your life is hid with Christ in God.
>
> When Christ, who is our life, shall appear, then shall ye also appear with him in glory.
>
> Mortify (kill, destroy) therefore your members which are upon the earth; fornication, uncleanness, inordinate affection, evil concupiscence, and covetousness, which is idolatry:
>
> For which things' sake the wrath of God cometh on the children of disobedience.
>
> In the which ye also walked some time, when ye lived in them.
>
> But now ye also put off all these; anger, wrath, malice, blasphemy, filthy communication out of your mouth.
>
> Lie not one to another, seeing that ye have put off the old man with his deeds;
>
> And have put on the new man, which is renewed in knowledge after the image of him that created him:
>
> Colossians 3:1–10 (KJV)

Jesus went on to speak of another one of God's commandments. The Mosaic law said, "whosoever shall put away his wife, let him give her a writing of divorcement." Jesus expanded the law to say that anyone who divorces his wife causes her to commit adultery, except if she had already committed adultery. Any man who marries a divorced woman commits adultery.

In the times of the Old Testament the law said that you should not break your promises (oaths). Keep the promises (vows) you make to God. Again Jesus magnified the law saying that no one should swear an oath at all. Don't swear by the heaven; it is God's throne. Don't swear by the earth; the earth belongs to God. Don't swear an oath using the name of Jerusalem; it is the city of the great King. Don't swear by your own head because you have no control over the color of your hair. Do not swear at all. Just say "yes" or "no". If you swear by anything, that is from the devil.

Jesus quoted another scripture. ""AN EYE FOR AN EYE AND A TOOTH FOR A TOOTH" (Ex. 21:24, Lev. 24:20, Deut.19:21). Jesus said to not resist or retaliate against evil that is done to you. If you are slapped on one cheek, turn and offer the other cheek. If someone wants to sue you in the court to take your shirt, let him take your coat too. If someone (a solider) forces you to carry his burdens for a mile, carry them for two miles. If someone asks you for something, give it to him. Don't refuse to loan if someone asks to borrow from you. You are acknowledging that God has control over everything. Let him decide who is right or wrong. Judgment and punishment are for him to choose.

> You have heard that it hath been said, "THOU SHALT LOVE THY NEIGHBOR AND HATE THINE ENEMY."
>
> But I say unto you, Love your enemies, bless them that curse you, do good to them that hate you, and pray for them which despitefully use you, and persecute you;
>
> That ye may be the children of your Father which is in heaven: for he maketh his sun to rise on the evil and on the good, and sendeth rain on the just and on the unjust.
>
> For if ye love them which love you, what reward have ye? Do not even the publicans the same?
>
> And if ye salute your brethren only, what do ye more than others? Do not even the publicans so?
>
> Be ye therefore perfect, even as your Father which is in heaven is perfect."
>
> Matthew 5:43–48 (KJV)

In the times of the Old Testament the law said, "Thou shalt love thy neighbor." But Jesus expanded the teaching to say that we should love our enemies. We should bless those people who curse us. We should do good things for someone who hates us. We should pray for someone who tries to injure us or to persecute us. We should do all these things because we are the children of God. God makes his sun to rise on the evil and the good. God sends rain for the unjust (unfair) man and the just man. Why would you receive a reward for loving people who love you? Don't the publicans do that?

If you share and speak politely to your friends, why would you be rewarded? Publicans do that too. You and your actions must be perfect because your Father, God, who lives in heaven is perfect. You should copy Him.

JESUS TEACHES ABOUT HYPOCRISY AND PRAYING

Take heed that ye do not your alms before men, to be seen of them: otherwise ye have no reward of your Father which is in heaven.

Therefore when thou doest thine alms, do not sound a trumpet before thee, as the hypocrites do in the synagogues and in the streets, that they may have glory of men. Verily I say unto you, They have their reward.

But when thou doest alms, let not thy left hand know what thy right hand doeth:

That thine alms may be in secret: and thy Father which seeth in secret himself shall reward thee openly.

And when thou prayest, thou shalt not be as the hypocrites are: for they love to pray standing in the synagogues and in the corners of the streets, that they may be seen of men. Verily I say unto you, They have their reward.

But thou, when thou prayest, enter into thy closet, and when thou hast shut thy door, pray to thy Father which is in secret; and thy Father which seeth in secret shall reward thee openly.

But when ye pray, use not vain repetitions, as the heathen do: for they think that they shall be heard for their much speaking.

Be not ye therefore like unto them: for your Father knoweth what things ye have need of, before ye ask him.

After this manner therefore pray ye: Our Father which art in heaven, Hallowed be thy name.

Thy kingdom come. Thy will be done in earth, as it is in heaven.

Give us this day our daily bread.

And forgive us our debts, as we forgive our debtors.

And lead us not into temptation, but deliver us from evil: For thine is the kingdom, and the power, and the glory, for ever. Amen.

For if ye forgive men their trespasses, your heavenly Father will also forgive you:

But if ye forgive not men their trespasses, neither will your Father forgive your trespasses.

Moreover when ye fast, be not, as the hypocrites, of a sad countenance: for they disfigure their faces, that they may appear unto men to fast. Verily I say unto you, They have their reward.

But thou, when thou fastest, anoint thine head, and wash thy face;

That thou appear not unto men to fast, but unto thy Father which is in secret: and thy Father, which seeth in secret, shall reward thee openly.

Matthew 6:1–18 (KJV)

JESUS CONTINUED TO teach the people. He admonished them to give their alms (money or food given to help the poor) privately or in secret. If you do it publically you will not be rewarded by God. The Pharisees had someone walk in front of them blowing a horn in the church or on the street. They did this so that men would admire them and treat them with respect. Jesus warned that the only reward they were going to receive was the notice of men not of God. When you are going to give to the poor, do it secretly. Your Heavenly Father, God, will see what you give secretly, and He will reward you openly.

When you pray, you should not do like the hypocrites (insincere) and pray standing up in the church or standing on the street corners. The hypocrites pray so that men will honor them; the only reward they will receive is the notice of men. As a devout Christian you should go into your closet (private place) and shut the door. You should pray to God in secret (privately), and God will reward (answer) your prayers openly (in public). Don't repeat the same prayers over and over like the heathen (people who do not worship the one true God) do. Jesus said that the heathens think that they will be rewarded according to how many times they pray the same prayer.

Don't pray with mindless repetition. Your Heavenly Father knows what you need even before you ask him. This is the way you should pray.

"Our Father which art in heaven, Hallowed be thy name."

We acknowledge that God is our spiritual Father. He is living in heaven where all things are done according to his will. When we say hallowed (holy) be thy name, we are declaring that God's name should always be sacred and honored (revered). "And he said, "Draw not nigh hither: put off thy shoes from off thy feet, for the place whereon thou standest in holy ground." (Exodus 3: 5 KJV) "Thou shalt not take the name of the LORD thy God in vain; for the LORD will not hold him guiltless that taketh his name in vain" (Exodus 20:7, KJV).

> Sanctify yourselves (set apart) therefore, and be ye holy: for I am the Lord your God.
>
> Leviticus 20:7 (KJV)

The Lord is righteous in all his ways, and holy in all his works.

Psalm 145:17 (KJV)

Only God is truly holy. Holy is perfect, commands absolute adoration and reverence, merits veneration.

We should proclaim that we desire (want) everything that is done on the earth to be done perfectly according to God's will. We ask that we live in a kingdom where there is no sin; where there is no rebellion against God; where God's Truth (Word) is never challenged. "Thy kingdom come. Thy will be done in earth as it is in heaven."

We acknowledge that all that we have is given to us by God. He provides for all our needs daily as the Children of Israel were fed daily with manna in the desert. We are also and more importantly being provided for spiritually; God is giving us not only physical life but also spiritual life constantly. "Give us this day our daily bread."

Jesus returned to the topic of mercy and forgiveness with this line from His prayer. We tend to ignore the importance of our forgiveness to others in regard to God's forgiveness for us. Jesus said that people who were merciful to others would be shown mercy by God. God created all things for his pleasure. God is entitled to all things. We must acknowledge that God has a plan for each of our lives. God's word says that all things work for good for those who love God and are called according to His purposes. That means if God allows something to happen, he is able to use the evil to make good. That does not mean that he wanted the evil to happen; it means that he can use it for good. "Forgive us our debts as we forgive our debtors."

> The Lord hath made all things for himself: yea, even the wicked for the day of evil.
>
> Everyone that is proud in heart is an abomination to the Lord: though hand join in hand, he shall not be unpunished.

By mercy and truth iniquity is purged: and by the fear of the Lord men depart from evil.

Proverbs 16:4–6 (KJV)

For by him were all things created, that are in heaven, and that are in earth, visible and invisible, whether they be thrones, or dominions, or principalities, or powers: all things were created by him, and for him.

And he is before all things, and by him all things consist.

Colossians 1:16–17 (KJV)

Our human natures inspire us to judge the actions of others. We must remember that all things belong to God. He alone has the right to judge our actions and our thoughts. When we forgive, we are acknowledging that God alone has the right to judge and set things right as He wills. "He hath shewed thee, O man, what is good; and what doth the Lord require of thee, but to do justly, and to love mercy, and to walk humbly with thy God?" (Micah 6:8, KJV).

Humble yourself as God sees you. Then God will lift you up. Do not say evil things about others. If you speak evil and judge your fellow Christian, you are judging God's law. You are not doing what God says; you are setting yourself to judge the laws of God. There is only one who has the right to make laws; who are you to judge God?

Humble yourselves in the sight of the Lord, and he shall lift you up.

Speak not evil one of another, brethren, He that speaketh evil of his brother, and judgeth his brother, speaketh evil of the law, and judgeth the law: but if thou judge the law, thou art not a doer of the law, but a judge.

There is one lawgiver, who is able to save and to destroy, who art thou that judgest another?

James 4:10–12 (KJV)

Jesus said to forgive others seventy times seven if they continue to come and ask your forgiveness. God has forgiven us great sin punishable by death; it is a debt so great that nothing could pay back the debt but the life of his own son. The sins that we must forgive others are insignificant in comparison. "And lead us not into temptation, but deliver us from evil."

We should acknowledge that God has power over our lives and all the beings that He created. He has authority over the devils. It is God who has made a plan for each of our lives. "Trust in the Lord with all your heart, and lean not to your own understanding. In all your ways acknowledge him, and he will direct your paths" (Proverbs 3:5–6, KJV).

We have a promise from the passage in Proverbs. If we will trust in God, and not try to seize power over our own lives, God will determine the circumstances in our lives. We ask God to plan our lives so that we are not tempted to sin against God. We ask God to deliver (save) us from the power of evil that is in the world. We should also remember to ask God to deliver other Christians from the power of evil which may have made them slaves to evil thoughts and actions. Deliver us from evil. Pray for those who despitefully use you.

We have acknowledged that God will deliver us from evil because heaven and earth are the kingdoms under God's authority. The power over all things is his alone. He alone has the right to be glorified. "For thine is the kingdom, and the power, and the glory, forever. Amen."

When we look at the Lord's Prayer it becomes evident that the prayer is not intended to change God. The prayer is intended to change our attitudes. The prayer confirms our beliefs about God and our relationship to him.

Jesus continued to stress to the people who were listening to him that they must forgive others if they want God to forgive their sins. He returns to that truth again and again. God will only forgive us if we forgive others who trespass against us.

He also returns to the topic of the Pharisees and their practices. God will not accept hypocrisy. God sees the intents of our hearts; he knows what we are secretly thinking. If you fast or make a sacrifice for God, don't announce to the world that you are making a sacrifice. Let your neat appearance hide your sacrifice and secret relationship with God. If you put on a show to impress men, the opinions of men are your only reward. If you fast or pray to please God in secret, God will know that you sincerely wanted to please him and not other people. He will see the desire of your heart to do his will, and he will reward you openly (publicly).

THE THINGS A CHRISTIAN VALUES AFFECT HIS RELATIONSHIP WITH GOD

Lay not up for yourselves treasures upon earth, where moth and rust doth corrupt (ruin), and where thieves break through and steal

But lay up for yourselves treasures in heaven, where neither moth nor rust doth corrupt, and where thieves do not break through nor steal:

For where your treasure is, there will your heart be also.

The light of the body is the eye: if therefore thine eye be single, thy whole body shall be full of light.

But if thine eye be evil, thy whole body shall be full of darkness. If therefore the light that is in thee be darkness, how great is that darkness!

No man can serve two masters: for either he will hate the one, and love the other; or else he will hold to the one, and despise the other. Ye cannot serve God and mammon.

Therefore I say unto you, Take no thought for your life, what ye shall eat, or what ye shall drink; nor yet for your body, what ye shall put on. Is not the life more than meat, and the body than raiment (clothing)?

Behold the fowls of the air: for they sow not, neither do they reap, nor gather into barns; yet your heavenly Father feedeth them. Are ye not much better than they?

Which of you by taking thought can add one cubit unto his stature?

And why take ye though for raiment Consider the lilies of the field, how they grow; they toil not neither do they spin:

And yet I say unto you, That even Solomon in all his glory was not arrayed like one of these.

Wherefore, if God so clothe the grass of the field, which to day is, and to morrow is cast into the oven, shall he not much more clothe you, O ye of little faith?

Therefore take no thought, saying, What shall we eat? Or, What shall we drink? Or, Wherewithal shall we be clothed?

(For after all these things do the Gentiles seek:) for your heavenly Father knoweth that ye have need of all these things.

But seek ye first the kingdom of God, and his righteousness; and all these things shall be added unto you.

Take therefore no thought for the morrow: for the morrow shall take thought for the things of itself. Sufficient unto the day is the evil thereof.

Matthew 6:19–34 (KJV)

JESUS ADMONISHED THE people who listened to him on the mountain to be mindful of what they treasured. He said not to concentrate on saving treasures of the earth where moths could eat cloth, metal could rust, or thieves could break into your house and steal. Christians should gather up heavenly treasures; spiritual treasures cannot be eaten by moths, caused to rust, or stolen by thieves. Whatever you treasure (value) will determine what is in your heart.

He said that your eyes are the lamp for the body. If your eyes are clear so that you can see well, your whole body is full of light. If your perceptions are spiritually healthy (clear) then your whole life will be guided by good values. But if your eyes are evil then your whole body will be filled with darkness. If your perceptions of live are not spiritually healthy clear, you will live in darkness (sin).

No person can serve two masters. The servant will despise (not faithfully serve to benefit) one master and love (eagerly serve to benefit) the other master. A servant with two masters will cheat (hate) one master and strive (work) to help the other master. You cannot serve God and serve mammon (worldly wealth and prosperity).

That is why Jesus said that you should not worry (concentrate) on saving and advancing your physical life.. Do not plan to depend on physical wealth. Do not concentrate on providing for your drink or food or clothing. Life (living) is more than what you feed your physical body or with what you clothe your physical body. Observe the birds. They do not plant seeds; harvest grain, or store food in barns. But your Heavenly Father feeds them. Aren't you more important than the birds?

Which one of you can make himself/herself taller by working or concentrating on changing yourself. Why do you worry about clothing? Observe the most beautiful flowers in the field; the flowers do not work or spin thread for cloth. But I say to you that even King Solomon's clothes were not as beautiful as the flowers. If God provides so abundantly for the beauty of the flowers which bloom briefly and then are burned in the fire, will he not provide clothing for his children? Can you not trust God for these things?

Don't think or worry about what you will drink, or what you will eat, or what you will wear. Depend upon your Heavenly Father to provide for your needs. Concentrating on obtaining food, clothing, and housing are the things that Gentiles (people who are not God's people) work to possess.

You, Jesus's followers, should work to become a part of God's spiritual kingdom as your primary goal. You should exert effort to become right with God (obtain righteousness). Everything that you need will be given to you by God.

Don't worry or plan for what you will need in the future; In the future you can think about what will happen in the future. It is sufficient (enough) for you to think about what happens today. The problems (evil) you work against today are all you need to strive to fix today.

DO NOT JUDGE OTHERS

Judge not that ye be not judged.

For with what judgment ye judge, ye shall be judged: and with what measure ye mete, it shall be measured to you again.

And why beholdest thou the mote that is in thy brother's eye, but considerest not the beam that is in thine own eye?

Or how wilt thou say to thy brother, Let me pull out the mote out of thine eye; and behold, a beam is in thine own eye?

Thou hypocrite, first cast out the beam out of thine own eye; and then shalt thou see clearly to cast out the mote out of thy brother's eye.

Matthew 7:1–5 (KJV)

JESUS SAID THAT we should not judge other people. Only God has the right to judge. All that is on the earth and in heaven are His. He alone can judge justly because only God can see the thoughts and intentions of a man or woman. If you judge others harshly then God will judge you harshly.

Why would you decide that a brother has a splinter in his eye (sin or injustice); you are not trying to remove the beam (large post) which is in your eye? The point can be made that both the splinter and the post keep the person from seeing clearly. No matter what we think or feel about our own ability to decide what is fair or accurate, we do not see (perceive) things as they really are. The lesson here is that if we are judging another person to decide what is wrong with him/her, we are sinning ourselves because we are commanded not to judge others.

If you are trying to remove the splinter from someone else's eye, that is correct their lives so that they will not sin, and you have not corrected the sin in your own life, you are a hypocrite. Hypocrisy is pretending to be what you are not and to believe what you do not believe. It is false appearance of virtue or religion. To be a hypocrite is to pretend to have more virtue or religious devotion than one actually possesses (has). God is able to see the heart of each person so He knows which people are actually followers who obey God and walk in his will. Jesus was very conscious of the people who pretended to love and obey God when they didn't. Those people liked to criticize others and judge them to be sinners.

JESUS TEACHES ABOUT GOD'S GIFTS AND FALSE PROPHETS

Give not that which is holy unto the dogs, neither cast ye your pearls before swine, lest they trample them under their feet, and turn again and rend (tear) you.

Ask and it shall be given you; seek, and ye shall find; knock and it shall be opened unto you.

For every one that asketh receiveth; and he that seeketh findeth; and to him that knocketh it shall be opened.

Or what man is there of you, whom if his son ask bread, will give him a stone?

Or if he ask a fish, will he give him a serpent?

If ye then, being evil, know how to give good gifts unto your children, how much more shall your Father which is in heaven give good things to them that ask him?

Therefore all things whatsoever ye would that men should do to you, do ye even so to them: for this is the law and the prophets.

Enter ye in at the strait gate: for wide is the gate, and broad is the way, that leadeth to destruction, and many there be which go in there at:

Because strait is the gate, and narrow is the way, which leadeth unto life, and few there be that find it.

Beware of false prophets, which come to you in sheep's clothing, but inwardly they are ravening (hungry) wolves.

Ye shall know them by their fruits. Do men gather grapes of thorns, or figs of thistles?

Even so every good tree bringeth forth good fruit; but a corrupt (bad) tree bringeth forth evil fruit.

A good (healthy) tree cannot bring forth evil fruit, neither can a corrupt tree bring forth good fruit.

Every tree that bringeth not forth good fruit is hewn down, and cast into the fire.

Wherefore by their fruits ye shall know them.

Not every one that saith unto me, Lord, Lord, shall enter into the kingdom of heaven; but he that doeth the will of my Father which is in heaven.

Many will say to me in that day, Lord, Lord, have we not prophesied in thy name? and in thy name have cast out devils? And in thy name done many wonderful works?

And then will I profess unto them, I never knew you: depart from me, ye that work iniquity.

Therefore whosoever heareth these sayings of mine, and doeth them, I will liken him unto a wise man, which built his house upon a rock:

And the rain descended, and the floods came, and the winds blew, and beat upon that house; and it fell not: for it was founded upon a rock.

And every one that heareth these sayings of mine, and doeth them not, shall be likened unto a foolish man, which built his house upon the sand:

And the rain descended, and the floods came, and the winds blew, and beat upon that house; and it fell: and great was the fall of it.

Matthew 7:6–27 (KJV)

JESUS SAID NOT to give things that are holy to dogs; he also said not to give your pearls to pigs. He was of course teaching with an analogy. Christians are of course given very valuable spiritual gifts when the will of God and His plan of salvation are given to us. It is true that we are admonished to preach the plan of salvation through Jesus Christ to all the world. Jesus is warning us to be careful; he had warned the followers earlier to guard themselves. He is warning the believers to be careful not to reveal spiritual truths to people who will use those truths in an evil world to destroy us. Remember that Jesus told the disciples to wait until the Holy Spirit came to help them. The Holy Spirit will tell us when we should share the messages of Jesus with other people. The Holy Spirit will speak to the people's hearts as we speak the words aloud. If we run ahead of God and try to reach people whose hearts are full of evil, those people will obey their father, the devil, and try to destroy us.

Continuing to teach, Jesus said that Christians should ask and we will receive; seek (search) and we will find; knock and the door will be opened. He is directing us to take an active role in learning more about God. If we just sit down passively and wait to see what we will receive, we will not find greater spiritual treasures. This is not the same as waiting on the Lord so that we will be given new strength to carry on. In Revelations we are warned not to become lukewarm. We must be actively involved in our own spiritual growth. "I know thy works, that thou art neither cold nor hot: I would thou wert cold or hot (one or the other). So then because thou art lukewarm, and neither cold or hot, I will spue (vomit) thee out of my mouth." (Revelations 3:15–16, KJV).

Sometimes the Holy Spirit will give us the question we need to ask before we are given the answer. Sometimes it seems that we have asked a question, and we didn't get an answer. We are not always prepared to receive the answer. The answer may be coming, but God needs to lead us to grow spiritually before we are ready to receive the answer.

We need to remain open to new revelations about God and his will. If we assume that we already know all there is to know, we won't be open to receive more spiritual truth.

> I love them that love me; and those that seek me early shall find me.
>
> Riches and honour are with me; yea, durable riches and righteousness.
>
> My fruit is better than gold, yea, than fine gold; and my revenue than choice silver.
>
> I lead in the way of righteousness, in the midst of the paths of judgment:
>
> Proverbs 8:17–20 (KJV)

God's people were always encouraged to try to find him and his truths. He has promised that if we seek after more of his truth, he will give it to us. He loves those people who try to find him. He has promised to lead us into righteousness.

Jesus reminded the people that any father will give his child bread if he asks for food not a rock; any father will give his child a fish if he asks for a fish to eat not a snake. If ordinary people who live in an evil world give good gifts to their children, how much more will God give gifts to the children he loves when they ask for things that God has to give.

Jesus went on to teach the people what they must do to receive God's gift of eternal life. Jesus told the listeners to treat other people as they wanted to be treated. God will be pleased if we treat others as we want to be treated. God has taught us that truth in the Mosaic Law and the words of the prophets; God's will as it is revealed in the words of the Old Testament emphasize repeatedly that God's will is for us to treat others with the same kindness and generosity that we desire for ourselves.

We should choose to enter the narrow gate into God's heavenly kingdom. There is a wide gate and a spacious (big) roadway leading to hell. But the gate is narrow and the road is narrow and difficult to follow that leads to eternal life in heaven. Only a few people will find and follow that narrow road and gate to the Father's kingdom.

Christians should be careful not to believe false prophets (people who teach untrue things about God and what He wants) so that the Christians are fooled into following the wide road into death (hell). Those false prophets will appear to be as innocent and gentle as lambs, but they are really as cruel as hungry wolves looking for believers to lead away and destroy.

You should identify the false prophets by looking at their own works and lives. You can't get good fruit from vines and trees that are not plants that grow food. A good vine or tree gives good food. A corrupt (bad) tree gives food that is not good to eat. If a vine or tree is not living and able to give good food, it is cut down and burned. You will know which prophets or teachers are sent from God by looking at the fruits (works and practices) in their own lives. Jesus was still warning the people about hypocrites. "But the fruit of the Spirit is love, joy, peace, longsuffering, gentleness, goodness, faith, Meekness, temperance: against such there is no law" (Galatians 5:22–23, KJV).

> Charity (love) suffereth long, and is kind; charity envieth not; charity vaunteth not itself, is not puffed up,
> Doth not behave itself unseemly, seeketh not her own, is not easily provoked, thinketh no evil;
> Rejoiceth not in iniquity, but rejoiceth in the truth;
> Beareth all things, believeth all things, hopeth all things, endureth all things.
>
> 1st Corinthians 13:4–7 (KJV)

God has always stressed that we are to love one another. In Corinthians LOVE is defined. Those who love show great patience with others; those who love are tolerant of the beliefs and behavior of others. Those who love are kind and compassionate. Those who love do not envy the lives and possessions of other people. Those who love do not try to show other people how great they are or how much God loves them above others. Those who love are not conceited; they don't take credit for what other people have done. Those who love don't behave in such a manner that God is shamed. Those who love don't try to make themselves greater than others. Those who love are not angry or vengeful against others. Those who love don't welcome iniquity which is unequal treatment of God's children. Those who love find great joy in God's truth. Those who love bear all things without retaliating. Those who love believe good things about God's other children. Those who love hope (believe in the future) for all things promised by God. Those who love endure all tribulation and suffering without blaming God or other people.

> Thou shalt not hate thy brother in thine heart: thou shalt in any wise rebuke thy neighbor, and not suffer sin upon him.
> Thou shalt not avenge, nor bear any grudge against the children of thy people, but thou shalt love thy neighbour as thyself: I am the Lord.
>
> Leviticus 19:17–18 (KJV)

Not everyone who calls to Jesus saying Lord, Lord, will be allowed to enter into the Kingdom of God (heaven). Only those who do the will (obey) of the Heavenly Father will be admitted into the Kingdom of God. Many people will tell Jesus that he is their Lord. They will claim to have prophesied in the name of Jesus (spoken his words to others); have cast out devils in the name of Jesus; and have done wonderful works in the name of Jesus. Jesus will tell these people who claim to be his servants that he never knew them.

Therefore the people of God should take note. Jesus requires that we listen to the words and commandments that he has given us. He will not tolerate the actions of people who are workers of iniquity (those who do evil things). "Depart from me, all ye workers of iniquity; for the Lord hath heard the voice of my weeping" (Psalm 6: 8, KJV).

Jesus used another parable to stress that God's people must obey the instructions that Jesus was speaking; his words were a rock to build their lives upon. He told a story about a man who built his house upon a rock. When the floods came and the wind (storm) blew the house with its foundation built on the rock (Jesus's teachings) stood firm. Another man built his house upon sand (false teachings and rebellion against God's laws); his house was destroyed when it was tested by adversity (the floods and storm). We must build our lives upon the teachings of Jesus so that our eternal lives will be preserved.

"And it came to pass, when Jesus had ended these sayings, the people were astonished at his doctrine: For he taught them as one having authority, and not as the scribes" (Matthew 7:28–29, KJV). When Jesus had finished teaching the people who sat around him on the mountain, the people were greatly impressed. They recognized that the Jewish teachers never taught them as Jesus did. He taught them with the authority of God; the Holy Spirit was confirming everything Jesus said in their hearts.

JESUS IS THE GREAT HEALER

When he was come down from the mountain, great multitudes (large crowds) followed him.

And, behold, there came a leper and worshipped him, saying, Lord, if thou wilt, thou canst make me clean.

And Jesus put forth his hand, and touched him, saying, *I will; be thou clean.* And immediately his leprosy was cleansed.

And Jesus saith unto him, See thou tell no man: but go thy way, shew thyself to the priest, and offer the gift that Moses commanded, for a testimony unto them.

And when Jesus was entered into Capernaum, there came unto him a centurion, beseeching him.

And saying, Lord, my servant lieth at home sick of the palsy (paralyzed) grievously tormented.

And Jesus saith unto him, I will come and heal him (make him well).

The centurion answered and said, Lord, I am not worthy that thou shouldest come under my roof: but speak the word only, and my servant shall be healed.

For I am a man under authority, having soldiers under me: and I say to this man, Go, and he goeth; and to another, Come, and he cometh; and to my servant, Do this, and he doeth it.

When Jesus heard it, he marvelled, and said to them that followed, Verily I say unto you, I have not found so great faith, no, not in Israel.

And I say unto you, That many shall come from the east and west, and shall sit down with Abraham, and Isaac, and Jacob, in the kingdom of heaven.

But the children of the kingdom shall be cast out into outer darkness: there shall be weeping and gnashing of teeth.

And Jesus said unto the centurion, Go thy way: and as thou hast believed, so be it done unto thee. And his servant was healed in the selfsame hour.

And when Jesus was come into Peter's house, he saw his wife's mother laid, and sick of a fever.

And he touched her hand, and the fever left her: and she arose, and ministered unto (waited on) them.

When the even was come, they brought unto him many that were possessed with devils (demons): and he cast out the spirits with his word, and healed all that were sick.

That it might be fulfilled which was spoken by Esaias the prophet saying, HIMSELF TOOK OUR INFIRMITIES AND BARE OUR SICKNESSES.

Matthew 8:1–17 (KJV)

WHEN JESUS CAME down from the mountain where he had taught the multitudes, large crowds followed him as he journeyed onward. As Jesus was traveling, a leper (one who has a skin disease) came and knelt down in front of Jesus. The man with leprosy told Jesus that he knew that Jesus could heal him if Jesus willed to do so. Jesus put out his hand and touched the man. He told the man that he willed to heal him; Jesus said, *"Be thou clean."* The man's leprosy disappeared, and he was healed immediately.

Jesus and the man both knew that Jesus was not supposed to touch a person with leprosy. The man told Jesus that he knew that Jesus could (had the power) heal him. The man's question to Jesus was did Jesus will (want) to heal him. The question was does God will (want) to heal us. Any doubt about God's intentions toward his created people reveals a very basic truth. God never intended for men to die or to suffer from diseases. God's will has always been to love his people and to provide for them. Man's own sin caused us to die and to be subject to diseases. God sent Jesus to us to give us eternal spiritual life and to heal all of our diseases.

> Bless the Lord, O my soul: and all that is within me, bless his holy name.
>
> Bless the Lord, O my soul, and forget not all his benefits:
>
> Who forgiveth all thine iniquities; who healeth all thy diseases;
>
> Who redeemeth thy life from destruction; who crowneth thee with lovingkindness and tender mercies.
>
> Psalms 103:1–4 (KJV)

> Surely he hath borne our griefs, and carried our sorrows: yet we did esteem him stricken, smitten of God, and afflicted.
>
> But he was wounded for our transgressions, he was bruised for our iniquities: the chastisement of our peace was upon him; and with his stripes we are healed.
>
> Isaiah 53:4–5 (KJV)

Please read Leviticus 14:1–21.

"But if the person is poor and unable to afford these offerings, he must take one male lamb for a guilt offering. It will be presented to the Lord to make him clean so he can belong to the Lord again" (Leviticus 14:21, KJV). The instructions for making a person clean after he has had a skin disease go on in verses twenty-two through thirty-two.

We can see that the instructions for making a person clean after he had a skin disease were very extensive and explicit. Jesus had told the people that he did not come to replace the Mosaic Law; he told the man who was cured of leprosy to go to the priest so that God's laws would be fulfilled.

If we examine the procedures specified for the cleansing of the man, we can find several significant items used in the sacrifices that coincide with the sacrifice that Jesus made when he was crucified. Water was required for cleansing. One bird died and its blood was shed. The blood of Jesus was used to offer a guilt offering to atone for our sins. One bird was set free; our souls were set free. The sacrifice required the use of a piece of a tree – the cross. The vinegar that was offered to Jesus as he hung on the cross was raised to him on a hyssop stick. When the soldiers struck Jesus in the side after he died, water and blood poured out. It is not possible for us to understand all the points of symbolism without enlightenment from the Holy Spirit, but there are certainly enough corresponding items used in the sacrifice for becoming clean so that a man could belong to God and what was fulfilled during Jesus's sacrifice upon the cross.

Jesus told the man with leprosy to go to the priests and fulfill the Law as it was given to Moses. This was to act as testimony about the healing. First of all the fact that Jesus sent the man to the priest meant that Jesus was not trying to replace the Jewish laws. He wanted the Mosaic Law to be fulfilled. Secondly, the priests would be given proof that the man was in fact healed by Jesus through God's power and according to God's will.

At Capernaum Jesus was approached by a centurion (Roman army officer). The centurion asked Jesus to heal his servant who was paralyzed and suffering greatly at the centurion's home. Jesus responded that he would come and heal the servant.

The centurion told Jesus that he, the centurion, was not worthy to have Jesus enter his home. The centurion knew that Jesus was a great Jewish teacher and healer. He also thought that Jesus would not want to enter the home of a Roman officer; the Jews would consider his home an unclean location. He asked Jesus if he would just say the words to heal the servant from the location where he was at the present time.

The centurion justified his request by explaining that as an officer he was accustomed to lines of authority. He gave orders to other men to go or come and to fulfill his orders. He knew that Jesus had great authority; he believed that Jesus's commands would be fulfilled without Jesus going to another location to achieve his goals.

Jesus was visibly surprised. He told his followers that he had not seen a faith as great as the centurion's in all the people of Israel. Jesus equated faith with the soldier's belief in authority. Jesus went on to tell his followers that many people from the countries far to the west and far to the east would come to God and share the places of Abraham, Isaac, and Jacob. They would be accorded that privilege because of their faith in God. " Now faith is the substance of things hoped for, the evidence of things not seen. For by it the elders obtained (won) a good report" (Hebrews 11:1–2, KJV).

> By faith Abraham, when he was called to go out into a place which he should after receive for an inheritance, obeyed; and he went out, not knowing whither he went.
>
> By faith he sojourned in the land of promise, as in a strange country, dwelling in tents with Isaac and Jacob, the heirs with him of the same promise.
>
> For he looked for a city which hath foundations, whose builder and maker is God.
>
> Hebrews 11:8–10 (KJV)

By faith Abraham, when he was tried, offered up Isaac: and he that had received the promises offered up his only begotten son.

Of whom it was said, That in Isaac shall thy seed be called.

Accounting that God was able to raise him up, even from the dead; from whence also he received him in a figure.

By faith Isaac blessed Jacob and Esau concerning things to come.

By faith Jacob, when he was a dying, blessed both the sons of Joseph; and worshipped leaning upon the top of his staff.

Hebrews 11:17–21 (KJV)

Jesus went on to say that the children of the kingdom (the Jews) would be thrown out into outer darkness where they would weep and cry and grind their teeth. The Jews would lose their places in heaven because they refused to believe God (have faith).

Jesus then addressed the centurion and told him to return to his home. Jesus had granted the soldier's request because the centurion had faith. The centurion did not question Jesus's authority. The servant was healed at the exact time that Jesus told the centurion he would be healed.

When Jesus came to Peter's house, Peter's mother-in-law was ill with a fever. Jesus touched her hand, and her fever went away. She got up from her bed and helped to serve the men at the table. Notice that no one asked Jesus to heal the woman; Jesus did not say anything aloud; he healed her instantly without speaking. We know that people were healed by Jesus without any words being spoken. The woman who touched the hem of Jesus's cloak as he walked through a crowd had not spoken to him; she believed that Jesus had the power to heal.

In the last day, that great day of the feast, Jesus stood and cried, saying, If any man thirst, let him come unto me, and drink.

He that believeth on me, as the scripture hath said, out of his belly shall flow rivers of living water.

John 7:37–38 (kjv)

Jesus is our living water that provides us with life eternally. Jesus is our River of Life.

In the forty-seventh chapter of Ezekiel, Ezekiel is taken to see the River of Life that flows out of the altar of God. It is a river whose depth cannot be measured because it is so great.

Then said he unto me, These waters issue out toward the east country, and go down into the desert, and go into the sea: which being brought forth into the sea, the waters shall be healed.

And it shall come to pass, that every thing that liveth, which moveth, whithersoever the rivers shall come, shall live: and there shall be a very great multitude of fish, because these waters shall come thither: for they shall be healed; and every thing shall live whither the river cometh.

And it shall come to pass, that the fishers shall stand upon it from Engedi even unto Eneglaim; they shall be a place to spread forth nets; their fish shall be according to their kinds, as the fish of the great sea, exceeding many.

But the miry places thereof and the marshes thereof shall not be healed; they shall be given to salt.

And by the river upon the bank thereof, on this side and on that side, shall grow all trees for meat, whose leaf shall not fade, neither shall the fruit thereof be consumed: it shall bring forth new fruit according to his months, because their waters they issued out of the sanctuary: and the fruit thereof shall be for meat, and the leaf thereof for medicine.

Ezekiel 47:8–12 (kjv)

Jesus is the River of Life. The life that he gives us flows out of the altar where he sacrificed his blood to atone for our sins. Everywhere the River flows is healed. On the banks of the River grow trees which provide constantly and eternally for us to be sustained with their life (fruit). The trees watered by the River of Life provide us not only with food (life); they provide us with leaves. The leaves represent our healing given to us by the life of Jesus.

Jesus is our Healer. He offers us cleansing. He offers us life. He offers us healing.

In the evening people brought people who were possessed with devils; Jesus spoke to the evil spirits and they were cast out of the people. He healed all the people who were brought to him because they were ill.

When Jesus saw great crowds of people were all around him, he ordered his disciples to leave and go to the other side of the sea.

JESUS REQUIRES SACRIFICE

A certain scribe came, and said unto him, Master, I will follow thee whithersoever thou goest.

And Jesus saith unto him, The foxes have holes, and the birds of the air have nests; but the Son of man hath not where to lay his head.

And another of his disciples said unto him, Lord, suffer me first to go and bury my father.

But Jesus said unto him, Follow me; and let the dead bury their dead.

Matthew 8:19–22 (KJV)

A JEWISH TEACHER CAME to Jesus and said that he wanted to go with Jesus. Jesus told him that the animals and birds had places to make homes. But Jesus had no place to call His home. One of the disciples who followed Jesus came to ask permission to go back to his home long enough to bury his father. Jesus told him to follow him without looking back. Jesus said that the spiritually dead would bury their dead. This might seem to be a callous answer. We need to remember that Jesus had warned that families would be torn apart. Some members of a family would follow Jesus; and some members of a family would reject Him. A follower must choose between staying with his family and home or following and believing in Jesus.

JESUS CALMS THE SEA AND CASTS OUT DEVILS

And when he was entered into a ship, his disciples followed him.

And, behold, there arose a great tempest in the sea, insomuch that the ship was covered with the waves: but he was asleep.

And his disciples came to him, and awoke him, saying, Lord, save us: we perish.

And he saith unto them, Why are ye fearful, O ye of little faith? Then he arose, and rebuked the winds and the sea; and there was a great calm.

But the men marveled, saying, What manner of man is this, that even the winds and the sea obey him?

And when he was come to the other side of the country of the Gergesenes' there met him two possessed with devils, coming out of the tombs, exceeding fierce, so that no man might pass by the way.

And, behold, they cried out, saying, What have we to do with thee, Jesus, thou Son of God? Art thou come hither to torment us before the time?

And there was a good way off from them an herd of many swine feeding.

So the devils besought him, saying, If thou cast us out, suffer us to go away into the herd of swine.

And he said unto them, Go. And when they come out, they went into the herd of swine: and, behold, the whole herd of swine ran violently down a steep place into the sea, and perished in the waters.

And they that kept them fled, and went their ways into the city, and told every thing, and what was befallen to the possessed of the devils.

And, behold, the whole city came out to meet Jesus: and when they saw him, they besought him that he would depart out of their coasts.

Matthew 8:23–34 (KJV)

JESUS'S DISCIPLES FOLLOWED him as he boarded a ship to go across the sea. While they were crossing the sea, a great storm began to blow the ship. The waves were covering the ship. Remember that several of the disciples were fishermen; they were accustomed to using boats; they would have been able to tell if the ship was about to sink. The disciples went to Jesus who was asleep. They woke Jesus, and begged him to save them because they were about to drown.

Jesus spoke to them when he was awake. He asked them why they were afraid; why did they have such a small amount of faith that he would take care of them? He stood up and rebuked (commanded) the storm and the sea. The wind and the waters became absolutely still. The disciples were astonished. They asked each other what kind of man was Jesus. Even though they had seen

Jesus perform so many miracles, they still didn't understand how much authority he had.

When the ship had reached the other side of the sea, they walked in the country of the Gergesenes (Gadarene people). It is the area starting at Gadara southeast of the Lake of Galilee. As Jesus was walking, two men who were possessed by devils came to meet him. The men lived in the tombs (caves) used to bury dead people. The men were so violent that no one tried to cross by the caves. The men began to yell; the demons were using the voices of the two men.

The devils living in the men began to scream asking Jesus why he was bothering them. The demons (who are spiritual beings not physical ones) recognized that Jesus was the Son of God and that he held authority over them. They wanted to know if he had come to torment them before the Judgment Day had come. Please note that the demons recognized Jesus and knew that He would command them at the Judgment Day; they did not question who he was or how much authority and power he commanded. Unlike men, their knowledge of God and Jesus had not been lost when man sinned and died.

In the distance a large herd of pigs were grazing. The devils begged Jesus to let them go into the pigs if He cast them out of the two men (ordered them to leave the two men). He spoke only one word; he told them to go. When the devils came out of the two men, they went into the herd of pigs. The whole herd of pigs ran frantically down a steep hill into the water. There the pigs all drowned.

The men who were herding the pigs ran into the city. There they told everyone what had happened to the two men who were demon possessed and the herd of pigs. Everyone living in the city came out to meet Jesus and begged Jesus to go far away from their city.

The people of the city were terrified of the two men possessed by the demons; they knew how powerful the demons were. They avoided any contact with the men and the demons. The people knew how much power Jesus must have to command the demons. For them Jesus was an unknown. They were afraid of what he could do to them. They already thought that Jesus was responsible for destroying their pigs. The pigs represented a large portion of their wealth. They begged Jesus to leave because they didn't know what he would do to them; they may have been afraid that more demons would come back to start a war with Jesus. Then they would be caught between two forces from which they were unable to protect themselves.

Please read Leviticus 11:3–8.

To the Jews, pigs were unclean; the Mosaic Law commanded Jews not to eat pigs. That may explain why Jesus allowed the demons to inhabit the swine. He would not have considered them fit for food. There may have been some justification for sending unclean spirits into unclean animals.

This passage and some others in the Bible may require a great leap of faith for some Christians. Some Christians believe that all of the Old Testament and the New Testament is the word of God (inspired and given to men through prophets and the words of Jesus). There are other Christians who believe (trust) God to give them salvation through Jesus Christ. They believe that some things that happened in the Bible no longer happen in modern times. They believe that other parts of the scriptures are only symbolic of God's truth. They believe that the creation of the universe had to have taken more than seven days. Jonah could not have lived inside a whale.

For the Christians who believe that all of the scriptures are the words given from God, the Bible's passages are received as being absolutely true. There is nowhere in the Bible where it says that there are no such things as demons and devils. Quite to the contrary, the Bible speaks frequently to the existence of angels and devils. They are not physical beings; they cannot be seen with man's physical eyes. Angels and devils (demons) are spiritual beings. The angels are spirits always doing God's will and serving God. The demons are evil spirits in rebellion against God always working to serve Satan and fulfill his agenda. Satan and the demons hate men. They want to destroy men. The Bible speaks of powers and principalities; there are legions of spiritual beings constantly at work to uphold God's will and legions of evil spiritual beings constantly trying to convince men that God's word is not true so that they can destroy mankind.

> And the priest shall sprinkle the blood upon the altar of the Lord at the door of the tabernacle of the congregation, and burn the fat for a sweet savour unto the Lord.
>
> And they shall no more offer their sacrifices unto devils, after whom they have gone a whoring. This shall be a statute for ever unto them throughout their generations.
>
> Leviticus 17:6–7 (KJV)

> When the unclean spirit is gone out of a man, he walketh through dry places, seeking rest, and findeth none.
>
> Then he saith, I will return into my house from whence I came out; and when he is come, he findeth it empty, swept, and garnished.
>
> Then goeth he, and taketh with himself seven other spirits more wicked than himself, and they enter in and dwell there; and the last state of that man is worse than the first. Even so shall it be also unto this wicked generation.
>
> Matthew 12:43–45 (KJV)

> And he said unto them, Go ye into all the world, and preach the gospel to every creature.
>
> He that believeth and is baptized shall be saved; but he that believeth not shall be damned.
>
> And these signs shall follow them that believe; In my name shall they cast out devils; they shall speak with new tongues;

They shall take up serpents; and if they drink any deadly thing, it shall not hurt them; they shall lay hands on the sick, and they shall recover.

Mark 16:15–18 (KJV)

If we go back and look at Chapter Eight of Matthew, there is one central theme weaving throughout the chapter. The man with leprosy had faith that Jesus could heal him; he was healed. The centurion had faith that Jesus could heal his servant from a distance; the servant was healed. Peter's mother-in-law had faith in Jesus; she was healed immediately. Jesus reprimanded the disciples because they did not have enough faith that he would save them; with faith they were saved. When we examine the casting out of devils, Jesus said that those who believed (trusted) on him could cast out devils. The believers needed faith. "But without faith it is impossible to please him: for he that cometh to God must believe that he is, and that he is a rewarder of them that diligently seek him" (Hebrews 11:6, KJV).

JESUS FORGIVES SINS

And he entered into a ship, and passed over, and came into his own city.

And, behold, they brought to him a man sick of the palsy, lying on a bed: and Jesus seeing their faith said unto the sick of the palsy; Son, be of good cheer; thy sins be forgiven thee.

And, behold, certain of the scribes said within themselves, This man blasphemeth.

And Jesus knowing their thoughts said, Wherefore think ye evil in your hearts?

For whether is easier, to say, Thy sins be forgiven thee, or to say, Arise, and walk?

But that ye may know that the Son of man hath power on earth to forgive sins, (then saith he to the sick of the palsy,) Arise, take up thy bed, and go into thine house.

And he arose, and departed to his house.

But when the multitudes saw it, they marveled, and glorified God, which had given such power unto men.

Matthew 9:1–8 (KJV)

AFTER JESUS HAD cast out the demons into the herd of pigs, he boarded a boat again. He came ashore at his own city. He was met there by people who brought a paralyzed man so that the man could be healed. Jesus saw that the man and the people who brought him had faith. He told the man to rejoice, because his sins were forgiven. Jesus was always specific about the necessity of faith in healing and in the forgiveness of sin. God requires that we believe what he says, and that we act upon that belief (faith).

> And he turned to the woman, and said unto Simon, Seest thou this woman? I entered into thine house, thou gavest me no water for my feet: but she hath washed my feet with tears, and wiped them with the hairs of her head.
>
> Thou gavest me no kiss: but this woman since the time I came in hath not ceased to kiss my feet.
>
> My head with oil thou didst not anoint: but this woman hath anointed my feet with ointment.
>
> Wherefore I say unto thee, Her sins, which are many, are forgiven; for she loved much: but to whom little is forgiven, the same loveth little.
>
> And he said unto her, Thy sins are forgiven.
>
> And they that sat at meat with him began to say within themselves, Who is this that forgiveth sins also?
>
> And he said to the woman, Thy faith hath saved thee; go in peace.
>
> Luke 7:44–50 (KJV)

We need to remember that God warned Adam and Eve not to eat from the Tree of the Knowledge of Good and Evil because they would die. They decided to not believe God, and they believed the devil instead. Mankind lost eternal life because men did not believe God. They called God a liar. It is necessary for each of us to make the decision to believe God and trust him to keep his word. He has promised to atone for our sins and give us eternal life in Jesus Christ. It is necessary for us to believe God and to act upon that belief (faith).

One of the Pharisees had invited Jesus to come to his home to eat. The Pharisee did not have faith in Jesus; he invited him to eat with him for a different reason. Jesus knew what the Pharisee, Simon, was thinking in his mind. A woman who was a notorious sinner came into the house seeking forgiveness of her sins. It was a sign of disrespect that Simon had not offered Jesus water to cleanse his feet. The people of that time wore sandals, and their feet were always soiled when they had been walking outside of the house. The woman had washed Jesus's feet with her tears; she had wiped his feet with her hair; and she had anointed his feet with perfumed oil. Jesus could see that she had faith in her heart, but she had also acted upon her faith by entering the house of the Pharisee and serving Jesus. God requires of us that we believe him and act upon our faith. Jesus told the woman that her sins were forgiven because she had faith. We are cleansed of our sins if we have faith.

The man who was paralyzed was brought to Jesus for healing; the people who brought him had acted in faith by bringing him. Jesus performed miracles so that the people would know that he was doing God's will. The miracles proved that Jesus had the power to forgive sins. He forgave the man's sins first so that the people would know that the sins had been forgiven when Jesus healed the man. We should also remember that all of us have sinned and that we all share the universal sin that came upon all people when Adam and Eve sinned. Jesus required that the man act upon his faith. He told the man to pick up his bed and go to his own home. God expects us to act upon our faith even if it is only by speaking; we publicly declare that we believe that Jesus is God's son and that we accept him as our personal savior. We actively have faith that our sins are atoned for and that we will have eternal life in union with Jesus. God has given us the power to heal; we choose not to use faith actively by healing in the name of Jesus. We are still bound by fear.

JESUS CAME TO SEEK AND FORGIVE SINNERS

But when the multitudes saw it, they marveled, and glorified God, which had given such power unto men.

And as Jesus passed forth from thence, he saw a man, named Matthew, sitting at the receipt of custom: and he saith unto him, Follow me. And he arose, and followed him.

And it came to pass, as Jesus sat at meat in the house, behold, many publicans and sinners came and sat down with him and his disciples.

And when the Pharisees saw it, they said unto his disciples, Why eateth your Master with publicans and sinners?

But when Jesus heard that, he said unto them. They that be whole need not a physician, but they that are sick.

But go ye and learn what that meaneth, I WILL HAVE MERCY AND NOT SACRIFICE; for I am not come to call the righteous, but sinners to repentance.

Then came to him the disciples of John, saying, Why do we and the Pharisees fast oft, but thy disciples fast not?

And Jesus said unto them, Can the children of the bridechamber mourn, as long as the bridegroom is with them? But the days will come, when the bridegroom shall be taken from them, and then shall they fast.

No man putteth a piece of new cloth unto an old garment, for that which is put in to fill it up taketh from the garment, and the rent is made worse.

Neither do men put new wine into old bottles: else the bottles break, and the wine runneth out, and the bottles perish: but they put new wine into new bottles, and both are preserved.

Matthew 9:8–17 (KJV)

W HEN THE MULTITUDES (great crowds of people) saw that Jesus could forgive sins and heal the sick, they were amazed. They knew that the power that Jesus used was given to him by God. They glorified God because he had given that power to a man.

As Jesus was walking he passed by a tax collector sitting at the place where people paid their taxes. Jesus spoke to the tax collector, Matthew. Jesus told Matthew to, *"Follow me."* Matthew got up immediately and followed Jesus. This was the Matthew who became a disciple, and who wrote the book of Matthew.

We do not know that it was Matthew's house where Jesus went to eat. It seems reasonable to assume that it was. The house was filled with tax collectors who had come to eat. When the Pharisees saw where Jesus was eating, they asked the disciples why Jesus would eat with publicans (tax collectors) and sinners. The Jews considered tax collectors as contemptible people because they took money from their own people (Jews) and gave it to the Romans who held their country captive. When Jesus heard the Pharisees criticizing him for eating with the tax collectors, he told them that people who were not sick didn't need a doctor. He told them to go and study the Old Testament to see what the quote he gave them meant. He quoted a line from Hosea that said "I will have mercy, and not sacrifice."

> O Ephraim, what shall I do unto thee? O Judah, what shall I do unto thee? For your goodness is as a morning cloud, and as the early dew it goeth away.
> Therefore have I hewed them by the prophets; I have slain them by the words of my mouth: and thy judgments are as the light that goeth forth.
> For I desired mercy and not sacrifice; and the knowledge of God more than burnt offerings.
> But they like men have transgressed the covenant: there have they dealt treacherously against me.
>
> Hosea 6:4–7 (KJV)

The passage that Jesus quoted was taken from a rebuke sent by the prophet to the leaders of the Jews. God said that their virtue (goodness) was like a morning mist; their virtue was a brief mist that disappeared quickly. He had rebuked them through the words of His prophets. God wanted them to be merciful instead of making blood sacrifices of animals. God wanted them seek after the wisdom and words of God; God didn't want burning sacrifices. Remember that Jesus is the Word of God so it was Jesus himself who had given those instructions to the people in the Old Testament. Jesus was telling the Pharisees that God wanted them to be merciful to those who had sinned so that they would be brought back to God. The Pharisees concentrated on making rules for other people to follow and condemned people who did not live as they did. They did not obey God themselves, but they wanted to decide how God would judge other people. The Pharisees did not want to bring the sinners to forgiveness (mercy) for their sins; they wanted to convict the people of sin so that they would die like a blood sacrifice.

The disciples of John the Baptist came to Jesus asking Him why the followers of John the Baptist and the Pharisees fasted, but Jesus's disciples did not fast. Jesus responded by telling them that members of a wedding celebration did not fast while the bridegroom was with them. Jesus was the groom who would join himself (marry) the bride of Christ (the church) when he offered himself as a sacrifice to pay for her sins. When Jesus was no longer with the disciples, they would fast.

Jesus reminded them that no one patches an old garment with new cloth because the new cloth would cause the old cloth to tear even more. He also said that no one puts new wine into old bottles (wine skins) because the new wine which is actively fermenting would tear apart the old wine skins. Symbolically he was saying that he was bringing about a new covenant with God that would replace the old covenant that was made with Abraham. The practices of the new church would not be the same as the ones of the old covenant. He would become our priest and the sacrifice for our sins. Jesus did not cancel the commandments of the Old Testament. He fulfilled them so that the new covenant would be different in some ways from the old.

JESUS CONTINUES TO HEAL AND RAISES A GIRL FROM DEATH

While he spake these things unto them, behold, there came a certain ruler, and worshipped him, saying, My daughter is even now dead: but come and lay thy hand upon her, and she shall live.

And Jesus arose, and followed him, and so did his disciples.

And behold, a woman, which was diseased with an issue of blood twelve years, came behind him, and touched the hem of his garment:

For she said within herself, If I may but touch his garment, I shall be whole.

But Jesus turned him about, and when he saw her, he said, Daughter, be of good comfort; thy faith hath made thee whole. And the woman was made whole from that hour.

And when Jesus came into the ruler's house, and saw the minstrels and the people making a noise,

He said unto them, Give place for the maid is not dead, but sleepeth. And they laughed him to scorn.

But when the people were put forth, he went in, and took her by the hand, and the maid arose.

And the fame hereof went abroad into all that land.

And when Jesus departed thence, two blind men followed him, crying, and saying, Thou son of David, have mercy on us.

And when he was come into the house, the blind men came to him: and Jesus saith unto them, Believe ye that I am able to do this? They said unto him, Yea, Lord.

Then touched he their eyes, saying, According to your faith be it unto you.

And their eyes were opened; and Jesus straitly charged them, saying, See that no man know it.

But they, when they were departed, spread abroad his fame in all that country.

Matthew 9:18–34 (KJV)

A RULER, A LEADER of the synagogue, came and bowed down in front of Jesus. The ruler told Jesus that his daughter had died, but he knew that Jesus could come and give her life again. Jesus stood up and followed the ruler with his disciples coming behind.

There is significance in the fact that the ruler was a leader of the Jewish church. Not all of the Jewish leaders and Pharisees rejected Jesus. The fact that the girl was dead (as we are all dead in sin and will die), but her father knew that Jesus could give her new life symbolizes the new birth (born again) experience all Christians receive when they believe (trust, act in faith) Jesus to give us eternal life.

As Jesus was walking, a woman, who was ill and had been bleeding for twelve years, came up behind Jesus and touched the fringe of his garment, cloak. She had silently told herself that she would be healed if she could just touch Jesus. The woman would have been considered unclean because she was having a menstrual cycle.

> Speak unto the children of Israel, and bid them that they make them fringes in the borders of their garments throughout their generations, and that they put upon the fringe of the borders a ribband of blue:
> And it shall be unto you for a fringe, that ye may look upon it, and remember all the commandments of the Lord, and do them; and that ye seek not after your own heart and your own eyes, after which ye use to go a whoring.
>
> Numbers 15:38–39 (KJV)

Please read Leviticus 15:19–28.

The woman knew that she was unclean; she had lived set apart from everyone for twelve years. She was not allowed to touch anyone, and everyone else was forbidden to touch her or anything she touched. In desperation she tried to touch the fringe at the bottom of Jesus's cloak; she thought she would be hidden in the crowd that followed Jesus. She had faith that he could heal her, but she was afraid that he would not because she was unclean. Jesus knew that healing power had gone out from him. When he turned around, he knew who had touched him and what her illness was. Again he said that her faith had healed her. He wanted her to be comforted and to be at peace. The woman was unclean. We are all soiled by our sin and unfit for God to accept us. When we place our faith in Jesus, we are cleansed of our sins by his sacrifice of blood and death. All that is necessary for us to be made clean from our sin is for us to believe (trust) Jesus, God's Word. She touched the fringe of his garment. The fringe was there to remind the wearer and everyone else that we must all obey God's commandments and submit to his will. We must believe God and submit to his will to be saved from sin.

When Jesus arrived at the ruler's house, He could see and hear the musicians, the singers, and all the people making a loud noise mourning the death of the girl. Her father was a leader of the church; there would have been many people mourning because of her death. Jesus told the people to step back. He said that the girl was only sleeping. The people taunted (mocked) him because they knew that she was dead.

When the people had been put outside, Jesus touched her hand, and the girl sat up. We should note that Jesus didn't need to say any significant words to heal the girl. He already knew that her father believed that Jesus could raise her to life again. The father had acted upon his faith by coming to ask Jesus to come. God does not need to show us an outward sign to bestow eternal life and union with Jesus's life when we become Christians. Our spiritual birth does not need to be seen physically. When we become one with Jesus, our eternal life has begun.

Because the girl's rebirth had been so dramatic, and there were so many people who witnessed it in a leader's home, the stories about the happening were repeated many, many times. When Jesus had left that place, he was followed by two blind men who were yelling at Jesus to have mercy upon them. They acknowledged Jesus as a descendent of King David thus stating that they knew his identity as the Messiah or one appointed by God. The men followed Jesus to the house where He was going.

> If our gospel be hid, it is hid to them that are lost:
> In whom the god of this world hath blinded the minds of them which believe not, lest the light of the glorious gospel of Christ, who is the image of God, should shine unto them.
> For we preach not ourselves, but Christ Jesus the Lord; and ourselves your servants for Jesus' sake.
> For God, who commanded the light to shine out of darkness, hath shined in our hearts, to give the light of the knowledge of the glory of God in the face of Jesus Christ.
>
> 2nd Corinthians 4:3–6 (KJV)

God had warned the children of Israel that they were not to hinder or take advantage of people who were blind. The Jews were warned not to cause a blind person to lose his/her way. "Cursed be he that maketh the blind to wander out of the way. And all the people shall say, Amen" (Deuteronomy 27:18, KJV).

In the New Testament we are taught about spiritual blindness. Paul teaches in Corinthians that the god of this physical world, Satan, has blinded the minds of those who are spiritually blind. It is Jesus Christ who is the Light of God. It is Jesus who enabled us to see God the Father and to know God's truth. Jesus has healed our blindness so that we can see the glory of God the Father.

Jesus asked the blind men if they believed that he was able to heal their eyes; they said that they did believe that. Jesus touched the blind men's eyes, but he did not tell them they were healed. He told them that they would receive what they had faith to receive. So much of what God gives us is dependent upon our own faith. It depends on how much we are willing to believe what God says. We have to trust him not to lie to us with an act of our free will. That is why it is necessary for us to act upon our faith. Faith is not a feeling. Faith is an act of our will to believe (trust) God.

Jesus told the men not to tell anyone about their healing. When they left Jesus, they told everyone anyway. Jesus became even more famous.

As the blind men were leaving, some people brought a man who could not speak to Jesus. The man could not speak because he was possessed by a demon. After Jesus cast out the demon (told the demon to leave), the man could talk. The large crowd of people told each other that no one of the Jews in Israel had ever been able to do all the miracles and cast out demons like Jesus did.

The Pharisees felt threatened that they would lose their power and authority over the people. To counteract the fame and approval that Jesus was gaining, the Pharisees told everyone that Jesus cast out devils because he received power from the prince of the demons, Satan.

And Jesus went about all the cities and villages, teaching in their synagogues, and preaching the gospel of the kingdom, and healing every sickness and every disease among the people.

But when he saw the multitudes, he was moved with compassion on them, because they fainted, and were scattered abroad, as sheep having no shepherd.

Then saith he unto his disciples, The harvest truly is plenteous, but the labourers are few;

Pray ye therefore the Lord of the harvest, that he will send forth labourers into his harvest.

Matthew 9:35–38 (KJV)

Jesus continued traveling through all the cities and villages. As he went he taught the Jewish people in their churches and preached about the kingdom of God that was coming. He healed all the people with every sickness and disease who were brought to him.

As Jesus saw the great crowds of people who came to him, He was filled with compassion because the people were so weak and unable to help themselves. The priests and spiritual leaders who should have been serving the people were not doing so. He said that they were like sheep who had no shepherd to protect and provide for them.

I am the good shepherd: the good shepherd giveth his life for the sheep.

But he that is an hireling, and not the shepherd, whose own the sheep are not, seeth the wolf coming, and leaveth the sheep, and fleeth: and the wolf catcheth them, and scattereth the sheep.

The hireling fleeth, because he is an hireling, and careth not for the sheep.

I am the good shepherd, and know my sheep, and am known of mine.

As the Father knoweth me, even so know I the Father: and I lay down my life for the sheep.

And other sheep I have, which are not of this fold;
them also I must bring, and they shall hear my voice; and
there shall be one fold, and one shepherd.

John 10:11–16 (kjv)

Jesus told his disciples that there were many, many people who
needed to be saved and taken care of, but there were not enough
people willing to care for them. He told them to ask God the
Father (the lord of the harvest) to send more harvesters (men) to
bring the people into his fold (group) of believers. He wanted all
of the peoples of the world to be brought into his group of believers so that he could protect and provide for them. The disciples
Jesus told to pray that God would send out more men to gather
the people in were in fact the ones that God would send. All but
one, John, gave their lives and were killed so that Jesus's message about salvation and eternal life could be spread. He commis-
sioned the disciples to "feed" his sheep.

JESUS SENDS OUT THE DISCIPLES TO HEAL AND CAST OUT DEMONS

And when he had called unto him his twelve disciples, he gave them power against unclean spirits, to cast them out, and to heal all manner of sickness and all manner of disease.

Now the names of the twelve apostles are these; The first, Simon, who is called Peter, and Andrew his brother; James the son of Zebedee, and John his brother;

Philip, and Bartholomew; Thomas, and Matthew the publican; James the son of Alphaeus, and Lebbaeus, whose surname was Thaddaeus;

Simon the Canaanite, and Judas Iscariot, who also betrayed him.

These twelve Jesus sent forth, and commanded them, saying, Go not into the way of the Gentiles, and into any city of the Samaritans enter ye not:

But go rather to the lost sheep of the house of Israel.

And as ye go, preach, saying, The kingdom of heaven is at hand.

Heal the sick, cleanse the lepers, raise the dead, cast out devils: freely ye have received, freely give.

Provide neither gold, nor silver, nor brass in your purses.

Nor scrip for your journey, neither two coats, neither shoes, nor yet staves: for the workman is worthy of his meat.

And into whatsoever city or town ye shall enter, enquire who in it is worthy; and there abide till ye go thence.

And when ye come into a house, salute it.

And if the house be worthy, let your peace come upon it: but if it be not worthy, let your peace return to you.

And whosoever shall not receive you, nor hear your words, when ye depart out of that house or city, shake off the dust of your feet.

Verily I say unto you, It shall be more tolerable for the land of Sodom and Gomorrha in the day of judgment, than for that city.

Behold, I send you forth as sheep in the midst of wolves: be ye therefore wise as serpents, and harmless (innocent) as doves.

Matthew 10:1–16 (KJV)

JESUS CALLED HIS twelve chosen disciples to him. He gave them power (authority) to cast out unclean spirits (demons) and to heal all kinds of sickness and disease. The names of the disciples were Simon, who Jesus called Peter, and his brother Andrew; James, the son of Zebedee, and his brother John; Phillip; Bartholomew; Thomas; Matthew, the tax collector; James, the son of Alphaeus; Lebbaeus, who was called Thaddaeus; Simon, who was a Canaanite; and Judas Iscariot. Judas Iscariot was the disciple who betrayed Jesus and led the soldiers to capture Jesus.

Jesus sent out the twelve disciples and commanded them to go to the cities and towns announcing that the Kingdom of Heaven was about to begin. He admonished them not to go to the cities of the Gentiles (people who were not Jews); they were not to go to any city in Samaria. The disciples were told to go to preach to the lost sheep (members) of the Jewish people.

When the disciples came to a new city, they were to heal the sick, cleanse the lepers (people with skin diseases), raise people from death, and cast out devils. They were to give these blessings freely (with no cost) just as they had received blessings from Jesus freely.

The twelve disciples were given instructions about what to take with them. These would be the instructions they would follow after Jesus had gone back to heaven. They were to take no kind of money. They were not to take extra clothes, extra shoes, or staves (staffs to help in walking). Jesus told them that a workman is entitled to his food (provision). They were to depend upon God to provide for their needs through the people to whom they ministered. When they entered a new town, they were to ask someone the identity of the most worthy (of God's blessings) person in that place. They were to go to that person's home and stay there until they left that town.

"And into whatsoever city ye enter, and they welcome you, eat such things as are set before you" (Luke 10:8, KJV). The disciples were to be fed by the person who was considered most worthy and who had welcomed them into their home.

> And David sent out ten young men, and David said unto the young men, Get you up to Carmel, and go to Nabal, and greet him in my name:
>
> And thus shall ye say to him that liveth in prosperity, Peace be both to thee, and peace be to thine house, and peace be unto all that thou hast.
>
> 1st Samuel 25:5–6 (KJV)

In the Old Testament King David sent ten of his servants to talk to Nabal. Nabal was extremely rude to them and would not welcome them. David was very angry because Nabal had not received (welcomed) the servants who came representing him. Later David was bringing an army to punish Nabal planning to kill him and all his family and servants. Nabal's wife, Abigail, convinced David not to kill Nabal and everyone with him. But Nabal was punished anyway. He had a heart attack and died ten days later. God had punished Nabal.

Jesus told the disciples to pray for a blessing of peace to be on the house that welcomed them. The disciples were to go in the name of Jesus representing him. If the people welcomed them and treated them well, the blessing of peace would stay with the people. If the people the disciples went to would not welcome them, the blessing of peace would be given to the disciples. When the disciples went in the name of Jesus, they would heal and preach in his name as his representatives. If they were rejected, it would be the same as if they had rejected Jesus himself.

If the disciples were not welcomed in a city, they were to shake off the dust of their shoes when they left signifying that they were not associated with the people of that city in anyway. They were not responsible for what would happen to the people of that city. God would punish the people of that city when the Judgment Day came. It would be worse for them than it was for the people of Sodom and Gomorrha when God punished them in the Old Testament.

Jesus warned the disciples that He was sending them out to preach and heal in a place filled with danger. They were as vulnerable as sheep would be in a pack of wolves. He warned them to be as wise as snakes in avoiding trouble. They were to be as innocent (harmless) as doves not causing any disturbances or fighting. Just as they were to depend on God to provide for them, they were to depend upon God to protect them and punish anyone who harmed them because they came in the name of Jesus.

JESUS TELLS THE DISCIPLES WHAT TO EXPECT AS HIS REPRESENTATIVES

But beware of men: for they will deliver you up to the councils, and they will scourge you in their synagogues;

And ye shall be brought before governors and kings for my sake, for a testimony against them and the Gentiles.

But when they deliver you up, take no thought how or what ye shall speak: for it shall be given you in that same hour what ye shall speak.

For it is not ye that speak, but the Spirit of your Father which speaketh in you.

And the brother shall deliver up the brother to death, and the father the child: and the children shall rise up against their parents, and cause them to be put to death.

And ye shall be hated of all men for my name's sake: but he that endureth to the end shall be saved.

But when they persecute you in this city, flee ye into another: for verily I say unto you, Ye shall not have gone over the cities of Israel, till the Son of man be come.

The disciple is not above his master, nor the servant above his lord.

It is enough for the disciple that he be as his master, and the servant as his lord. If they have called the master of the house Beelzebub, how much more shall they call them of his household.

Matthew 10:17–25 (KJV)

JESUS WARNED THE disciples that they would be taken to the Sanhedrin and charged with crimes. They would be beaten in the synagogues (churches). They would be taken to appear in front of kings and governors because they preached about Jesus. All these things would happen to them so that there would be proof at the Judgment Day about what the people had done to the disciples who came representing Jesus.

The disciples were told not to worry about what they would say; they should not plan what to say when they were challenged. The Holy Spirit would speak through them when they were called upon to speak.

There would be a great division among the Jews. Some would believe (trust) in Jesus and accept him as their savior. Some would reject him and act violently against his followers. A brother would bring charges against his brother (sibling) so that the brother was killed. A father would testify against his own child, and children would testify against their own parents. The testimonies would cause the family members to be killed.

The disciples would be hated because they came in the name of Jesus. Anyone who resisted and refused to turn against Jesus would be saved from eternal death. Jesus told them that when they were persecuted in a city to go on to the next city and preach there. They would not run out of places to spread the gospel of Jesus Christ before Jesus returned to them.

Jesus reminded the disciples that a servant is not greater (more important) than his master. It is enough that the disciples of Jesus will be treated the same as Jesus was treated. If the master of the house (Jesus who rules in heaven and earth) is called Beelzebub (Satan), then what will the disciples (servants, followers) of Jesus be called?

JESUS'S DISCIPLE MUST FOLLOW HIM AND SHARE HIS EXPERIENCES

Fear not therefore: for there is nothing covered, that shall not be revealed; and hid, that shall not be known.

What I tell you in darkness, that speak ye in light: and what ye hear in the ear, that preach ye upon the housetops.

And fear not them which kill the body, but are not able to kill the soul: but rather fear him (God) which is able to destroy both soul and body in hell.

Are not two sparrows sold for a farthing (1/16 of a day's wage)? And one of them shall not fall on the ground without your Father.

But the very hairs of your head are all numbered.

Fear ye not therefore, ye are of more value than many sparrows.

Whosoever therefore shall confess me before men, him will I confess also before my Father which is in heaven.

Think not that I am come to send peace on earth: I came not to send peace, but a sword.

For I am come to set a man at variance against his father, and the daughter against her mother, and the daughter-in-law against her mother-in-law.

And a man's foes shall be they of his own household.

He that loveth father or mother more than me is not worthy of me: and he that loveth son or daughter more than me is not worthy of me.

And he that taketh not his cross, and followeth after me, is not worthy of me.

He that findeth his life shall lose it: and he that loseth his life for my sake shall find it.

He that receiveth you receiveth me, and he that receiveth me receiveth him that sent me.

He that receiveth a prophet in the name of a prophet shall receive a prophet's reward; and he that receiveth a righteous man in the name of a righteous man shall receive a righteous man's reward.

And whosoever shall give to drink unto one of these little ones a cup of cold water only in the name of a disciple, verily I say unto you, he shall in no wise lose his reward.

Matthew 10:26–42 (KJV)

JESUS TOLD THE disciples not to be afraid because there is nothing that is hidden (secret) that won't be revealed (seen), and there is nothing hidden that won't be known. At the Judgment Day everything will be seen openly, and we will all be judged for the things we did in secret and what we thought to ourselves.

He told them to listen for God's voice when it seems to be spiritually dark around you; then speak what you have heard to others. What God teaches you in your spirit, ye should preach from the housetops.

Don't be afraid of someone who can kill your body; that person cannot kill your soul. You should be afraid (respect and obey) of God; He is able to destroy your soul and your body.

Aren't two sparrows sold for pennies? Not one sparrow falls to the ground that your Heavenly Father does not know it. You are so important to God that every hair on your head is numbered. So don't be afraid. You are of more worth many sparrows.

If someone says that I am God's son, the Messiah, and that they claim me as their saviour in front of other people, I will claim that person as my own when we stand in front of God the Father. If someone says that I am not the Messiah and that they do not claim me as their savior in front of other people, I will not claim that person as my own when we stand in front of God the Father who is in heaven.

Don't think that I came to bring peace over all the earth between all people. I didn't come to bring peace; I came bringing a sword to divide. I came to set a man against his father, to set a daughter against her mother, and a daughter-in-law against her mother-in-law. A man's enemies will be his family.

> Trust ye not in a friend, put ye not confidence in a guide: keep the doors of thy mouth from her that lieth in thy bosom.
>
> For the son dishonoureth the father, the daughter-in-law against her mother-in-law; a man's enemies are the men of his own house.
>
> Therefore I will look unto the Lord; I will wait for the God of my salvation: my God will hear me.
>
> Micah 7:5–7 (KJV)

Micah had prophesized in the Old Testament that families would make war upon themselves. Every person must make his/her own decision to believe (trust) Jesus to give them salvation and eternal life. No one can look to someone else to make that decision for them. Some of the Jews would believe that Jesus was the Messiah, God's promised one, and some of the Jews would try to kill everyone who proclaimed that he/she believed in Jesus. Those who would be saved from eternal death would need to depend upon God to identify the Messiah who brought salvation from sin.

Jesus said that anyone who loved his/her father or mother more than he/she loved Jesus was not worthy of being Jesus's disciple. It is required that each one of us stop letting our family decide what we will believe. If we want Jesus to be loyal to us, we must be loyal to Jesus.

Jesus recognized that turning away from their family and the teachings of the Jewish religion was a great sacrifice. They had to die to dependence on physical methods to please God. The Jews depended on the priests to make sacrifices to God to pay for their sins. Every Jew would need to step out in faith to abandon their old beliefs and trust Jesus. We still make that decision. We need to decide to act on our faith as an act of our free will to accept that everything that God has said in the Bible is true. We can't trust in what we see and hear in the physical world. We must choose to believe what God says in order to be given eternal spiritual life with Jesus. We have to die to dependence on our own works to save us from sin and eternal death.

The person who gains eternal life will lose their physical life; they will need to give up dependence on physical senses. Anyone who loses his physical life will receive eternal spiritual life. For those living when Jesus was on earth, many would actually be put to death to prove their belief in Jesus so that they could have eternal spiritual life.

If anyone welcomed the disciples of Jesus, he/she was welcoming Jesus; anyone who welcomed Jesus was welcoming God the Father. Jesus said that anyone who welcomed a prophet (one who speaks God's messages) would receive from God the reward that God gives to his prophets. Anyone who welcomed a righteous man because the righteous man obeyed God's commandments would receive the reward given to a righteous man from God. Anyone who gave a cup of cold water to Jesus's disciples because that person was a disciple of Jesus would not lose his/her reward from God. We must all look to God to reward us; we should not work to receive approval from other men. God rewards the people who serve God, and God rewards the people who help and minister to the people who serve as God's messengers.

JESUS REBUKES THOSE WHO CRITICIZED JOHN THE BAPTIST

And it came to pass, when Jesus had made an end of commanding his twelve disciples, he departed thence to teach and to preach in their cities.

Now when John had heard in the prison the works of Christ, he sent two of his disciples,

And said unto him, Art thou he that should come, or do we look for another?

Jesus answered and said unto them, Go and show John again those things which ye do hear and see.

The blind receive their sight, and the lame walk, the lepers are cleansed, and the deaf hear, the dead are raised up, and the poor have the gospel preached to them.

And blessed is he, whosoever shall not be offended in me.

And as they departed, Jesus began to say unto the multitudes concerning John, What went ye out into the wilderness to see? A reed shaken with the wind?

But what went ye out to see? A man clothed in soft raiment? Behold, they that wear soft clothing are in kings' houses.

But what went ye out to see? A prophet? Yea, I say unto you, and more than a prophet.

For this is he, of whom it is written, BEHOLD, I SEND MY MESSENGER BEFORE THY FACE WHICH SHALL PREPARE THY WAY BEFORE THEE. Behold, I send my messenger before thy face which shall prepare thy way before thee.

Verily I say unto you, Among them that are born of women there hath not risen a greater than John the Baptist: notwithstanding he that is least in the kingdom of heaven is greater than he.

And from the days of John the Baptist until now the kingdom of heaven suffereth violence, and the violent take it by force.

For all the prophets and the law prophesized until John.

And if ye will receive it, this is Elias, which was for to come.

He that hath ears to hear, let him hear.

But whereunto shall I liken this generation? It is like unto children sitting in the markets, and calling unto their fellows,

And saying, We have piped unto you, and ye have not danced, we have mourned unto you, and ye have not lamented.

For John came neither eating nor drinking, and they say, He hath a devil.

The Son of Man came eating and drinking, and they say, Behold a man gluttonous, and a winebibber, a friend of publicans and sinners. But wisdom is justified of her children.

Then began he to upbraid (accuse) the cities wherein most of his mighty works were done, because they repented not:

Woe unto thee, Chorazin! Woe unto thee, Bethsaida! For if the mighty works, which were done in you, had been done in Tyre and Sidon, they would have repented long ago in sackcloth and ashes.

But I say unto you; it shall be more tolerable for Tyre and Sidon at the day of Judgment, than for you.

And thou, Capernaum, which art exalted unto heaven, shalt be brought down to hell: for if the mighty works, which have been done in thee, had been done in Sodom, it would have remained until this day.

But I say unto you, That it shall be more tolerable for the land of Sodom in the day of judgment, than for thee.

Matthew 11:1–24 (KJV)

AFTER JESUS HAD given the disciples their instructions, He sent them away to preach and heal in his name. He left that place to preach and teach in other cities. John the Baptist, who was in prison, sent two of his disciples (followers) to talk to Jesus. John had heard about all the works that Jesus did; he wanted to know if Jesus was the Messiah, or if they should wait for another messenger from God. Jesus answered John's disciples. He told them to return to John and tell him what they had observed Jesus doing. They were to tell John that they had seen Jesus give sight to the blind, cure the lame so they could walk, cleanse the lepers, help the deaf to hear, and raise people from the dead. They were to tell John that the good news sent from God was preached to the poor. Jesus wanted John to decide for himself that Jesus was the Messiah after John knew about all the things that Jesus was doing. John would know that Jesus was sent from God because no one else had ever been able to do those things. It may seem strange to us that John the Baptist did not know that Jesus was the Messiah. John was a man. He had served God faithfully doing what God told him to do and saying what God told him to say. But he was not supernatural; he only knew what God told him. He wanted clarification from Jesus because he believed that Jesus was chosen by God to do what he did and that God gave Jesus great power. He knew that Jesus was led by the Holy Spirit. Jesus wanted John to welcome Jesus as the Messiah and believe (trust) on Him of his own free will. Jesus wanted the same thing from John that Jesus wants from us. Jesus sent word to John that John would be blessed by God if he did not falter in his walk of faith. We can only have salvation if we believe God. Jesus did not condemn John because his experiences had caused John to doubt. He told John what he needed to think about and remember so that John could believe (trust) Jesus to give him salvation.

As John's disciples were leaving, Jesus turned to address the great crowd that always followed him. He asked them what they went out into the wilderness (desert) to see when they went to see John the Baptist. Did they go to see a weak man who wavered in his belief and resolve to serve God? Did they go out to see a man dressed in fine expensive clothing? Only men who lived in king's palaces wore those kinds of clothing. Did they go out to the desert to see and listen to a prophet? Yes, Jesus said to the people. Jesus said John was even more than a prophet.

Jesus quoted from the Old Testament identifying John the Baptist as the messenger that would go in front of the Son of God to prepare the way for the arrival of Jesus Christ.

> Isaiah 40:3–5 The voice of him that crieth in the wilderness, Prepare ye the way of the Lord, make straight in the desert a high way for our God.
>
> Every valley shall be exalted, and every mountain and hill shall be made straight, and the rough places plain:
>
> And the glory of the Lord shall be revealed, and all flesh shall see it together: for the mouth of the Lord hath spoken it.
>
> Isaiah 40:3–5 (KJV)

Jesus continued to speak saying in God's truth there was no one who had been born as the child of a woman who was greater than John the Baptist. Even so, as great as John was, the person of least importance in the Kingdom of Heaven would be greater than John was. From the days when John began preaching to prepare for the coming of God, the Kingdom of Heaven had been attacked. Satan, the king of the world and the spreader of evil, was trying to seize the Kingdom of Heaven where God's will is always done. In the Old Testament all the prophets and the Mosaic Law spoke of the Saviour who was coming. If the people would only accept it, John was Elijah whom God had promised to send. Let anyone who had the ability to hear God and understand God recognize that John the Baptist was Elijah coming to prepare the way for the Messiah.

Continuing to speak to the crowd, Jesus told them that they were like children playing in the marketplace yelling at one another. One group shouted that they had played music, but the other children did not dance. When John came to preach, he didn't drink wine or eat food prepared for him. You said he had a devil because he abstained from your food and wine. Then the Son of man (Jesus) came, and he ate your food and drank wine. You still were not satisfied. You said the Son of man was a glutton (one who stuffs himself with food) and a drunkard. You complained because he ate with tax collectors and sinners. You justify (defend) your own wisdom. You say that your reasoning makes sense when it does not.

Then Jesus began to accuse (criticize) the cities of that region. He said that even though he had done many great works (miracles) in their cities, the cities still refused to repent (to be sorry and stop sinning) and to turn to God. He said that the cities of Chorazin and Bethsaida would be punished and would have great sorrow and suffering.

Tyre was a large seaport city; ships from all over the known world came there to trade cargoes. During the reign of King

Solomon, Hiram of Tyre provided workers and building materials to build an armory, a palace, and the temple in Jerusalem. Most of the vast wealth and treasures that King Solomon acquired came through Tyre. After the Babylonians destroyed Jerusalem in 586 BC many people from Israel were taken to Babylonia as slaves. With Jerusalem in a weakened position, Tyre stopped serving Jerusalem, and its people gloated over the fall of Jerusalem. Part of the covenant that God made with Abraham was to bless those that blessed Abraham's descendants, and to curse those that cursed Abraham's descendants.

> Thus saith the Lord; For three transgressions of Tyrus, and for four, I will not turn away the punishment thereof; because they delivered up the whole captivity to Edom, and remembered not the brotherly covenant:
> But I will send a fire on the wall of Tyrus, which shall devour the palaces thereof.
>
> Amos 1:9–10 (KJV)

> Yea, and what have ye to do with me, O Tyre, and Zidon, and all the coasts of Palestine? Will ye render me a recompence? And if ye recompense me, swiftly and speedily will I return your recompence upon your own head,
> Because ye have taken my silver and my gold, and have carried into your temples my goodly precious things.
>
> Joel 3:4 (KJV)

There is a lengthy description of the destruction of Tyre which would happen as God's punishment of Tyre in the 26th chapter of Ezekiel.

From several passages in the Old Testament it seems that God punished Tyre because they loved the world (monetary success) instead of God; they also worshiped a Phoenician god. The people were arrogant and believed that they were self-sufficient without God. They were full of pride. They treated God's people (Israel) cruelly.

Nebuchadnezzar of Babylon conquered Tyre; the people of Tyre fled to an island across the water from Tyre where they built another city and named it Tyre. 250 years later Alexander the Great came to conquer Tyre. He had no ships so he could not seize the island city. Alexander ordered his men to gather and scrape up the ruins of the old city of Tyre; they threw them into the sea to build a causeway to the island city of Tyre. Thus Alexander was able to reach the new Tyre and destroy it again.

Jesus said that at the Judgment Day the cities of Tyre and Sidon would be judged less harshly than the cities of Chorazin and Bethsaida. The people of Tyre and Sidon had been full of pride and arrogance; they had worshiped other gods and persecuted the Jews. But the people of Chorazin and Bethsaida had witnessed the arrival and miracles of Jesus. They had rejected the Son of God when God sent Jesus to call them to repentance. They had refused to accept or obey God himself.

He continued teaching saying that the area surrounding Capernaum would be judged more harshly than Sodom which God had destroyed with fire and brimstone. The people of Capernaum refused to obey God and worship God because they were full of pride and self-importance.

In Genesis Chapter 18 we read that God and two angels had appeared at Abraham's tent. He greeted them and prepared a feast for them. God told Abraham that Sarah, Abraham's wife, would have a son even though they were both very elderly. God sent the two angels ahead to survey Sodom, and he talked to Abraham. Abraham's nephew, Lot, lived in Sodom, and Abraham did not want him to be killed. He persuaded God to spare Lot and his family because Lot was a righteous man. Homosexuality is an abomination to God. All of the men of Sodom were homosexual. "If a man also lie with mankind, as he lieth with a woman, both of them have committed an abomination: they shall surely be put to death, their blood shall be upon them" (Leviticus 20:13, kjv).

Ezekiel tells us that the city of Sodom had other sins as well.

> Behold, this was the iniquity of thy sister Sodom, Pride, fullness of bread, and abundance of idleness was in her and in her daughters, neither did she strengthen the hand of the poor and needy.
>
> And they were haughty, and committed abomination before me therefore I took them away as I saw good.
>
> Ezekiel 16:49–50 (KJV)

The people of Sodom were full of pride; they did not acknowledge God. They were self-indulgent and lazy. They did not help those who were poor. They believed that they were full of worth and superiority. They committed homosexual acts even though they knew that God said that it was an abomination. God does not allow people to be prideful. He wants his people to be humble and to be obedient. God destroyed Sodom and Gomorrah by sending down brimstone and fire. He consumed the cities with the same punishment which is in hell.

Jesus said that Sodom and Gomorrah would be less harshly judged at the Judgment Day than Capernaum would be judged. The people of Capernaum had witnessed the healing and the casting out of devils and the raising from the dead. They knew that God was with them. They still refused to acknowledge God and to repent of their sins; they refused to accept the Son of God and obey God's commandments.

> At that time Jesus answered and said, I thank thee, O Father, Lord of heaven and earth, because thou hast hid these things from the wise and prudent, and hast revealed them unto babes.
>
> Even so, Father: for so it seemed good in thy sight.
>
> All things are delivered unto me of my Father, and no man knoweth the Son, but the Father; neither knoweth any man the Father, save the Son, and he to whomsoever the Son will reveal him.
>
> Come unto me, all ye that labour and are heavy laden, and I will give you rest.

> Take my yoke upon you, and learn of me; for I am meek
> and lowly in heart: and ye shall find rest unto your souls.
> For my yoke is easy, and my burden is light.
>
> Matthew 11:25–30 (KJV)

The next line of scripture may seem to be a little puzzling. In the King James version of text, it says that Jesus answered; the literal translation in Greek uses the word for answered as well. If we go back and look at the words telling what Jesus said, we don't see a question that Jesus was answering. Was he responding to what he heard from the Holy Spirit or God the Father? Or did someone in the crowd ask Jesus a question? We can't really tell.

Jesus began to address God the Father directly. He thanked God the Father acknowledging that He is the ruler of the Kingdom of Heaven and the earth. He thanked God the Father for hiding the truth about spiritual life from the wise and the prudent. He thanked him for revealing (showing) those truths to babies (people who were not admired for their learnedness and intelligence). Still continuing to speak to the Father, he said that it was God the Father's decision to arrange circumstances in that way.

> And he said unto me, My grace is sufficient for thee: for
> my strength is made perfect in weakness. Most gladly
> therefore will I rather glory in my infirmities, that the
> power of Christ may rest upon me.
>
> 2 Corinthians 12:9 (KJV)

Accordingly, we can see that Jesus thanked God the Father that the great truths about God and salvation were not given to noted teachers or Rabbis. The truths were given to simple, powerless people so that no man could take credit for God's wisdom.

At that point Jesus began to talk to the crowd. He told them that all truth and authority is given to Jesus by God the Father. No person is able to identify the Son of God or know what He is doing but God the Father. No person is able to see (identify, understand) God the Father unless Jesus reveals (shows) God the Father to that person. Only those who see (recognize) God because Jesus has shown them who He is are able to know God the Father.

Jesus called the people to come to him if they were carrying a heavy load and working very hard. The Jewish leaders and the Pharisees had made rules that were very hard (impossible) for the people to follow. The Pharisees told the people that God would not accept them if they did not obey the Pharisees. The people were also carrying the burden of trying to obey the Mosaic Law. No one can be good (righteous) enough to please God but Jesus.

> Even the righteousness of God which is by faith of Jesus Christ unto all and upon on them that believe: for there is no difference.
>
> For all have sinned, and come short of the glory of God;
>
> Being justified freely by his grace through the redemption that is in Christ Jesus:
>
> Whom God hath set forth to be a propitiation through faith in his blood, to declare his righteousness for the remission of sins that are past, through the forbearance of God.
>
> Romans 3:22–25 (KJV)

Jesus promised to give rest to those people who came to him. If they would take His yoke (become the servants of Jesus) upon themselves, they would learn from him. Jesus said that he was meek and lowly in heart: He meant that he was not a great Jewish leader or Pharisee. He was meek; he did not elevate himself above God the Father. Jesus was not filled with pride and self-importance. The people could trust Jesus to bring peace with God to their souls. Being Jesus's follower and a believer in Jesus to give them salvation would free them from the great load of carrying their own sin. The people were being weighed down with their own sins and the inability to pay for them. The people were bound by death because of their sin. Jesus told them to trust Him to pay for their sins (give them salvation) and to give them eternal spiritual life. They would still need to follow God's commandments, but they would be one with Jesus. He would help them to obey God's commandments and to become righteous. They would still have a burden; they would be responsible for following the commandments and the Mosaic Law; but they would have Jesus to help them.

JESUS OBSERVES THE SABBATH LAW

At that time Jesus went on the Sabbath day through the corn; and his disciples were an hungred, and began to pluck the ears of corn, and to eat. But when the Pharisees saw it, they said unto him, Behold, thy disciples do that which is not lawful to do upon the Sabbath day.

But he said unto them, Have ye not read what David did, when he was an hungred, and they that were with him;

How he entered into the house of God, and did eat the showbread, which was not lawful for him to eat, neither for them which were with him, but only for the priests?

Or have you not read in the law, how that on the Sabbath days the priests in the temple profane the Sabbath, and are blameless?

But I say unto you, That in this place is one greater than the temple.

But if ye had known what this meaneth, I will have mercy and not sacrifice, ye would not have condemned the guiltless.

For the Son of man is Lord even of the Sabbath day.

And when he was departed thence, he went into their synagogue:

And, behold, there was a man which had his hand withered. And they asked him, saying, Is it lawful to heal on the Sabbath days? That they might accuse him.

And he said unto them, What man shall there be among you, that shall have one sheep, and if it fall into a pit on the Sabbath day, will he not lay hold on it, and lift it out?

How much then is a man better than a sheep? Wherefore it is lawful to do well on the Sabbath days.

Then saith he to the man, Stretch forth thine hand. And he stretched it forth; and it was restored whole, like as the other.

Then the Pharisees went out and held a council against him, how they might destroy him.

Matthew 12:1–14 (KJV)

AT A LATER time when the disciples had returned to Jesus, they were walking through a corn field. His disciples were hungry so they began to pick the ears of corn and to eat them. "When thou comest into the standing corn of thy neighbor, then thou mayest pluck the ears with thine hand; but thou shalt not move a sickle unto thy neighbour's standing corn" (Deuteronomy 23:25, KJV)

According to the Mosaic Law it was within their rights to eat the corn in someone else's field. The Pharisees saw the disciples eating, and they used it as an opportunity to condemn Jesus because the disciples were harvesting the corn on the Sabbath day. Jesus asked them if they had not read in the Old Testament scriptures that David and his men went into God's house and ate the showbread which was there for the priests to eat. Jesus also asked them if they had read that the priests in the temple are exempted from following the laws concerning the Sabbath day. Jesus told them that there was someone there in that place who was greater than God's temple. He was speaking of himself because He was God, and the temple was just a building dedicated to God.

Jesus told them again as he had before that they did not understand what a passage in the Old Testament meant. The passage was "I will have mercy and not sacrifice." If the Pharisees recognized the true meaning of the scripture, they would not have criticized the disciples. The passage means that God prefers for people to be forgiven of their sins rather than to condemn them to death because they have sinned. Jesus told them that he was the Lord (ruler) over the Sabbath day.

> I saw in the night visions, and, behold, one like the Son of man came with the clouds of heaven, and came to the Ancient of days, and they brought him near before him.
>
> And there was given him dominion, and glory, and a kingdom, that all people, nations, and languages, should serve him: his dominion is an everlasting dominion, which shall not pass away, and his kingdom that which shall not be destroyed.
>
> Daniel 7:13–14 (kjv)

When Jesus left that place, He went into the synagogue (church). In the church was a man who had a withered (badly injured, shrunken) hand. The Pharisees were still trying to find a reason to discredit Jesus in front of the people. The Pharisees asked Jesus if it was lawful (by the Mosaic Law) to heal someone on the Sabbath day. No one was to work on the Sabbath day according to the law.

Jesus answered them by asking them a question. He asked them what man would find his sheep fallen into a pit (deep hole) on the Sabbath day, and the man would not reach into the pit to save the sheep? Then Jesus asked them a second question. How much more valuable was a man than a sheep? It was therefore acceptable to do good on the Sabbath day.

Jesus said to the man with the withered hand to hold his hand out. The man could not be condemned by the Pharisees because all he did was stretch out his hand. Jesus had not said anything to the man about healing. The hand was healed (restored) instantly because the man acted upon his faith in Jesus by reaching out his hand. Now the Pharisees could say nothing. If they broadcasted the story to the people, the healing would be a testimony that Jesus healed with the power of God.

The Pharisees went out of the temple and held a meeting to discuss among themselves how they could destroy (kill) Jesus.

JESUS CONTINUES TO HEAL AND PREACH; THE PHARISEES CONTINUE TO HARASS

But when Jesus knew it, he withdrew himself from thence: and great multitudes followed him, and he healed them all;

And charged them that they should not make him known:

That it might be fulfilled which was spoken by Esaias the prophet saying,

BEHOLD MY SERVANT, WHOM I HAVE CHOSEN; MY BELOVED, IN WHOM MY SOUL IS WELL PLEASED: I WILL PUT MY SPIRIT UPON HIM, AND HE SHALL SHEW JUDGMENT TO THE GENTILES.

HE SHALL NOT STRIVE, NOR CRY; NEITHER SHALL ANY MAN HEAR HIS VOICE IN THE STREETS.

A BRUISED REED SHALL HE NOT BREAK, AND SMOKING FLAX SHALL HE NOT QUENCH, TILL HE SEND FORTH JUDGEMENT UNTO VICTORY.

AND IN HIS NAME SHALL THE GENTILES TRUST.

Then was brought unto him one possessed with a devil, blind, and dumb: and he healed him, insomuch that the blind and dumb both spake and saw.

And all the people were amazed, and said, Is not this the son of David?

But when the Pharisees heard it, they said, This fellow doth not cast out devils, but by Beelzebub the prince of the devils.

And Jesus knew their thoughts, and said unto them, Every kingdom divided against itself is brought to desolation (ruin); and every city or house divided against itself shall not stand.

And if Satan cast out Satan, he is divided against himself; how shall then his kingdom stand?

And if I by Beelzebub cast out devils, by whom do your children cast them out? Therefore they shall be your judges.

But if I cast out devils by the Spirit of God, then the kingdom of God is come unto you.

Or else how can one enter into a strong man's house, and spoil (take away) his goods, except he first bind the strong man? And then he will spoil (rob) his house.

He that is not with me is against me; and he that gathereth not with me scattereth abroad.

Wherefore I say unto you, All manner of sin and blasphemy shall be forgiven unto men: but the blasphemy against the Holy Ghost shall not be forgiven unto men.

And whosoever speaketh a word against the Son of man, it shall be forgiven him: but whosoever speaketh against the Holy Ghost, it shall not be forgiven him, neither in this world, nether in the world to come.

Either make the tree good, and his fruit good; or else make the tree corrupt, and his fruit corrupt: for the tree is known by his fruit.

O generation of vipers, how can ye, being evil, speak good things? For out of the abundance of the heart the mouth speaketh.

A good man out of the good treasure of the heart bringeth forth good things: and an evil man out of the evil treasure bringeth forth evil things.

But I say unto you, That every idle word that men shall speak, they shall give account thereof in the day of judgment.

For by thy words thou shalt be justified, and by thy words thou shalt be condemned.

Then certain of the scribes and of the Pharisees answered, saying, Master, we would see a sign from thee.

But he answered and said unto them, An evil and adulterous generation seeketh after a sign; and there shall no sign be given to it, but the sign of the prophet Jonas:

For as Jonas was three days and three nights in the whale's belly; so shall the Son of man be three days and three nights in the heart of the earth.

The men of Nineveh shall rise in judgment with this generation, and shall condemn it: because they repented at the preaching of Jonas; and behold, a greater than Jonas is here.

The queen of the south shall rise up in the judgment with this generation, and shall condemn it: for she came from the uttermost parts of the earth to hear the wisdom of Solomon; and behold, a greater than Solomon is here.

When the unclean spirit is gone out of a man, he walketh through dry places, seeking rest, and findeth none.

Then he saith, I will return into my house from whence I came out; and when he is come, he findeth it empty, swept, and garnished.

Then goeth he, and taketh with himself seven other spirits more wicked than himself, and they enter in and dwell there: and the last state of that man is worse than the first. Even so shall it be also unto this wicked generation.

Matthew 12:15–45 (KJV)

J ESUS KNEW THAT the Pharisees were meeting together to find a way to kill him. He went away from the synagogue (church). The multitudes (great crowds of people) still followed him. He healed all of the sick people who were brought to him.

Jesus told the people who were healed not to tell other people about the miracles. This seems to be just the opposite of what we would expect Jesus to do. Jesus did the miracles so that the people could believe that God sent him and gave Jesus power to heal and cast out devils. Why wouldn't he want people to spread the good news? He was fulfilling scriptures from the Old Testament.

> Behold my servant, whom I uphold; mine elect, in whom my soul delighteth; I have put my spirit upon him: he shall bring forth judgment to the Gentiles.
> He shall not cry, nor lift up, nor cause his voice to be heard in the street.
> A bruised reed shall he not break, and the smoking flax shall he not quench: he shall bring forth judgment unto truth.
> He shall not fail nor be discouraged, till he have set judgment in the earth: and the isles shall wait for his law.
>
> Isaiah 42:1–4 (KJV)

A bruised reed is used to show weakness in a message sent by God to Hezekiah, King of Judah. The king was trusting Egypt to save him instead of trusting God. "Now behold, thou trustiest upon the staff of this bruised reed, even upon Egypt, on which if a man lean, it will go into his hand, and pierce it: so is Pharaoh King of Egypt unto all that trust on him" (2nd Kings 18: 21, KJV).

The same message (prophecy) is seen in Isaiah 36:6 and Ezekiel 29:6.

The prophecy about Jesus told what and how God the Father would send Jesus to fulfill His word. Jesus is God's servant. He serves God the Father. God the Father upholds (strengthens, gives authority to) Jesus. God the Father's soul delights (rejoices) in Jesus, God's son. God himself sent the Holy Spirit to stay with Jesus and strengthen him. Jesus will bring judgment to the Gentiles; they will be saved and given eternal life through Jesus. He would not cry (shout, make loud noises in public) to draw attention to himself. Jesus would not use God's power to destroy or injure; symbolically, Jesus would not damage the very weakest reed. Jesus would not fight (make war upon) the established Jewish leaders. Jesus would not put out the smoking flax; he would not diminish the light of God. Jesus would proclaim God's truth. Jesus would not fail to bring about God's will. Jesus would rule over all the world.

A man who was blind and dumb (unable to see or speak) because he was possessed by a devil was brought to Jesus. Jesus healed the man who could then see and speak. All the people in the crowd were amazed that any man could heal as Jesus did. They began to ask one another if he was the Messiah, the descendent of King David.

When the Pharisees heard what the people were saying, they tried to discredit Jesus so that the people would not follow and believe Jesus. The Pharisees told the people that Jesus cast out devils so that people were healed by using the power of Beelzebub, the prince of all the demons.

Jesus knew what the Pharisees thought, and he began to speak to the Pharisees. He told them that every kingdom (nation) that fights against itself will be destroyed. One part of a city can not fight to destroy another part of a city or the whole city will be destroyed. If Satan (the devil) was fighting against Satan, he would be fighting against himself; how could Satan's kingdom

survive? Jesus asked them if he used the power of the devil to cast
out demons, whose power did the Jews use to cast out demons?
The fact that the Jews themselves called on the power of God to
cast out demons proved that demons were not cast out with the
power of Satan.

He continued reasoning with the Pharisees. If Jesus cast out
demons with the power of the Holy Spirit, then the Kingdom
of God was beginning. How can a criminal go into the house
of a strong man and steal his belongings unless he ties up the
strong man first? After the strong man is tied up, the criminal
can take the man's possessions. Anyone who does not believe in
Jesus (who is not Jesus's follower) will not be drawn to Jesus; that
person who refuses to believe Jesus will be scattered away from
the Kingdom of God. No one can be neutral. A person is a part
of the Kingdom of God with Jesus, or that person is an enemy of
God's kingdom.

Jesus reminded the Jews that any sin or blasphemy (lies, rejection, and rebellion) which were committed against Jesus could
be forgiven. But blasphemy (lies, rejection, rebellion) committed
against the Holy Spirit will never be forgiven. Anyone who sees,
knows that a miracle has been done by the power of the Holy
Spirit, and then says that the miracle was not done by God is
damned and cannot be forgiven.

> But a certain man named Ananias, with Saphira his wife,
> sold a possession (some property).
> And kept back part of the price, his wife also being
> privy to it, and brought a certain part, and laid it at the
> apostles' feet.
> But Peter said, Ananias, why hath Satan filled thine
> heart to lie to the Holy Ghost, and to keep back part of
> the price of the land?
> Wiles it remained, was it not thine own? And after it
> was sold, was it not in thine own power? Why hast thou
> conceived this thing in thine heart? Thou hast not lied unto
> men, but unto God. And Ananias hearing these words fell

down, and gave up the ghost: and great fear came on all them that heard these things.

And the young men arose, wound him up, and carried him out, and buried him.

And it was about the space of three hours after, when his wife, not knowing what was done, came in.

And Peter answered unto her, Tell me whether ye sold the land for so much? And she said, Yea, for so much.

Then Peter said unto her, How is it that ye have agreed together to tempt the Spirit of the Lord? Behold, the feet of them which have buried thy husband are at the door, and shall carry thee out.

Then fell she down straightway at his feet, and yielded up the ghost: and the young men came in, and found her dead, and carrying her forth, buried her by her husband.

Acts 5:1–10 (KJV)

When the early church was first organized, many of the believers sold their possessions and gave the money to the apostles so that all of the believers' needs could be met. They were not required to make that sacrifice. Ananias and his wife were Christians. Ananias and his wife wanted the other Christians to believe that they had given all that they had to the body of believers. They sold their possession and gave part of the money to Peter. They thought no one would know that they had misrepresented their gift. The Holy Spirit did know; so Peter knew too. Peter did not condemn them to death. Committing blasphemy against the Holy Spirit caused their deaths.

As Christians living in the time we live in, we must be careful that we do not commit blasphemy against the Holy Spirit. If you know that you have seen a miracle done through the power of the Holy Spirit, you must give the Holy Spirit credit for the healing or miracle. We cannot lie about what God has done or about what we have done for God's people. If God gives us a scripture to share, and we are asked how we found the scripture, we must give the Holy Spirit credit. Sometimes it is easier to not tell Christians who do not believe in miracles that we have witnessed a miracle because they do not believe. It is more important that we do not commit blasphemy against the Holy Spirit than make other people happy. God knows what you know and think and feel. Be careful what you say.

Jesus continued to speak to the Pharisees. He said that they must be consistent. If a tree is healthy and good, it will give good fruit; if the tree is not healthy and rotten, it will produce fruit that is spoiled and not fit to eat. Jesus called them a generation of snakes. How could they speak truthfully when their hearts were full of evil? Whatever is in a person's heart will determine what comes out of their mouths. A good person who treasures God and God's words in his heart will speak about righteous things. An evil man who treasures evil thoughts and abominations in his heart will speak of blasphemous things and words that are not pleasing to God.

Jesus told them that every person who has spoken evil words or words that are not pleasing to God (words that are contradictory to God's will and commandments) must explain those words to God at the Judgment Day. On that day a person's words will show that he is fit to live in God's heavenly kingdom. But if the person's words are not excusable, the words that were spoken will cause that person to be condemned to eternal death and separation from God.

One of the teachers who was a member of the Pharisee group spoke to Jesus. He said that he wanted Jesus to do some trick (miracle) to prove that Jesus was speaking for God. Jesus answered the Pharisee. Jesus said that an evil generation (group) of people who were adulterous to God because they did not follow God's commandments was asking for a miraculous sign to prove that God was speaking to them. There would be no sign given by God to the Pharisees.

The only sign that the Pharisees would see was the sign of Jonas. Jonas the prophet was sent to warn God's people that they must repent and obey God. Jonas lived for three days and nights inside a whale's stomach before he delivered God's message to the people of Nineveh. (Jonas 1:17) Jesus meant that the sign that the Pharisees would see was His death and burial for three days in the tomb (heart of the earth). He said that the men of Nineveh will rise up and accuse the Pharisees at the Judgment Day. Those men of Nineveh repented and obeyed God after they heard the words of Jonah. The Pharisees would not repent and obey God even after they heard God's word from someone much greater than Jonah (Jesus).

> And when the queen of Sheba heard of the fame of Solomon, she came to prove Soloman with hard questions at Jerusalem, with a very great company, and camels that bare spices, and gold in abundance, and precious stones: and when she was come to Solomon, she communed with him of all that was in her heart.
>
> 2 Chronicles 9:1 (KJV)

The queen of Sheba heard about the great wisdom of King Soloman. She traveled a great distance bringing priceless gifts to Soloman so that she could hear Soloman speak. She asked Soloman questions and shared the personal thoughts that she had in her heart. Jesus (speaking about himself) told the Pharisees that someone greater than King Solomon was with them, and they refused to listen to the wisdom and teachings that Jesus could share with them.

Still speaking to the Pharisees Jesus spoke to them about unclean spirits (demons). We should remember that Jesus had said that they were a generation of vipers (snakes). In the Garden of Eden Adam and Eve listened and believed the lies of Satan rejecting the words of God. The implication here is that the Pharisees believed the lies about Jesus told to them by evil spirits and rejected the words of God.

Jesus said that when an unclean spirit (demon) is cast out of a person, the spirit goes and wanders around in the desert because the spirit cannot find a place to live. Then the spirit says to himself that he will return to the man with whom he lived before. When he comes back to the man, the man has been cleansed of evil spirits. So the evil spirit that was cast out of the man brings seven demons more evil than he is, and all of them inter into the man. The man is more possessed by evil than he was before the first spirit was cast out of him. Jesus came to save the Jews. He was casting out the evil spirits who held them captive with their lies. They would not accept Jesus. So after Jesus was gone back to heaven, those evil spirits would come back with more spirits to torment the Jews who rejected Jesus.

MARY AND THE BRETHREN OF JESUS VISIT

While he yet talked to the people, behold, his mother and his brethren stood without, desiring to speak with him.

Then one said unto him, Behold, thy mother and thy brethren stand without, desiring to speak with thee.

But he answered and said unto him that told him, Who is my mother? And who are my brethren?

And he stretched forth his hand toward disciples, and said, Behold my mother and my brethren!

For whosoever shall do the will of my Father which is in heaven, the same is my brother, and sister, and mother.

Matthew 12:46–50 (KJV)

EVEN WHILE JESUS was still speaking to the people who followed him, someone came to tell him that his mother and his family had come. His family had sent word to him that they wanted to talk with him. Jesus answered the man who brought him the message. He asked the man who were his mother and family? Jesus stretched out his hand and pointed to His disciples. He said that his disciples were his family. Jesus said that anyone who does the will of God the Father, who lives in heaven, is a member of Jesus's family. He was speaking of his spiritual family. When we become one with Jesus, we are the children of God. Thus we are all members of the spiritual family of Jesus.

JESUS TEACHES THE DISCIPLES IN PARABLES

The same day went Jesus out of the house, and sat by the sea side.

And great multitudes were gathered together unto him, so that he went into a ship, and sat; and the whole multitude stood on the shore.

And he spake many things unto them in parables (illustrations), saying, Behold, a sower went forth to sow;

And when he sowed, some seeds fell by the way side, and the fowls came and devoured them up:

Some fell upon stony places, where they had not much earth: and forthwith they sprung up, because they had no deepness of earth:

And when the sun was up, they were scorched; and because they had no root, they withered away.

And some fell among thorns; and the thorns sprung up, and choked them:

But other fell into good ground, and brought forth fruit, some an hundredfold, some sixtyfold, some thirtyfold.

Who hath ears to hear, let him hear.

And the disciples came and said unto him, Why speakest thou unto them in parables?

He answered and said unto them, Because it is given unto you to know the mysteries (hidden truths) of the kingdom of heaven, but to them it is not given.

For whosoever hath, to him shall be given, and he shall have more abundance; but whosoever hath not, from him shall be taken away even that he hath.

Therefore speak I to them in parables: because they seeing see not; and hearing they hear not, neither do they understand.

And in them is fulfilled the prophecy of Esaias, which saith, by hearing ye shall hear, and shall not understand; and seeing ye shall see, and shall not perceive.

For this people's heart is waxed gross, an their ears are dull of hearing, and their eyes they have closed; lest at any time they should see with their eyes and hear with their ears, and should understand with their heart, and should be converted, and I should heal thee.

But blessed are your eyes, for they see: and your ears, for they hear.

For verily I say unto you, That many prophets and righteous men have desired to see those things which ye see, and have not seen them; and to hear those things which ye hear, and have not heard them.

Hear ye therefore the parable of the sower.

When any one heareth the word of the kingdom, and understandeth it not, then cometh the wicked one, and catcheth away that which was sown in his heart. This is he which received seed by the way side.

But he that received the seed into stony places, the same is he that heareth the word, and anon with joy receiveth it;

Yet hath he not root in himself, but dureth for a while: for when tribulation or persecution ariseth because of the word, by and by he is offended.

He also that received seed among the thorns is he that heareth the word; and the care of this world and the deceitfulness of riches, choke the word, and he becometh unfruitful.

But he that received seed into the good ground is he that heareth the word, and understandeth it; which also beareth fruit, and bringeth forth, some an hundredfold, some sixty, and some thirty.

Another parable put he forth unto them, saying, The kingdom of heaven is likened unto a man which sowed good seed in his field:

But while men slept, his enemy came and sowed tares among the wheat, and went his way.

But when the blade was sprung up, and brought forth fruit, then appeared the tares also.

So the servants of the householder came and said unto hi, Sir, didst not thou sow good seed in thy field? From whence then hath it tares?

He said unto them, An enemy hath done this. The servants said unto him, Wilt thou then that we go and gather them up?

But he said, Nay; lest while ye gather up the tares, ye root up also the wheat with them.

Let both grow together until the harvest: and in the time of harvest I will say to the reapers, Gather ye together first the tares, and bind them in bundles to burn them: but gather the wheat into my barn.

Another parable put he forth unto them, saying, The kingdom of heaven is like to a grain of mustard seed, which a man took, and sowed in his field:

Which indeed is the least of all seeds: but when it is grown, it is the greatest among herbs, and becometh a tree, so that the birds of the air come and lodge in the branches thereof.

Another parable spake he unto them; The kingdom of heaven is like unto leaven, which a woman took, and hid in three measures of meal, till the whole was leavened.

All these things spake Jesus unto the multitude in parables; and without a parable spake he not unto them:

That it might be fulfilled which was spoken by the prophet, saying, I will open my mouth in parables; I will utter things which have been kept secret from the foundation of the world.

Then Jesus sent the multitude away, and went into the house: and his disciples came unto him, saying, "Declare unto us the parable of the tares of the field."

He answered and said unto them, He that soweth the good seed is the Son of man;

The field is the world; the good seed are the children of the kingdom; but the tares are the children of the wicked one;

The enemy that sowed them is the devil; the harvest is the end of the world; and the reapers are the angels.

As therefore the tares are gathered and burned in the fire; so shall it be in the end of this world.

The Son of man shall send forth his angels, and they shall gather out of his kingdom all things that offend, and them which do iniquity:

And shall cast them into a furnace of fire: there shall be wailing and gnashing of teeth.

Then shall the righteous shine forth as the sun in the kingdom of their Father, Who hath ears to hear, let him hear.

Again, the kingdom of heaven is like unto treasure hid in a field; the which when a man hath found, he hideth, and for joy thereof goeth and selleth all that he hath, and buyeth that field.

Again, the kingdom of heaven is like unto a merchant man, seeking goodly pearls:

Who, when he had found one pearl of great price, went and sold all that he had, and bought it.

Again, the kingdom of heaven is like unto a net, that was cast into the sea, and gathered of every kind:

Which, when it was full, they drew to shore, and sat down, and gathered the good into vessels, but cast the bad away.

So shall it be at the end of the world: the angels shall come forth, and sever the wicked from among the just,

And shall cast them into the furnace of fire: there shall be wailing and gnashing of teeth.

Jesus saith unto them, "Have ye understood all these things? They say unto him, Yea, Lord."

Then said he unto them, "Therefore every scribe which is instructed unto the kingdom of heaven is like unto a man that is an householder, which bringeth forth out of his treasure things new and old."

Matthew 13:1–52 (KJV)

O N THE SAME day that Mary and Jesus's brethren came to see him, he went out of the house and sat by the sea. Even going out of the house did not allow room for all of the great crowd of people to hear Jesus. So Jesus entered into a ship and sat down. The great crowd of people who had come to see Jesus stood on the shore close to the ship where Jesus sat.

Jesus began to teach the people using parables (illustrations). He began to tell them a story about a sower (planter) who went out to plant seed. The sower would have been sowing by tossing the seed out as he walked. Some of the seeds fell on the side of the road, and the birds came and ate those seeds. Some of the seeds fell on ground that had many stones mixed in with the dirt; those seeds sprouted and started to grow, but the plants died because there was not enough soil to sustain life. When the sun shone on the plants, the plants died because there was not enough soil to develop a good root system. Some of the seeds fell where there were thorns (weeds) growing. The thorns grew where the seeds had fallen and choked out the plants from the seeds. But some of the seeds fell on good ground. Those seeds sprouted and grew strong, healthy plants. Some of the seeds in the good ground produced a hundred times more grain than was planted. Some of the seeds produced sixty times more grain than was planted. Some of the seeds produced thirty times more grain than was planted. After Jesus had told the story, he said that those who could hear the story and understand its meaning should learn from it.

His disciples came to Jesus and asked him why he was using parables (stories) to teach the people. Jesus answered them that God had given them the ability to understand the teachings behind the stories. The disciples were given the ability to understand the mysteries of the Kingdom of God. The people who had come to see Jesus were not given that knowledge.

People who understand the truths and teachings of God will increase their understanding of God's secrets and know more about God. The people who did not understand the significance of the parables would lose the understanding that they possessed. That was the reason why Jesus taught with parables. The people on the shore did not see the truth of God; they did not spiritually hear the truth about God; they did not understand what Jesus was teaching in their spirits. Isaiah had spoken about those people in Isaiah 6:8–10.

> Also I heard the voice of the Lord, saying, Whom shall I send, and who will go for us? Then said I, Here am I; send me.
>
> And he said, Go, and tell this people, Hear ye indeed, but understand not; and see ye indeed, but perceive not.
>
> Make the heart of this people fat, and make their ears heavy, and shut their eyes; lest they see with their eyes, and hear with their ears, and understand with their heart, and convert, and be healed.
>
> Isaiah 6:8–10 (KJV)

The people had grown callous. Jesus saw their hearts, and He knew that they would not receive (value) what he was teaching. The eyes and ears of the disciples were blessed by God because they could understand the spiritual truths that they saw and heard. Jesus told the disciples that many prophets and righteous men had longed to hear and see the spiritual truths that the disciples were able to perceive (understand). He began to explain to the disciples the truths (meaning) behind the parable of the sower (planter).

When anyone hears the truth (word) of God's kingdom and does not understand it, the devil comes and takes the truth from the heart of the hearer. These are the seeds that were thrown beside the road which the birds ate.

The seed that landed on stony soil was like the people who heard the word of God and understood it. They received the word of God and rejoiced because they understood it. They held the truth of God in their hearts until they were tried with tribulation and persecution which came to them because they knew the truth of God's word. Then those people turned aside from God like the seeds that fell on rocky ground and died because their faith was not deeply rooted.

The seeds that fell on ground where thorns (weeds) grew were like the people who understood the words of God but the troubles (stress) of their earthy life choked out the truth of God. Those people began to value earthly wealth so that their lives did not produce the fruit of the spirit.

The seeds that fell on good ground were like the people who heard and understood God's truths. They took those truths into their hearts and were strongly rooted in God's truth. Their lives produced the fruits that God values. Some of their lives yielded a hundredfold; they lived and taught the truth about God so that others were converted. Some of their lives yielded sixty times as much; they sought God's truth and lived in such a manner that other people turned to God because of what they saw in the disciples. Some of their lives yielded thirty times as much; they were an example (of love and generosity) to others of the lives that God wills for us to live.

Jesus continued to tell another parable. The Kingdom of God is like a man who planted good seed in his fields. While the man was sleeping, his enemy came and planted weeds in the first man's fields with the good seeds. When the good seeds sprouted and began to grow, the weeds began to grow too. The man's servants went to the man and asked him if he did not plant good seed. The servants asked him why there were weeds in the fields. The man told his servants that his enemy had planted the weeds. The servants asked him if they should go and pull up the weeds. The man answered them telling them to leave the grain and the weeds to grow because they would damage the grain crop while they were pulling up the weeds. He told them that when the grain was harvested, he would tell the reapers (harvesters) to gather up the weeds first, tie them up, and burn them. Then the harvesters would gather the grain and put it in his barns.

Jesus told the people a third parable. The kingdom of heaven is like a mustard seed that a man planted in his field. A mustard seed is the smallest of all the seeds. When the mustard seed grows, it becomes a great tree where the birds come and make their nests. When a person receives the truth about Jesus, that truth produces great faith in the person. The person's life and faith become so evident (great) that many other people are drawn to Jesus and salvation.

Jesus taught another parable to the great crowd. He said that the kingdom of heaven is like a small bit of leaven (yeast) which a woman placed in three measures of flour. As the leaven grew the whole dough mixture was expanded. When the word of God is taught it expands the understanding of many people.

Speaking to the great crowd, Jesus told them these parables. He did not teach them any truth without using a parable. Again He was fulfilling the scriptures from the Old Testament spoken by the prophet. "I will open my mouth in a parable: I will utter dark sayings of old" (Psalms 78:2, KJV).

The scriptures said that Jesus would speak in parables. He would tell things that had been kept secret even from the creation of the world. After Jesus finished telling the parables to the people, he sent them away. He returned to the house where He was staying. His disciples came to Him, and they asked Him to explain the parables that He taught to the people.

Answering the disciples, Jesus told them that the man who planted the good seed was the Son of man (Jesus). The field was the world. The good seed planted by Jesus were the children of God's kingdom (Jesus's followers). The weeds were the people who obeyed the devil. The enemy was the devil. The harvest was the end of the world. The harvesters were the angels.

Just as the weeds were gathered and burnt, the things that offend God and the people who do iniquity are the weeds. Jesus will send the angels to gather up all the people and things that are offensive to God. The angels will throw them into a furnace of fire. There will be terrible crying and gnashing of teeth from those who have disobeyed God.

Those who are righteous because Jesus is their redeemer and savior will shine like suns (stars) in the Kingdom of God the Father. Those who are able to understand God's truth should accept it.

The kingdom of heaven is like a treasure that was buried in a field. A man found the treasure, and hid it. He went and sold everything he had so that he could buy the piece of ground where the treasure was hidden. We should give up everything of value by worldly values to obtain a place in the Kingdom of Heaven for eternity.

The kingdom of heaven is like a merchant (buyer) who found a priceless pearl that was more valuable than anything else; the buyer sold everything that he had so that he could buy that pearl.

The kingdom of heaven is like a net that was thrown into the sea and caught fish of every kind. When the net was full, the fishermen drug it to the shore. They sat down and separated what was good from the net into containers. The fishermen threw away what was not good. At the end of the world, the angels will do the same thing separating the wicked (evil) from the just (pleasing to God). Those who are not justified by their faith in Jesus Christ will be thrown into the great furnace of fire. Jesus asked the disciples if they understood everything that He had taught them. They responded that they did understand.

Then Jesus said to the disciples that it was best if every scribe (scholar, teacher) who teaches about the Kingdom of Heaven should be like the man who brings out from his treasures both old and new things. He meant that the new teachings that Jesus gave them did not replace the teachings of the Old Testament. A smart man would value the teachings of the Old Testament and the new teachings given by Jesus himself.

THE PEOPLE ASK THEMSELVES WHO JESUS IS

And it came to pass, that when Jesus had finished these parables, he departed thence.

And when he was come into his own country, he taught them in their synagogue, insomuch that they were astonished, and said, Whence hath this man this wisdom, and these might works?

Is not this the carpenter's son? Is not his mother called Mary? And his brethren, James, and Joses, and Simon, and Judas?

And his sisters, are they not all with us? Whence then hath this man all these things?

And they were offended in him. But Jesus said unto them, A prophet is not without honour, save in his own country, and in his own house.

And he did not many mighty works there because of their unbelief.

Matthew 13:53–58 (KJV)

AFTER JESUS HAD finished teaching the people with parables, he returned to the town where He grew up, Nazareth. In his hometown, Jesus taught in the church. The people who lived in that place were greatly surprised. They asked one another where Jesus had gotten his wisdom and the power to do miracles. They asked if he was a local carpenter's son. They asked if he was the son of a local woman named Mary. They knew his brothers, James and Joseph and Simon and Judas. They asked if his sisters didn't live in their village. Where could Jesus being a local man of no great wealth or family reputation have learned the things that he taught? Where did he obtain power to work miracles?

The local people were offended (upset, indignant) because he did not know his place in their society. He tried to make himself great when he was not great. Jesus said to his critics that a prophet (one who speaks words given to him by God) would be honored everywhere except in his own country or village. A prophet was never supported, encouraged, or honored by his own family. Because these people living in Nazareth did not believe or place their faith on Jesus as God's son and the Messiah, he did not do great miracles in Nazareth.

Again we are reminded that God requires that we have faith (Do God the honor of believing Him) if our prayers are going to be answered.

JOHN THE BAPTIST IS BEHEADED BY HEROD

At that time Herod the tetrarch heard of the fame of Jesus,

And said unto his servants, This is John the Baptist; he is risen from the dead; and therefore mighty works do shew forth themselves in him.

For Herod had laid hold on John, and bound him, and put him in prison for Herodias' sake, his brother Philip's wife.

For John had said unto him, It is not lawful for thee to have her.

And when he would have put him to death, he feared the multitude, because they counted him as a prophet.

But when Herod's birthday was kept, the daughter of Herodias danced before them, and pleased Herod.

Whereupon he promised with an oath to give her whatsoever she would ask

And she, being before instructed of her mother, said, Give me here John Baptist's head in a charger.

And the king was sorry: nevertheless for the oath's sake, and them which sat with him at meat, he commanded it to be given her.

And he sent, and beheaded John in the prison.

And his head was brought in a charger, and given to the damsel: and she brought it to her mother.

And his disciples came, and took up the body, and buried it, and went and told Jesus.

Matthew 14:1–12 (KJV)

KING HEROD HEARD that Jesus had become famous. Herod said to his servants that he believed that Jesus was really John the Baptist who had come back from the dead. He believed that Jesus could do the great miracles that he did because he was John the Baptist.

Herod believed that Jesus was really John the Baptist because Herod had ordered his servants to kill John. At a previous time, Herod had told his men to seize John and put him in prison. He did this to please Herodias who was the wife of his brother, Philip. Herodias hated John because John had told Herod that it was not lawful for him to marry his brother's wife. John's statement to Herod was fully in keeping with John's ministry. John had been sent by God to call people to repentance. John preached that people should admit their sins, ask God for forgiveness, and stop sinning.

Herod had not killed John because he was afraid of what the people would do if he killed him. The people believed that John was a prophet sent to them by God. Herod held a great feast (party) to celebrate his own birthday. He was greatly pleased with the dance Herodias's daughter performed at the party. Herod feeling great pride and being influenced by the riotous party promised with an oath (a solemn vow) that he would give Herodias' daughter anything that she wanted. Herodias had told her daughter before the party that the girl was to ask Herod for John the Baptist's head on a platter. Herod was not willing to kill John, but he had made the solemn vow in front of all his guests. Herod felt that he had no choice but to do what he had promised to do. So he sent his servants to the prison with orders to behead John. John's head was brought to the party on a platter and given to the girl. She took the head and gave it to Herodias.

John's disciples took John's body and buried it properly according to Jewish law. Then John's disciples went to Jesus and told him what had happened to John.

JESUS FEEDS THE MULTITUDE

When Jesus heard of it, he departed thence by ship into a desert place apart: and when the people had head thereof, they followed him on foot out of the cities.

And Jesus went forth, and saw a great multitude, and was moved with compassion toward them, and he healed their sick.

And when it was evening, his disciples came to him, saying, This is a desert place, and the time is now past; send the multitude away, that they may go into the villages, and buy themselves victuals.

But Jesus said unto them, They need not depart; give ye them to eat.

And they say unto him, We have here but five loaves, and two fishes.

He said, Bring them hither to me.

And he commanded the multitude to sit down on the grass, and took the five loaves, and the two fishes, and looking up to heaven, he blessed, and brake, and gave the loaves to his disciples, and the disciples to the multitude.

And they did all eat, and were filled: and they took up of the fragments that remained twelve baskets full.

And they that had eaten were about five thousand men,
beside women and children.

And straightway Jesus constrained his disciples to get
into a ship, and to go before him unto the other side, while
he sent the multitudes away.

Matthew 14:13–22 (KJV)

WHEN JESUS HAD been told that John had been killed, He got into
a ship and went to an isolated desert place. He went to a place
where he could be alone to grieve for John. But when the people
heard where he had gone, they followed him walking on foot from
the cities. Jesus went out of seclusion and saw all the great crowd
of people who were following him because they had no one else to
go to for healing. Seeing their great need and despair, Jesus healed
the sick people that they had brought to him.

As it became evening, the disciples came to Jesus. They asked
him to send the people away. They reminded him that they were
in a deserted area; the people would need to walk some distance
to reach a city where they could buy food.

Jesus told the disciples to feed the people. He asked them to
bring to him the small amount of food that they had. Jesus gave
thanks to God acknowledging that God the Father is the pro-
vider of all we receive. Then he told the disciples to step out in
faith and begin feeding the great crowd of people. The disciples
did not see the huge amount of food that would be consumed
before they started feeding the people. They just obeyed Jesus and
believed that he would provide. They did not refuse to act because
they couldn't see the physical evidence first. They didn't question
whether he was telling them the truth. They began to act upon
Jesus'commandment believing that he would provide the means
of completing the task.

We are reminded here that in Revelation 22:1–2, John was
shown a river of pure water that came from the throne of God

and the Lamb, Jesus. This perfectly pure river was bordered by trees which provided fruit eternally. When the people came to Jesus he provided them with food. The trees which were sustained by the living water bore not only fruit that changed with each season but also leaves which provided healing. The great crowds of people had come to Jesus because they knew that he could heal them. Jesus, who is the River of Life, fed and healed the people who followed him.

When Moses was leading the people of Israel through the desert, God provided food for them; they gathered manna each morning (Exodus 16). And God provided flesh for the people to eat in the eleventh chapter of Numbers. God had fed the children of Israel in the Old Testament; Jesus provided food for the people when they came to him for healing.

There is significance in the fact that there were only five loaves when they brought the food to Jesus. He multiplied the loaves so that there was enough for five thousand men and their families. There is also significance in the fact that the leftover food that was gathered after the meal filled twelve baskets. Even after salvation was given to the Gentiles, there will always be provision enough left for the twelve tribes of Israel, the descendants of Abraham, to receive salvation through Jesus.

Finally there is significance in the manner in which Jesus provided for the great number of people who came to Him because they believed in Him. The disciples asked Jesus to send the people away because they had nothing to give them.

As Christians we have nothing to give those who come searching for Jesus. We are not the ones who provide the bread of life and salvation for these people. It is Jesus himself who performs the miracle providing the salvation which will give them eternal life. We have nothing to give from our own powers. It is Jesus who provides eternal life. We are only the disciples who deliver the message of salvation through Jesus. There will always be enough to provide everyone who comes seeking Jesus with salvation and eternal life.

JESUS WALKS ON WATER

And when he had sent the multitudes away, he went up into a mountain apart to pray; and when the evening was come, he was there alone.

But the ship was now in the midst of the sea, tossed with waves; for the wind was contrary.

And in the fourth watch of the night Jesus went unto them, walking on the sea.

And when the disciples saw him walking on the sea, they were troubled, saying, it is a spirit, and they cried out for fear.

But straightway Jesus spake unto them, saying, Be of good cheer; it is I; be not afraid.

And Peter answered him and said, Lord, if it be thou, bid me come unto thee on the water.

And he said, Come. And when Peter was come down out of the ship, he walked on the water, to go to Jesus.

But when he saw the wind boisterous, he was afraid; and beginning to sink, he cried, saying, Lord, save me.

And immediately Jesus stretched forth his hand, and caught him, and said unto him, O thou of little faith, wherefore didst thou doubt?

And when they were come into the ship, the wind ceased.

Then they that were in the ship came and worshipped him, saying, Of a truth thou art the Son of God.

And when they were gone over, they came into the land of Gennesaret.

And when the men of that place had knowledge of him, they sent out into all that country round about, and brought unto him all that were diseased;

And besought him that they might only touch the hem of his garment: and as many as touched were made perfectly whole.

Matthew 14:23–36 (KJV)

AFTER JESUS HAD fed the five thousand men and their families, he directed his disciples to get into a boat and go to the opposite side of the sea. He would stay to send the great crowd of people away from that place. When Jesus had sent the people away, he went up on the mountain by Himself to pray. Jesus had not had a time by himself since he was told that John the Baptist was dead. He needed a time apart from everyone else to communicate with God the Father. When it became dark Jesus was alone up on the mountain.

The ship that the disciples had set out in across the Sea of Galilee was now in the middle of the sea. The ship was being tossed about because there was a great wind blowing. Jesus came to the disciples when they needed him. Between three and six o'clock in the morning, Jesus approached the boat walking on the water. The disciples saw Jesus walking on the water, and they were very frightened. They thought that they were seeing a ghost, and they began to scream in fear. Jesus told them to be filled with courage; He told them not to be afraid. Jesus identified himself saying, "It is I." This could have been translated as "I am". Jesus and God frequently identified themselves as "I am" indicating that they were eternal beings with no beginning or ending of their lives.

Peter answered Jesus and told Jesus that if it was truly Jesus they were seeing, Peter wanted Jesus to tell Peter to come to him walking on the water. Jesus told Peter to come to him. There is a very powerful lesson in this passage.

In 1st Corinthians 13:13 we are told that faith, hope, and charity (love) will never end. Sometimes we mistake the definition of hope for faith. We learn in Hebrews 11:6 "But without faith it is impossible to please him: for he that cometh to God must believe that he is, and that he is a rewarder of them that diligently seek him." Paul goes on in the book of Hebrews to site all of the people in the Bible who acted on their faith.

Faith is an action word. Hope is a belief in the future. But faith is an action taken by the act of the person's will. Faith is not a feeling. Faith is deciding to believe God and to take an action because you believe God. Peter's walk on the water is a great example of faith. Peter believed Jesus when Jesus told him that he could come walking on the water. It wasn't faith until Peter got out of the boat. Peter had no physical evidence that he could walk on the water. He could sit in the boat and believe Jesus. It was an act of faith when Peter got out of the boat and walked on the water. Peter actually did walk on the water. Jesus did not say that Peter did not have faith. Jesus said that Peter had too little faith. Peter had faith and could walk on the water as long as he kept his eyes and attention on Jesus. Peter's faith faltered, and he began to sink when he looked at the physical evidence of the waves and stopped concentrating on Jesus. Faith isn't faith until you get out of the boat ignoring physical evidence and believing that Jesus will do what he says he will do. Jesus did not say that Peter would always lack faith because his faith was too small then. Peter's faith did grow; he developed great faith. His faith enabled him to perform many miracles in the name of Jesus and to die for his faith in Jesus without renouncing Jesus. Man's stumbling block with God is that we still don't believe him enough. If we don't believe, we are calling him a liar.

When Peter faltered, Jesus reached out and saved him. Jesus will always do the same for us. When we need him, he is always there. When Jesus and Peter entered into the ship, the storm stopped. It doesn't say that Jesus rebuked the winds, but we know that in other passages in the Bible all of God's creation is subject to the orders of Jesus. The disciples who were on the ship and had witnessed what had happened to Peter and Jesus walking on the water and the storm stopping when Jesus wished it to do so. They fell on their knees and worshipped Jesus declaring that Jesus was truly the Son of God.

The ship continued across the sea and docked at the land of Gennesaret. The men of Gennesaret knew about Jesus so they sent messages to all the people living around their town telling the people that Jesus was at Gennesaret. The people in all the towns around that area came to Gennesaret bringing their family members who were ill. We know that God never intended that man would have illness and pain and die. Illness and evil and death came into the world, and man became subject to them because Adam and Eve did not believe God. They did not obey God. But the first and greatest step in their sinning was that they did not believe God. Adam and Eve believed that God lied to them. All illness is subject to Jesus's authority. Jesus has authority over all of heaven and earth. There is no sickness and pain in the Kingdom of Heaven.

The people even begged Jesus to allow them to touch the hem (fringe) of his garment (clothes) believing that they would be healed.

> Speak unto the children of Israel, and bid them that
> they make them fringes in the borders of their garments

throughout their generations, and that they put upon the fringe of the borders a ribband of blue:

And it shall be unto you for a fringe, that ye may look upon it, and remember all the commandments of the Lord, and do them; and that ye seek not after your own heart and your own eyes, after which ye use to go a whoring:

That ye may remember, and do all my commandments, and be holy unto your God.

I am the Lord your God which brought you out of the land of Egypt, to be your God: I am the Lord your God.

Numbers 15:38–41 (KJV)

When the people of Gennesaret touched the fringes of Jesus's clothing, they were acknowledging that they recognized that they were God's own people and that they must obey God's commandments. They believed that the healings that Jesus performed came from God. They believed that Jesus was sent by God. All of the people who touched the fringe of Jesus's garment (clothing) were healed.

JESUS ANSWERS THE PHARISEES AND EXPLAINS SCRIPTURE

Then came to Jesus scribes and Pharisees, which were of Jerusalem, saying, Why do thy disciples transgress the tradition of the elders? For they wash not their hands when they eat bread.

But he answered and said unto them, Why do ye also transgress the commandment of God by your tradition?

For God commanded, saying, Honour THY FATHER AND MOTHER: AND HE THAT CURSETH FATHER OR MOTHER, LET HIM DIE THE DEATH.

But ye say, Whosoever shall say to his father or his mother, It is a gift, by whatsoever thou mightiest be profited by me;

And honour not his father or his mother, he shall be free. Thus have ye made the commandment of God of none effect by your tradition.

Ye hypocrites, well did Esaias prophesy of you saying,
THIS PEOPLE DRAWETH NIGH UNTO ME
WITH THEIR MOUTH, AND HONOURETH ME
WITH THEIR LIPS, BUT THEIR HEART IS FAR
FROM ME.

BUT IN VAIN THEY DO WORSHIP
ME, TEACHING FOR DOCTRINES THE
COMMANDMENTS OF MEN.

And he called the multitude, and said unto them, Hear, and understand:

Not that which goeth into the mouth defileth a man; but that which cometh out of the mouth, this defileth a man.

Then came his disciples, and said unto him, Knowest thou that the Pharisees were offended, after they heard this saying?

But he answered and said, Every plant, which my heavenly Father hath not planted, shall be rooted up.

Let them alone: they be blind leaders of the blind. And if the blind lead the blind, both shall fall into the ditch.

Then answered Peter and said unto him, Declare unto us this parable.

And Jesus said, Are ye also yet without understanding?

Do not ye yet understand, that whatsoever entereth in at the mouth goeth into the belly, and is cast out into the draught?

But those things which proceed at out the mouth come forth from the heart; and they defile the man.

For out of the heart proceed evil thoughts, murders, adulteries, fornications, thefts, false witness, blasphemies:

These are the things which defile a man: but to eat with unwashen hands defileth not a man.

Matthew 15:1–20 (KJV)

JEWISH TEACHERS AND Pharisees from Jerusalem had traveled to speak to Jesus. They began to test Jesus and criticize the disciples. They asked Jesus why his disciples disobeyed the rules set by the elders (past leaders) of the Jews. The scribes and Pharisees charged that the disciples ate food without first washing their hands.

Jesus answered them by asking why their people established customs that disobeyed the commandments of God. He said that God had commanded them to honour their parents. "Honour thy father and thy mother: that thy days may be long upon the land which the Lord thy God giveth thee." (According to Ephesians 6: 2—3, this is the first commandment given by God with a promise.) (Exodus 20:12, KJV).

> Honour thy father and thy mother, as the Lord thy God hath commanded thee; that thy days may be prolonged, and that it may go well with thee, in the land which the Lord thy God giveth thee.
>
> Deuteronomy 5:12 (KJV)

> And ye shall keep my statutes, and do them: I am the Lord which sanctify you.
> For every one that curseth his father or his mother shall be surely put to death: he hath cursed his father or his mother; his blood shall be upon him.
>
> Leviticus 20:8–9 (KJV)

"And he that curseth his father, or his mother, shall surely be put to death" (Exodus 21: 17, KJV). God's law as he gave it to Moses stated that every person should honour (respect) their parents. Anyone who slandered (cursed, shamed) his parent should be put to death. The Jewish leaders had developed a custom that said that a person could tell a parent that the son or daughter had something which could be used to provide for the parent but that the son or daughter had given that thing (money, provision) to God instead. That custom was called Corban.

> And he said unto them, Full well ye reject the commandment of God, that ye may keep your own tradition.
>
> For Moses said, "Honour thy Father and thy Mother; and whoso curseth father or mother, let him die the death."
>
> But ye say, If a man shall say to his father or mother, It is Corban, that is to say, a gift, by whatsoever thou mightiest be profited by me; he shall be free.
>
> And ye suffer him no more to do ought for his father or his mother;
>
> Making the word of God of none effect through your tradition, which ye have delivered: and many such like things do ye.
>
> Mark 7:9–13 (KJV)

Jesus said that the Jewish leaders and Pharisees were hypocrites because they pretended to honour and obey God making a great show of their holiness, but they established laws that taught people to disobey God. "Wherefore the Lord said, Forasmuch as this people draw near me with their mouth, and with their lips do honour me, but have removed their heart far from me, and their fear toward me is taught by the precept of men" (Isaiah 29:13, KJV).

Isaiah had prophesized that the Jewish people had spoken as though they were honoring God, but they were not obeying the real meaning of God's words. They did not show respect to God or his commandments; they established laws that were contrary to God's commandments.

Jesus called out to the multitude (great crowd) that He wanted them to listen and understand what He was teaching them. What a man (person) eats or drinks does not defile (make unholy before God). It is what comes out of a person's mouth, what he says, that defiles a person before God.

The disciples of Jesus then asked Him if He did not understand that the Pharisees were angry about what He had said to them. He answered the disciples by saying that every plant that was not planted according to the will of God the Father would be destroyed. Every person who was not chosen by God the Father would be condemned in the day of Judgment. He told the disciples not to try to change the Pharisees and scribes. The Pharisees were blind to (did not understand) the will of the Heavenly Father. They were people who did not see what God was doing or what God wanted; they (the leaders) were leading other people who did not understand God (who were blind to God's will). If a blind person leads another blind person both of them will fall into the ditch (be destroyed).

Peter asked Jesus to explain the parable that Jesus had taught. Jesus asked Peter if he still did not understand what Jesus was saying. Whatever enters the mouth of a person (is eaten or drunk) is thrown away (disposed of) in the waste disposal. It is the things that come out of a person's mouth (what he or she says) that defile (soil, make unholy) in the eyes of God. Whatever a person thinks, desires, believes, or proclaims in his or her words will reveal what is in that person's heart. If a person's heart and mind are full of evil thoughts, murder, adultery, fornication, stealing, telling lies (giving false witness), and speaking against God or disobeying God, those things will defile a person when he speaks of them. God sees our secret thoughts, desires, plans, and values. He sees everything about us. A person must control what that person says; the person will be judged for what that person says. Eating food without washing a person's hands does not condemn a person in God's eyes.

JESUS HEALS A GENTILE DAUGHTER

Then Jesus went thence, and departed into the coasts of Tyre and Sidon.

And, behold, a woman of Canaan came out of the same coasts, and cried unto him, saying, Have mercy on me, O Lord, thou son of David; my daughter is grievously vexed with a devil.

But he answered her not a word. And his disciples came and besought him, saying, Send her away; for she crieth after us.

But he answered and said, I am not sent but unto the lost sheep of the house of Israel.

Then came she and worshipped him, saying, Lord, help me.

But he answered and said, It is not meet to take the children's bread, and to cast it to dogs.

And she said, Truth, Lord: yet the dogs eat of the crumbs which fall from their masters' table.

Jesus answered and said unto her, O woman, great is thy faith: be it unto thee even as thou wilt. And her daughter was made whole from that very hour.

Matthew 15:21–28 (KJV)

JESUS LEFT THAT place and went to the area around the towns of Tyre and Sidon. As he and the disciples walked down the road, a Canaan woman (person who was not a Jew) began to follow them crying out loudly for Jesus to help her. The woman was begging Jesus to have mercy on her. She acknowledged that she knew that Jesus was a descendant of King David; this probably indicates that she knew that he was the Messiah or sent from God. She had come to plead with Jesus to heal her daughter who was troubled greatly by a demon.

Jesus did not answer her. His disciples encouraged him to send the woman away because she was making an embarrassing scene wherever they went. We know that Jesus had healed and cast out demons for hundreds of people. We know that the disciples were accustomed to seeing him heal all those who came to him for healing. There was a reason why Jesus did not answer her. There was a reason why the disciples did not expect Jesus to help her. First of all, Jesus only did what God the Father told him to do. Secondly, everyone including people who were not Jewish knew that Jesus had been sent to call the Jewish people to repentance; to save them from sin; and to give them eternal life. The Jews were the chosen people of God. We can remember at this time that Jesus had offered salvation to the woman at the well in Samaria; she came from people who were despised by the Jews. This woman came from a people who were not even remotely related to the Jews and their God.

When Jesus finally acknowledged her, He told her that he wasn't sent by God the Father to gather people who were not of the Jewish faith or worshippers of their God. She came and knelt down before Jesus. The woman begged Jesus to help her. Jesus told her that it was not appropriate for him to give the blessings that he had been sent to give to people who were not believers in the Jewish God. She told him that he spoke the truth, but that even the puppies were allowed to eat the crumbs (garbage)

THOU SHALL CALL HIS NAME JESUS

beneath the master's table. She was willing to take less blessings from Jesus than he gave to the Jews. But she wanted just a small portion of the blessings given to the Jews. She wanted to receive the blessing that the Jews had rejected.

When Jesus answered her again, He said that her great faith had gained his favor. She believed that Jesus was sent by God. She believed that Jesus would and could help her daughter. Again we are reminded that God rewards people who believe in Jesus's power and depend upon Jesus (trust Jesus). She had taken an action based upon her faith; she came to Jesus and begged for his help. Jesus rewarded her faith. He gave her what she begged to receive. Jesus cast out the demon and healed her daughter from that exact hour in time.

JESUS HEALS AND FEEDS THE MULTITUDES

And Jesus departed from thence, and came nigh unto the Sea of Galilee; and went up into a mountain, and sat down there.

And great multitudes came unto him, having with them those that were lame, blind, dumb, maimed, and many others, and cast them down at Jesus's feet; and he healed them:

Insomuch that the multitude wondered, when they saw the dumb to speak, the maimed to be whole, the lame to walk, and the blind to see: and they glorified the God of Israel.

Then Jesus called his disciples unto him, and said, I have compassion on the multitude, because they continue with me now three days, and have nothing to eat: and I will not send them away fasting, lest they faint in the way.

And his disciples say unto him, Whence should we have so much bread in the wilderness, as to fill so great a multitude?

And Jesus saith unto them, How many loaves have ye? And they said, Seven, and a few little fishes.

And he commanded the multitude to sit down on the ground.

And he took the seven loaves and the fishes, and gave thanks, and brake them, and gave to his disciples, and the disciples to the multitude.

And they did eat, and were filled: and they took up of the broken meat that was left seven baskets full.

And they that did eat were four thousand men, beside women and children.

And he sent away the multitude, and took ship, and came into the coasts of Magdala.

Matthew 15:29–39 (KJV)

JESUS LEFT THAT area and went close to the Sea of Galilee where he climbed up towards the top of a mountain. He sat down at that height so that He could be heard and seen by more people. Again great crowds of people came to Him bringing their family members to be healed of all kinds of illness. They brought people who were lame (unable to walk), blind (unable to see), dumb (unable to speak), maimed (with arms, legs, hands, or feet missing), or ill with many sicknesses. The crowds came believing that Jesus had the power to heal and make a person whole.

All of the ill and disabled were set down in front of Jesus. He healed them all. The lame could walk; the blind could see; the dumb could talk; the ones with missing limbs had new body parts; everyone was healed. Note that whatever the person needed, Jesus would and could heal and provide for that person's needs. Jesus still has that power and willingness to provide for all of our needs. He is still able to heal us physically, mentally, and spiritually. He has enough power and love to care for each of us no matter what our need might be.

When the great crowd of people saw that Jesus had the power to heal all of the people brought to him, they began to wonder about who Jesus was and why he was able to do what no other man could do. They recognized why Jesus had so much compassion and power; the crowd glorified (praised and attributed the miracles) the God of Israel. "Therefore when he was gone out, Jesus said, Now is the Son of man glorified, and God is glorified in him. If God be glorified in him, God shall also glorify him in himself, and shall straightway glorify him" (John 13: 31–32, KJV)

> Believe me that I am in the Father, and the Father in me; or else believe me for the very works' sake.
>
> Verily, verily, I say unto you, He that believeth on me, the works that I do shall he do also; and greater works than these shall he do; because I go unto my Father.
>
> And whatsoever ye shall ask in my name, that will I do, that the Father may be glorified in the Son.
>
> If ye shall ask anything in my name, I will do it.
>
> John 14:11–14 (KJV)

> If ye abide in me, and my words abide in you, ye shall ask what ye will, and it shall be done unto you.
>
> Herein is my Father glorified, that ye bear much fruit; so shall ye be my disciples.
>
> John 15:7–8 (KJV)

The 31st verse of the 15th chapter of Matthew reveals the real purpose of the miracles that Jesus performed. Jesus performed miracles so that God the Father might be revealed and glorified. At the last supper that Jesus shared with the disciples before Jesus died on the cross, He spoke to the disciples about his purpose in glorifying God the Father. When Jesus performed miracles, he glorified God the Father. Jesus came to reveal God the Father to men. God the Father sent him to rescue men from sin and death.

All of the miracles that Jesus performed gave the people physical evidence that they could see and understand so that God the Father would be revealed to them. Jesus's miracles had an eternal purpose; they had a greater purpose than the physical healing of sickness. The miracles proved to the people that Jesus had come from God and that he spoke the words of God. Jesus repeatedly said that he only did and said what God the Father told him to do and say.

Jesus went on to tell the disciples that they were to continue to perform miracles in Jesus's name so that God the Father would be revealed and glorified. If the disciples believed Jesus, they would do as he instructed them. They would perform miracles in the name of Jesus so that other people would believe in Jesus and be saved from eternal death. If Jesus performed miracles in obedience to God the Father's will, then the disciples of Jesus (past and present) should perform miracles in obedience to the will of God the Father and Jesus, the Son of God. Jesus committed himself to do the miracles if they were done in his name. Thus God the Father will be glorified in Jesus and the disciples who perform miracles in the name of Jesus. We must also remember that Jesus said that he did only what God the Father told him to do. We must be constantly led by the Holy Spirit so that we will know if Jesus and God the Father will us to perform a miracle. Without Jesus we are nothing; without the vine the branches cannot bear fruit. If we want to comply with the will of God the Father, we must be constantly listening for the direction of the Holy Spirit.

Jesus felt great compassion for the people who had walked so far to see and hear him. The great crowd had been following and listening to Him for three days. The people had not eaten for all that time. He called the disciples and told them that he would not send the people away without feeding them because they were so weak from hunger that they would faint as they walked.

The disciples wanted to obey Jesus, but they told him that they did not have resources to feed the people in the deserted place where they were located. Jesus asked them how many loaves of bread that they had. They replied that they had seven loaves of bread and a few fish.

Jesus told the great crowd of people to sit down on the ground. He took the loaves and the fish and gave thanks to God for the food he had provided. Jesus blessed the food. He spoke a blessing over the food in God the Father's name. He divided the food among the disciples and instructed them to feed the great crowd of people. Jesus is the Bread of Life. We receive life from him (We are one with him.) so that we have eternal life. When Jesus fed the five thousand men and their families, he taught his disciples to perform the miracle of salvation for all men. Jesus taught the disciples the truth of God the Father's plan of salvation for all men. The disciples taught the truth of God the Father's plan to other believers. The miracle is still being performed. The believers who have learned the plan of salvation given by God the Father through Jesus Christ is still being distributed to new believers after more than 2,000 years. When all the people had eaten as much as they wanted, the disciples gathered up left over food to fill seven baskets. There is no limitation on the salvation offered by God the Father through Jesus Christ. There will always be enough salvation to provide anyone who believes (trusts) in Jesus with eternal life in union with Jesus.

After Jesus had fed the huge crowd of people, He went on board a ship and traveled to the coast of Magdala.

JESUS ADDRESSES THE BELIEFS OF THE PHARISEES AND THE SADDUCEES

The Pharisees also with the Sadducees came, and tempting desired him that he would shew them a sign from heaven.

He answered and said unto them, When it is evening, ye say, It will be fair weather: for the sky is red.

And in the morning, It will be foul weather today: for the sky is red and lowering. O ye hypocrites, ye can discern the face of the sky; but can ye not discern the signs of the times?

A wicked and adulterous generation seeketh after a sign; and there shall no sign be given unto it, but the sign of the prophet Jonas. And he left them and departed.

And when his disciples were come to the other side, they had forgotten to take bread.

Then Jesus said unto them, Take heed and beware of the leaven of the Pharisees and of the Sadducees.

And they reasoned among themselves, saying, It is because we have taken no bread.

Which when Jesus perceived, he said unto them, O ye of little faith, why reason ye among yourselves, because ye have brought no bread?

Do ye not yet understand neither remember the five loaves of the five thousand, and how many baskets ye took up?

Neither the seven loaves of the four thousand, and how many baskets ye took up?

How is it that ye do not understand that I spake it not to you concerning bread, that ye should beware of the leaven of the Pharisees and of the Sadducees?

Then understood they how that he bade them not beware of the leaven of bread, but of the doctrine of the Pharisees and of the Sadducees.

Matthew 16:1–12 (KJV)

A GROUP OF Pharisees and Sadducees came as a group to test Jesus. They asked Him to show them a sign from heaven so that they would know that God had sent him. The Pharisees and the Sadducees were trying to discredit Jesus (prove that Jesus was a fake). They challenged him to do a magic trick so that they would know that he spoke as God told him to speak.

The Pharisees were a powerful Jewish sect. They believed that they were the ones who should translate God's laws for all Jews. Their doctrine and laws did not agree with the commandments of God. Jesus's most frequent criticism of the Pharisees was that they were hypocrites. They made extensive laws to govern the behavior and beliefs of all the Jews. They made displays to prove how holy they were. They had men blow horns in the streets so that everyone would see them when they prayed on the street corners or gave offerings. But they ignored the commandments of God and made laws of their own. The Pharisees held authority over all the Jews saying that they had the authority to judge others and make laws on God's behalf. The Pharisees tried repeatedly to prove that Jesus did not come from God because they wanted to rule and have power over all Jews. They fought against Jesus even though they knew that he represented God so that they could keep their power and authority.

At this point we should remember what the original sin of Adam and Eve was. The devil convinced Eve that she could be a god. In believing the devil instead of believing God, Adam and Eve called God a liar. They wanted to take God's place as God. Man's original sin repeats itself over and over. People still want to be god. People still want to decide what is right and wrong (good and evil). People still want to rule over other people and judge other people. The yeast of the Pharisees that Jesus spoke about repeatedly was the desire and actions of people who want to stand in the place of God and make commandments for other people to follow. We still see this human characteristic in people who organize cults and groups who want to establish doctrines for all churches to follow. Only God has the right to judge others and give commandments to people.

The Sadducees were a group made up of the ruling class of priests. They rejected the doctrines not specifically found in the Jewish law such as resurrection from death, punishment in a future life, and existence of angels. Just as the Pharisees did, the Sadducees fought to have dominance over the beliefs and actions of all of God's people.

Jesus responded to the demands of the Pharisees and the Sadducees to do a magic trick by telling them that they recognized the sign of a red sky in relationship to what future weather would be. They had not read the signs which had come from God in establishing his support of Jesus. They ignored the hundreds of miracles that Jesus had performed in God's name. He said that they were an evil and adulterous generation. They were evil because they chose the evil of the devil instead of God's truth. They were adulterous because they belonged to God, but they chose to embrace (give loyalty to) the ways of the devil.

> If there be found among you, within any of thy gates which the Lord thy God giveth thee, man or woman, that hath wrought wickedness in the sight of the Lord thy God, in transgressing his covenant,
>
> And hath gone and served other gods, and worshipped them, either the sun, or moon, or any of the host of heaven, which I have not commanded;
>
> And it be told thee, and thou hast heard of it, and enquired diligently, and behold, it be true, and the thing certain, that such abomination is wrought in Israel:
>
> Then shall thou bring forth that man or that woman, which have committed that wicked thing, unto thy gates, even that man or that woman, and shalt stone them with stones, till they die.
>
> Deuteronomy 17:2–5 (KJV)

The scripture from the Old Testament used by the Jews to show what should happen to an adulterous woman was actually a passage which spoke of the adultery of a person when that person worshipped a false god.

> They say, If a man put away his wife, and she go from him, and become another man's, shall he return unto her again? Shall not that land be greatly polluted? But thou hast played the harlot with many lovers; yet return again to me, saith the Lord.
>
> Lift up thine eyes unto the high places, and see where thou hast not been lien with. In the ways hast thou sat for them, as the Arabian in the wilderness; and thou hast polluted the land with thy whoredoms and with thy wickedness.
>
> Jeremiah 3:1–2 (KJV)

The Lord said also unto me in the days of Josiah the king, Hast thou seen that which backsliding Israel hath done? She is gone up upon every high mountain and under every green tree, and there hath played the harlot.

And I said after she had done all these things, Turn thou unto me, But she returned not. And her treacherous sister Judah saw it.

And I saw, when for all the causes whereby backsliding Israel committed adultery I had put her away, and given her a bill of divorce; yet her treacherous sister Judah feared not, but went and played the harlot also.

And it came to pass through the lightness of her whoredom, that she defiled the land, and committed adultery with stones and with stocks.

Jeremiah 3:6–9 (kjv)

As often happened when Jesus spoke, he was not speaking about physical things. He was speaking of spiritual adultery. Jesus declared that the Pharisees and the Sadducees were guilty of being evil and adulterous because they did not keep their covenant with God. They had become loyal and obedient to other gods – wealth and power and pride.

Jesus went on to tell them that they would receive no sign from God other than the sign of Jonas.

Jonah was a man who was sent by God to warn the people of Nineveh to stop their evil way of life. Jonah did not want to go to Nineveh so he got on a ship going to another place. The Lord God sent a great storm on the sea that was strong enough to wreck the ship. The sailors were very frightened. They threw their possessions off of the ship to keep it from sinking. Jonah was asleep down inside the ship. The ship's captain came and told Jonah to come and pray to his god for their safety. The men on the ship cast lots to decide with whom God was angry. The lots showed that Jonah was responsible for the storm. The sailors asked Jonah who he was. Jonah told them that he was a Hebrew, some one who worshipped the God of heaven and of earth. He told them that he had disobeyed God. They asked Jonah what they should do with him to appease God so that the ship would not be wrecked. Jonah told the sailors to throw him in the sea. The sailors did not want to throw Jonah overboard so they tried to row the boat to shore, but they could not do it. The men prayed to God to save their lives and threw Jonah into the sea. The great storm stopped.

The Lord God had sent a huge fish to swallow Jonah. Jonah was in the fish's belly for three days and three nights. Even though Jonah had sunk to the depth of the sea, he did not die. Jonah told God that God had brought up his life from corruption (death). After Jonah had agreed to sacrifice to God with thanksgiving and to keep the vow that he had taken, Jonah said that salvation comes from God. God caused the huge fish to vomit Jonah up on the shore.

Again God told Jonah to go to Nineveh, a great city, and tell the people there what God told Jonah to say. Jonah warned the people of Nineveh that their city would be destroyed in forty days. The people believed what God told Jonah to tell them. They proclaimed a fast and put on sack cloth to show their repentance. They cried out to God and God did not destroy them.

Jonah was angry because the Lord had forced him to go and tell the people of Nineveh that their city would be destroyed. And then God did not destroy the city. Jonah told God to just kill Jonah. God asked Jonah if Jonah should be angry. So Jonah went outside the city and built a shack. He sat down to wait and see what God would do. God caused a plant to grow and give Jonah shade. But the next day God sent a worm to kill the plant. God sent a sultry (hot, humid) wind to blow, and the sun beat down on Jonah. Again Jonah told God that he would be better off if he was dead. Then God told Jonah that Jonah felt sorry for the gourd plant that had shaded him and then died the next day. God asked Jonah if God should not be sorry for the six score thousand people of Nineveh who didn't know right from wrong.

THOU SHALL CALL HIS NAME JESUS

When those people knew that they were sinning against God, they had repented.

God had saved Jonah when Jonah had disobeyed God. He had forgiven Jonah and given him a second chance. Jonah had no right to be angry when God forgave the people of Nineveh after they repented for their disobedience and prayed to God for forgiveness.

Jesus told the Sadducees and the Pharisees that the only proof they would be given that Jesus was sent by God was the sign of the prophet Jonah. God sent Jonah to warn the people of Nineveh to repent of their sins and obey God. God sent Jesus to warn the Jewish people to repent and stop sinning against God. Jonah was in the belly of the fish three days and nights. Jesus was in the tomb for three days. Jesus rose from death just as Jonah was delivered from death after three days. The people that Jonah warned about their destruction repented about their sins and obeyed God. The Jews who believed Jesus's words, repented of their sins, and obeyed God so that they could have salvation through Jesus. They were not not destroyed (sentenced to eternal death).

After Jesus had left the Pharisees and Sadducees, He and his disciples went to the other side of the sea. The disciples had forgotten to take bread for them to eat. Jesus told them to be careful and to be warned that they should not accept the yeast of the Pharisees and of the Sadducees. The disciples discussed what Jesus had said and decided that he was talking about the bread that they had forgotten to take.

Jesus knew what they thought and told them that they had not understood his warning. Again he said that they had little faith; he meant that they did not judge what his words meant spiritually. They kept looking to physical, earthly things to understand his words.

He asked them if they did not remember that he had fed five thousand people with five loaves of bread. Did they not remember that he had fed four thousand people with seven loaves of bread? He asked them why they did not understand the spiritual truth of what he said to them. Then they understood that he had not warned them about yeast in bread. He had warned them about the doctrines (teachings) of the Pharisees and Sadducees. If they were not alert and watchful the message of God that anyone could receive salvation through Jesus would be corrupted and ruined by the doctrines and teachings of the Pharisees and the Sadducees.

JESUS ASKS THE DISCIPLES WHO HE IS AND WARNS THEM ABOUT THE FUTURE

When Jesus came into the coasts of Caesarea Philippi, he asked his disciples, saying, Whom do men say that I the Son of man am?

And they said, Some say that thou art John the Baptist: some, Elias; and others, Jeremias or one of the prophets.

He saith unto them, But whom say ye that I am?

And Simon Peter answered and said, Thou art the Christ, the Son of the living God.

And Jesus answered and said unto him, Blessed art thou, Simon Barjona: for flesh and blood hath not revealed it unto thee, but my Father which is in heaven.

And I say also unto thee, That thou art Peter, and upon this rock I will build my church; and the gates of hell shall not prevail against it.

And I will give unto thee the keys of the kingdom of heaven: and whatsoever thou shalt bind on earth shall be bound in heaven: and whatsoever thou shalt loose on earth shall be loosed in heaven.

Then charged he his disciples that they should tell no man that he was Jesus the Christ.

From that time forth began Jesus to shew unto his disciples, how that he must go unto Jerusalem, and suffer many things of the elders and chief priests and scribes, and be killed, and be raised again the third day.

Then Peter took him, and began to rebuke him, saying, Be it far from thee, Lord: this shall not be unto thee.

But he turned, and said unto Peter, Get thee behind me, Satan: thou art an offence unto me: for thou savourest not the things that be of God, but those that be of men.

Then said Jesus unto his disciples, If any man will come after me, let him deny himself, and take up his cross, and follow me.

For whosoever will save his life shall lose it: and whosoever will lose his life for my sake shall find it.

For what is a man profited, if he shall gain the whole world, and lose his own soul? Or what shall a man give in exchange for his soul?

For the Son of man shall come in the glory of his Father with his angels, and then he shall reward every man according to his works.

Verily I say unto you, There be some standing here, which shall not taste of death, till they see the Son of man coming in his kingdom.

Matthew 16:13–28 (KJV)

W HEN JESUS HAD traveled to the sea coasts of Caesarea Philippi, he asked his disciples whom did men say that Jesus was? Please note that he refers to himself as the Son of Man; He makes a distinction between his identity as a human man and his identity as the Son of God. His person, who was human (mortal), would die. His person as God will live eternally.

His disciples answered Jesus. Some say that you are John the Baptist. Some say that you are Elijah. Some say that you are Jeremiah. Some say that you are one of the other prophets.

Jesus asked them whom did they say that He was. Simon Peter answered and told Jesus that Jesus was the Christ, the Son of the living God. Jesus told Peter that Peter was blessed by God the Father because Peter did not learn the truth about who Jesus was from mortal understanding. Peter knew who Jesus was because God the Father had given Peter that knowledge. Jesus told Peter that Peter was the rock upon which Jesus would build his church. Satan (the Devil) and his group of evil spirits would never win over (defeat) the church established by Jesus. Jesus said that he would give Peter the authority to bind (limit, tie) things on earth and those things would be bound in heaven. Peter would have the authority to loose (release, take away the bindings) things on earth and they would be freed in heaven.

There is a double meaning in this passage. Peter was chosen by Jesus to be the leader of the new church that Jesus would establish. After Jesus returned to heaven Peter was given authority to bind up (stop, hold captive) things on earth and in heaven. Peter was given authority to release (free) things on earth and in heaven. We should remember that Peter would be led by the Holy Spirit so Peter would be fulfilling the will of God the Father.

We know that Jesus established an eternal church. Peter did not live eternally (physically) as the head of the church on earth. When Jesus gave this authority to Peter, he meant this authority to pass on to those who would follow Peter as Christians. Peter and the new church were given the power to bind and release because they believed that Jesus is the Christ, the Son of God. The church made up of people who share eternal life with Jesus and who are the adopted children of God still has this power.

Jesus instructed His disciples not to tell anyone outside of their group that Jesus was the Christ, the Son of God. God the Father told Jesus what to say and do and when to do it. God the Father would decide when it was time for Jesus to go to Jerusalem to be judged by the Pharisees.

Starting from that time, Jesus began to teach the disciples about what was going to happen in the future. Jesus told the disciples that he would go to Jerusalem where the Jewish elders and the Jewish chief priests and the Jewish scribes (teachers) would cause Jesus to suffer greatly; they would work to kill Jesus; and Jesus would come back to life on the third day. We know that Jesus's life wasn't taken from Him on the cross. Jesus gave up his life of his own will.

Peter was horrified that Jesus would be treated in the manner that Jesus described. Peter took Jesus aside and began to correct Jesus. Peter said that he knew that God would forbid all those things to be done to Jesus. It was not proper for Jesus to be treated in such a manner. Remember that Peter refused to let Jesus wash Peter's feet; Peter was very outspoken and impetuous.

Jesus turned toward Peter and strongly corrected Peter. He commanded Peter to get behind Jesus. The words Peter was speaking were from the Devil and rebelled against God. Jesus was telling Peter that Peter had no right to correct Jesus. He said that Peter smelled of human desires and reasoning. The things that Peter was saying were not approved by God. Peter was setting himself up to pass judgment about whether God's will (commands) should be followed.

Jesus spoke very plainly to the disciples. If any person wanted to be a disciple (follower) of Jesus, that person must put his own plans and desires away and pick up his cross and follow Jesus. That person must die to his own will and choose to do God's will. The person who wanted to save his mortal life (live according to his own desires and choices) would lose eternal life. If the person was willing to sacrifice his own plans, desires, values, and choices to do God's will, then that person would gain eternal life.

What did a person gain if he received all that the world had to offer that person, but the person lost his/her soul? How much would you pay for your soul? What would you trade your soul to receive?

Jesus said that He would come back with the glory of God the Father surrounded by the angels of God. He will reward every person in relation to what that person has done during his/her mortal life. Jesus will judge what each one of us have said and done.

In God's truth, Jesus said there were some people standing there at that time who would not die until they saw the Son of man crowned as the King of all heaven and earth. Jesus said that we who choose to follow Him and do God the Father's will would never die.

JESUS IS TRANSFIGURED AND ACKNOWLEDGED BY GOD THE FATHER

And after six days Jesus taketh Peter, James, and John his brother, and bringeth them up into an high mountain apart.

And was transfigured (changed) before them: and his face did shine as the sun, and his raiment was white as the light.

And, behold, there appeared unto them Moses and Elias talking with him.

Then answered Peter, and said unto Jesus, Lord, it is good for us to be here: if thou wilt, let us make here three tabernacles; one for thee, and one for Moses, and one for Elias.

While he yet spake, behold, a bright cloud overshadowed them: and behold a voice out of the cloud, which said, This is my beloved Son, in whom I am well pleased; hear ye him.

And when the disciples heard it, they fell on their face, and were sore afraid.

And Jesus came and touched them, and said, Arise, and be not afraid.

And when they had lifted up their eyes, they saw no man, save Jesus only.

And as they came down from the mountain, Jesus charged them, saying, Tell the vision to no man, until the Son of man be risen again from the dead.

And his disciples asked him, saying, Why then say the scribes that Elias must first come?

And Jesus answered and said unto them, Elias truly shall first come, and restore all things.

But I say unto you, that Elias is come already, and they knew him not, but have done unto him whatsoever they listed. Likewise shall also the Son of man suffer of them.

Then the disciples understood that he spake unto them of John the Baptist.

Matthew 17:1–13 (KJV)

SIX DAYS LATER Jesus took Peter, James, and John, James' brother, high up on a mountain away from anyone else. On the mountain Jesus was transfigured (changed) right before their eyes. We can assume that Jesus was in his glorified state at that time; his face was shining with a light bright as the sun's rays and his clothing was so white that it appeared to be light. After Jesus was transfigured, Moses and Elijah appeared and were talking with Jesus. We should remember that God had honored these two prophets. Moses went up on the mountain, and he was never seen again. Elijah was taken up into heaven in a chariot in the sky. The disciples were devote Jews; they knew how highly esteemed Moses and Elijah were to the Jewish people.

Peter, as he usually did impulsively, tried to think of something he could do to honor Jesus, Moses, and Elijah. Peter spoke to Jesus offering to build three tabernacles: one for Moses, one for Elijah, and one for Jesus. The tabernacle was a very holy place;

only the priests were authorized to approach God in the tabernacle. "And thou shalt rear up the tabernacle according to the fashion thereof which was shewed thee in the mount" (Exodus 26: 30, KJV).

> And thou shalt hang up the vail under the taches, that thou mayest bring in thither within the vail the ark of the testimony: and the vail shall divide unto you between the holy place and the most holy.
>
> Exodus 26:33 (KJV)

> And thou shalt bring Aaron and his sons unto the door of the tabernacle of the congregation, and wash them with water.
>
> And thou shalt put upon Aaron the holy garments, and anoint him, and sanctify him; that he may minister unto me in the priest's office.
>
> And thou shalt bring his sons, and clothe them with coats;
>
> And thou shalt anoint them, as thou didst anoint their father, that they may minister unto me in the priest's office: for their anointing shall surely be an everlasting priesthood throughout their generations.
>
> Exodus 40:12–15 (KJV)

God the Father himself corrected Peter on that occasion. God the Father's voice spoke out from a bright cloud that was over their heads. He told them that Jesus was his beloved Son in whom God was very pleased. The disciples were to honor Jesus alone and listen to what he told them.

As Jews the disciples were very frightened because they knew that only a few people were ever authorized to see God face to face. When the disciples heard God's voice, they fell to the ground on their faces, and they were terrorized.

Jesus came to the disciples and touched each one of them. He told them to stand up and not to be afraid. Jesus does not want any of us to be afraid to approach him. On numerous occasions he told the disciples to not be afraid and to be at peace. When the disciples looked up, they saw no one but Jesus.

While they came down from the mountain, Jesus told the disciples not to tell anyone what they had seen until after Jesus had risen from the dead. His three disciples asked him why the scribes (teachers) said that Elijah had to come to the Jewish people before the Messiah would come. Jesus replied that it was true that Elijah had to come before the Messiah would come. Then He told them that Elijah had already come, and that the Jews did not recognize or accept him. They had treated Elijah with disrespect and violently injured him. Elijah had been killed because he told the people to repent and turn away from sin to prepare the way for the Messiah. Jesus told the disciples that the Jewish leaders and people would abuse the Son of man, Jesus, in the same way. Then the disciples knew that the Elijah that Jesus spoke about was John the Baptist.

We might note at this time that there was significance in the choice of disciples that Jesus took with him to the mountain where he was transfigured. Peter had been chosen by Jesus to lead the followers of Christ and establish Christ's new church. Jesus recognized the strength and fervor that Peter would exhibit as the "rock" that Jesus chose to build the church. James was the first of the disciples to sacrifice his own life to spread the gospel of salvation. James was the one whose faith in Jesus enabled him to set the example for the other Christians to follow. John was the disciple who called himself the one who Jesus loved. John understood the love of God expressed in Jesus better than anyone else. John was the only disciple who stood at the cross as Jesus suffered and died. John's love for Jesus overcame his fear; he focused on Jesus and not on himself. Of all the disciples, John was the one God chose to leave on earth until he was old so that he could teach the new Christians about God's love. Peter and John were the first disciples to run to the tomb and witness the resurrection of Jesus.

JESUS TEACHES THE DISCIPLES ABOUT FAITH

And when they were come to the multitude, there came to him a certain man, kneeling down to him, and saying,

Lord, have mercy on my son: for he is lunatic, and sore vexed: for oftimes he falleth into the fire, and oft into the water.

And I brought him to thy disciples, and they could not cure him.

Then Jesus answered and said, O faithless and perverse generation, how long shall I be with you? How long shall I suffer you? Bring him hither to me.

And Jesus rebuked the devil; and he departed out of him: and the child was cured from that very hour.

Then came the disciples to Jesus apart, and said, Why could not we cast him out?

And Jesus said unto them, Because of your unbelief: for verily I say unto you, If ye have faith as a grain of mustard seed, ye shall say unto the mountain, Remove hence to yonder place; and it shall remove; and nothing shall be impossible unto you.

Howbeit this kind goeth not out but by prayer and fasting.

And while they abode in Galilee, Jesus said unto them, The Son of man shall be betrayed into the hands of men:

And they shall kill him, and the third day he shall be raised again. And they were exceeding sorry.

Matthew 17:14–23 (KJV)

WHEN JESUS CAME to speak to the great crowd of people who followed him, a man came and knelt down in front of Him. The man pleaded with Jesus to have mercy on his son. His son was insane (lunatic, demented); the son was so greatly afflicted that he had seizures and fell into the fire or fell into the water where he would drown. The man told Jesus that he had taken his son to Jesus's disciples, but they could not cure the son.

Jesus did not rebuke his disciples; he knew that they had done the best that they could for the boy. He spoke to the crowd in general. He called them a generation of people who were without faith and who were obstinate (stubborn, headstrong). He asked how long he would be with them to help them. How long would he be able to teach them with patience? Jesus told them to bring the boy to Him.

Jesus rebuked (cast out, sent away) the devil that was tormenting the boy, and the devil left. The boy was healed immediately. The disciples came to Jesus privately and asked him why they had been unable to cast out the demon. He told them that it was because their faith (belief) was not strong enough. Jesus continued to talk to the disciples telling them that if they only had a little faith, faith as small as a mustard seed, they could do great things. A mustard seed is an extremely small seed that grows to be a great, large tree. He said that they could move mountains to another location if they had faith. Nothing would be impossible for them to do if they had faith.

Jesus added that that particular kind of demon could only be cast out if the disciples prayed and fasted. The prayer and fasting was to increase their faith.

When we pray for healing or cast out an illness, too often we lose sight of what we are doing. We heal or pray in the name of Jesus. Jesus is the one who does the healing; it is his authority that causes the demons to obey. If we look at the physical impossibility of what we are praying for, we diminish our faith. We should be concentrating on the promises and power of Jesus, not on whether we are holy enough or correct in our process. We cannot concentrate upon our own abilities or on the nature of the physical circumstance. We must concentrate on Jesus. We cannot concentrate on the quality of our faith. We have to believe his promises and trust him to do what he promised to do. We will never be worthy of Jesus performing miracles that we have spoken in his name. We will never be worthy of Jesus's love; he loves us because of who he is. The miracles will happen because of who he is.

Jesus told the disciples that they must fast in order to cast out some demons. We don't really understand what fasting is. We think in modern times that God is pleased when we don't eat for a given period of time. The act of doing without food is the smallest part of fasting. Fasting is about our relationship with God. Fasting is always accompanied by prayer.

> And I set my face unto the Lord God, to seek by prayer and supplications, with fasting, and sackcloth, and ashes:
> And I prayed unto the Lord my God, and made my confession, and said, O Lord, the great and dreadful God, keeping the covenant and mercy to them that love him, and to them that keep his commandments;
>
> Daniel 9:3–4 (KJV)

It is accompanied by confession (acknowledgement) of sin. "And they gathered together to Mizpeh, and drew water, and poured it out before the Lord, and fasted on that day, and said there. We have sinned against the Lord. And Samuel judged the children of Israel in Mizpeh" (1st Samuel 7:6, KJV).

Fasting is accompanied by humbling oneself before God. Fasting is accompanied by the reading of God's word.

> Now in the twenty and fourth day of this month the children of Israel were assembled with fasting, and with sackclothes, and earth upon them.
>
> And the seed of Israel separated themselves from all strangers, and stood and confessed their sins, and the iniquities of their fathers.
>
> And they stood up in their place, and read in the book of the law of the Lord their God one fourth part of the day; and another fourth part they confessed, and worshipped the Lord their God.
>
> Nehemiah 9:1–3 (KJV)

So we can see that fasting is not presenting to God our sacrifice of doing without food in exchange for God answering our prayers. As it is with all prayer, we must align ourselves with the will of God. It is impossible for God to change. He is eternal. He is without change. When we pray we must align ourselves with his will not try to change his will to match ours. Fasting is a process of aligning ourselves with God's will. We must be subject to his commandments and listen for the leading of the Holy Spirit. When we pray in the name of Jesus, we must be fully conscious of the fact that he performs the miracle; we only serve as his hands and his voice. When we fast, we must pray, confess our sins, read the word of God, and humble ourselves. Fasting aligns us with God's will so that we can speak and act as he would have us to do. We must realize in our hearts that he alone is God.

While Jesus and the disciples were staying in Galilee, He warned them that the Son of man, Jesus, would be betrayed and taken prisoner by men. He told them that men would kill Him, and on the third day he would be raised from the dead. The disciples were very sad and depressed about his sayings. He was preparing them for what would happen to him in Jerusalem so that their faith would not be destroyed.

JESUS INSTRUCTS THE DISCIPLES TO PAY TAXES

And when they were come to Capernaum, they that received tribute money came to Peter, and said, Doth not you master pay tribute?

He saith, Yes. And when he was come into the house, Jesus prevented him, saying, What thinkest thou, Simon? Of whom do the kings of the earth take custom or tribute? Of their own children, or of strangers?

Peter saith unto him, Of strangers. Jesus saith unto him, Then are the children (citizens) free.

Not withstanding, lest we should offend them, go thou to the sea, and cast an hook, and take up the fish that first cometh up; and when thou hast opened his mouth, thou shalt find a piece of money: that take, and give unto them for me and thee.

Matthew 17:24–27 (KJV)

WHEN JESUS AND the disciples reached Capernaum, the tax collectors who collected tribute money for the Romans came to Peter. The Romans collected this tribute (tax) requiring the people to acknowledge that they were under the rule of the Romans. Those people who collected the tribute money asked Peter if Jesus paid tribute money to the Romans. Did he acknowledge the authority of the Romans over him. Peter told them that Jesus did pay.

When Peter entered the house, Jesus stopped him and asked Peter a question. Please note that Jesus did not address Peter as Peter; He addressed him as Simon. He was not speaking to Peter as the leader of his new church. Jesus was speaking to Peter as Simon, his student and follower. Jesus asked Peter if kings took tribute money from strangers or from their own children (citizens). Peter answered him that kings require tribute money from strangers. The king's children (citizens) are free (not required to pay). Jesus meant that they as children (citizens) of God the Father's kingdom in heaven and on earth, they did not owe tribute money to the kings of the earth.

Even though they did not owe the Romans tribute money, Jesus told Peter to pay it anyway. Jesus did not want to cause a confrontation with the Romans at that time. Jesus sent Peter to the sea to fish. He told Peter to pick up the first fish that Peter caught. Peter was to open the fish's mouth, and Peter would find the coin that he needed to pay tribute to the Romans for Peter and Jesus.

Although Jesus did not owe any tribute money to the Romans, he paid it. We are citizens of the Kingdom of God; we recognize God as our ruler. We pay taxes to our government because we live in an earthly kingdom and are subject to the government's authority while we live on the earth. Even though Jesus was not subject to the authority of the Romans, God the Father provided the tribute money. God provides for all our needs, even taxes. It is interesting that Matthew related this incident. Matthew himself had been a tax collector; he would have been greatly interested in what Jesus said about taxation.

JESUS EXPLAINS CITIZENSHIP IN GOD'S KINGDOM

At the same time came the disciples unto Jesus, saying, Who is the greatest in the kingdom of heaven?

And Jesus called a little child unto him, and set him in the midst of them.

And said, Verily I say unto you, Except ye be converted, and become as little children, ye shall not enter into the kingdom of heaven.

Whosoever therefore shall humble himself as this little child, the same is greatest in the kingdom of heaven.

And whoso shall receive one such little child in my name receiveth me.

But whoso shall offend (hurt) one of these little ones which believe in me, it were better for him that a millstone were hanged about his neck, and that he were drowned in the depth of the sea.

Woe unto the world because of offences! For it must needs be that offences come; but woe to that man by whom the offence cometh!

Wherefore if thy hand or thy foot offend thee, cut them off, and cast them from thee: it is better for thee to enter into life halt or maimed, rather than having two hands or two feet to be cast into everlasting fire.

And if thine eye offend thee, pluck it out, and cast it from thee: it is better for thee to enter into life with one eye, rather than having two eyes to be cast into hell fire.

Take heed that ye despise not one of these little ones; for I say unto you, That in heaven their angels do always behold the face of my Father which is in heaven.

For the Son of man is come to save that which was lost.

How think ye? If a man have an hundred sheep, and one of them be gone astray, doth he not leave the ninety and nine, and goeth into the mountains, and seeketh that which is gone astray?

And if so be that he find it, verily I say unto you, he rejoiceth more of that sheep, than of the ninety and nine which went not astray.

Even so it is not the will of your Father which is in heaven, that one of these little ones should perish.

Matthew 18:1–14 (KJV)

AT THE SAME time that Jesus had spoken to Peter about the tribute, the disciples came to Jesus to ask him a question. They asked him who was the greatest in the kingdom of heaven. Jesus called a little child to come to him, and he stood the little child in the middle of the disciples. The Jesus told them that in truth unless they were changed (transformed) so that they became like a little child they could not enter the kingdom of heaven. A person must be as humble as that child was to be the greatest in the Kingdom of Heaven. A little child does not try to take power

THOU SHALL CALL HIS NAME JESUS

or authority or self- worth so that he will be greater than others are. So long as we retain (keep) a very small part of our pride and sense of importance, we cannot be pleasing to God. So long as we continue to think of ourselves as being worthy to judge and rule others, we cannot be pleasing to God. We cannot decide what is right or wrong. We cannot take pride in our accomplishments; we must recognize that God gave us the ability and opportunity to reach accomplishment. A little child does not try to be God. He knows that he is not independent; he is dependent on others.

Anyone who treats a little child with compassion and gentleness in the name of Jesus, is giving compassion and gentleness to Jesus. Woe to the person who says that he comes representing Jesus and hurts a little child. It would be better for that person who claims to be Jesus's servant if a giant stone were tied around his neck, and he was drowned in the bottom of the sea. If a person claims to be a Christian and hurts a little child so that the child believes that Jesus does not love the child, that one who claims to be a Christian has destroyed himself. If a Christian shows partiality or refuses to help a child or acts in such a way that the child believes that he has been judged and condemned, that person is answerable to God because he caused that child to believe that God does not love him. Woe to the world we live in because there will always be people who hurt and injure other people. But let every individual be warned that he/she is in danger of being judged by God if he or she is the one who injures (hurts) someone else. If we call ourselves Christians, we must be very sure that we do not shame Jesus or diminish Jesus in someone's eyes.

Jesus spoke about cutting off a hand or foot if that hand or foot caused a person to sin. He spoke of plucking out (pulling out) an eye if the eye caused a person to sin. What he was saying was not about hands, or feet, or eyes. He used those as examples because people knew how much they valued them. Anything in a person's life that causes them to sin should be avoided in the future. No matter how important something or someone is to a Christian, it or they are not important enough to cause a Christian to disobey God and cause that person to lose eternal life with God.

Jesus went on to caution (warn) his disciples again. Be very, very careful that you do not treat some people as if they have more value than other people. Do not devalue little children. Remember that the angels responsible for taking care of children are always standing right in front of God the Father. You may not believe that little children are as worthy of respect as adults are worthy of consequence. God regards little children as the most important of God's believers.

Jesus came to save the people who were lost. God is always greatly concerned about his children (people) who are lost. Those who have been separated from God are of primary importance. Jesus asked them what they thought. If a man had one hundred sheep, and he lost one, wouldn't he leave the ninety-nine and go look for the lost sheep? If the man found his lost sheep, wouldn't he rejoice (be happier) more about the one saved sheep than all the other ninety-nine sheep which were not lost?

That is how it is in the Kingdom of Heaven. God rejoices more over the lost person who returns to God than he does over the ones who were not lost. God knew that the people who were not lost were safe from eternal death; God was concerned for the lost person who was in danger of losing eternal life. God does not will that any of his little children should be lost from eternal life because some Christian was careless in the way he treated a child.

JESUS TEACHES ABOUT DISPUTES AND FORGIVENESS

Moreover if thy brother shall trespass against thee, go and tell him his fault between thee and him alone: if he shall hear thee, thou hast gained thy brother.

But if he will not hear thee, then take with thee one or two more, that in THE MOUTH OF TWO OR THREE WITNESSES EVERY WORD BE ESTABLISHED.

And if he shall neglect to hear them, tell it unto the church: but if he neglect to hear the church, let him be unto thee as an heathen man and a publican.

Verily I say unto you, Whatsoever ye shall bind on earth shall be bound in heaven: and whatsoever ye shall loose on earth shall be loosed in heaven.

Again I say unto you, That if two of you shall agree on earth as touching anything that they shall ask, it shall be done for them of my Father which is in heaven.

For where two or three are gathered together in my name, there am I in the midst of them.

Then came Peter to him, and said, Lord, how oft shall my brother sin against me, and I forgive him? Till seven times?

Jesus saith unto him, I say not unto thee, Until seven times: but, Until seventy times seven.

Therefore is the kingdom of heaven likened unto a certain king, which would take account of his servants.

And when he had begun to reckon, one was brought unto him, which owed him ten thousand talents.

But forasmuch as he had not to pay, his lord commanded him to be sold, and his wife, and children, and all that he had, and payment to be made.

The servant therefore fell down, and worshipped him, saying, Lord, have patience with me, and I will pay thee all.

Then the lord of that servant was moved with compassion, and loosed him, and forgave him the debt.

But the same servant went out, and found one of his fellowservants, which owed him an hundred pence: and he laid hands on him, and took him by the throat, saying, Pay me that thou owest.

And his fellowservant fell down at his feet, and besought him, saying, Have patience with me, and I will pay thee all.

And he would not: but went and cast him into prison, till he should pay the debt.

So when his fellow servants saw what was done, they were very sorry, and came and told unto their lord all that was done.

Then his lord, after that he had called him, said unto him, O thou wicked servant, I forgave thee all that debt, because thou desiredst me:

Shouldest not thou also have had compassion on thy fellowservant, even as I had pity on thee?

And his lord was wroth, and delivered him to the tormentors, till he should pay all that was due unto him.

So likewise shall my heavenly Father do also unto you, if ye from your hearts forgive not every one his brother their trespasses.

Matthew 18:15–35 (kjv)

Jesus gave instructions about what should be done if one Christian trespassed against another. It is not God's will that there should be bitter feelings and unforgiveness between two of God's people. The person who feels that another Christian has trespassed against him should go to the other person and try to settle the disagreement between the two of them. If the disagreement is settled between the two of them, then they have built a sense of brotherhood between them.

If the two cannot reach an agreement between them, then the injured person should take the dispute to two or three other Christians. The settlement of disputes between God's people had been covered in the Mosaic Law.

Thou shalt not remove thy neighbor's landmark, which they of old time have set in thine inheritance, which thou shalt inherit in the land that the Lord thy God giveth thee to possess it. One witness shall not rise up against a man for any iniquity, or for any sin, in any sin that he sinneth: at the mouth of two witnesses, or at the mouth of three witnesses, shall the matter be established.

If a false witness rise up against any man to testify against him that which is wrong;

Then both the men, between whom the controversy is, shall stand before the Lord, before the priests and the judges, which shall be in those days;

And the judges shall make diligent inquisition: and, behold, if the witness be a false witness, and hath testified falsely against his brother;

Then shall ye do unto him, as he had thought to have
done unto his brother: so shalt thou put the evil away from
among you.

Deuteronomy 19:14–19 (KJV)

Jesus quoted from this part of the Law when he taught about
the settlement of disagreements between Christians. He continued to speak about the acceptable process to be followed in the
settlement of disputes. If the accused person will not listen to
the two or three witnesses, then the question should be taken to
the complete church of believers. If the person who has wronged
another Christian refuses to alter his behavior and admit his
wrong, then the church should treat that person as they would
treat someone who is not a Christian.

At this point Jesus speaks of something that he had already
taught. He said whatever was bound on earth by Christians is
bound in heaven as well. He said whatever is loosed on earth by
Christians is loosed in heaven. Jesus is specifically talking about
forgiveness. He said that when a trespass is forgiven by two or
more Christians, it is forgiven in heaven. Jesus said that when a
trespass is not forgiven by two or three Christians, then that trespass is not forgiven in heaven. This puts a much heavier responsibility upon the Christians who are called to mediate between two
other Christians. Jesus reminds the disciples again that whatever
two or three believers bind or loose on earth will be bound or
loosed in heaven by God the Father. Where ever two or three
believers are gathered together in the name of Jesus, Jesus himself
is present in that place with them.

Jesus saw forgiveness as a commandment and an obligation
for those who believe on Jesus and who become his disciples. All
of the four gospels show us that Jesus viewed forgiveness as one
of His primary goals in coming to earth as a human. He came so
that we might have God the Father's forgiveness. He also com-

manded us to forgive others as God has forgiven us. Our own forgiveness is dependent upon our obedience in forgiving others.

Peter came to Jesus and asked how many times a person had to forgive a brother (follower of Jesus). Jesus responded that it was not enough to forgive seven times.

He should forgive 490 times. Jesus taught Peter a parable about forgiveness. He said that the Kingdom of Heaven was similar to a king who began to inventory the debts that were owed to him. When the king began to add up the totals, a servant was brought before him who owed the equivalent of $3,840,000,000 in silver. The servant could not pay the debt so the king ordered that the man, his wife, and his children be sold as slaves; the money paid for them was to be joined with all the property that the man had so that the resulting funds could be applied to the man's debt. The servant fell down before the king and pleaded with the king to give him some more time, and he would pay the king the money that he owed. The king felt sorry for the man and released him and canceled the great debt.

That same man went out of the king's court and found one of his fellow servants. That servant owed the first servant about $3200. The second servant begged the first servant to give him more time to pay the debt. The first servant refused to show mercy to the second servant; the first servant had the second servant put in jail until the debt was paid. When the king's other servants saw what the first servant had done to the second servant, they went and told the king what had happened. The king called the first servant to appear before the king again. The king told him that he was an evil, cruel man. The king had forgiven a huge debt for the first servant because the man asked the king to forgive him. The king asked the man if he should not show the same mercy on the second servant just as the king had shown mercy on the first servant. The king was very angry; he ordered that the first servant be sent to the tormentors (torturers) until the servant had paid every penny that he owed the king.

Jesus told Peter that his heavenly Father, God, would do the same thing the king did. If Christians did not forgive others in their hearts, their Father, God would not forgive their sins either.

THE PHARISEES TEST JESUS ABOUT DIVORCE

And it came to pass, that when Jesus had finished these sayings, he departed from Galilee, and came into the coasts of Judaea beyond Jordan:

And great multitudes followed him; and he healed them there.

The Pharisees also came unto him, tempting him, and saying unto him, Is it lawful for a man to put away his wife for every cause?

And he answered and said unto them, Have ye not read, that he WHICH MADE THEM AT THE BEGINNING MADE THEM MALE AND FEMALE.

And said, FOR THIS CAUSE SHALL A MAN LEAVE FATHER AND MOTHER, AND SHALL CLEAVE TO HIS WIFE; AND THE TWAIN SHALL BE ONE FLESH?

Wherefore they are no more twain, but one flesh. What God hath joined together, let not man put asunder.

They say unto him, Why did Moses then command to give a writing of divorcement, and to put her away?

He saith unto them, Moses because of the hardness of your hearts suffered you to put away your wives: but from the beginning it was not so.

And I say unto you, Whosoever shall put away his wife, except it be for fornication, and shall marry another, committeth adultery: and whoso marrieth her which is put away doth commit adultery.

His disciples say unto him, If the case of the man be so with his wife, it is not good to marry.

But he said unto them, All men cannot receive this saying, save they to whom it is given.

For there are some eunuchs, which were so born from their mother's womb: and there are some eunuchs, which were made eunuchs of men: and there be eunuchs, which have made themselves eunuchs for the Kingdom of Heaven's sake. He that is able to receive it, let him receive it.

Matthew 19:1–12 (KJV)

WHEN JESUS WAS finished teaching, He left Galilee and went to the coast of Judaea which is beyond the Jordan River. Great crowds of people still followed him, and he healed those who came at the place where he went.

Again the Pharisees came to him trying to trick him so that he would say something that they could use to discredit him. They asked him if it was lawful for a man to divorce his wife for any cause. He answered them as he frequently did. Jesus asked them if they did not know what the Old Testament said about divorce. He reminded them that God himself had made people to be male and female when he created them. The Mosaic Law said that the fact that God had created them to be man and woman was the reason that the Law said that a man should leave his father and mother and remain only with his wife. The man and his wife would become one flesh (person). Therefore the man and his wife were no longer two people because God had caused them to be one person. Since God had created them to be one person, it was not right that anyone should split them apart.

The Pharisees asked him if that was so then why did Moses give them a law that said that the man could give his wife a written statement of divorce and put her out of his house? Jesus replied that Moses gave them that law of divorcement because their hearts were too hard (unyielding) to accept God's Law. In the beginning when God created Adam and Eve, God's Law did not allow divorcement.

Jesus continued to teach them. He said that any man who divorced his wife for any reason other than the fact that she had committed adultery with another man was sinning. The man who divorced his wife and married another wife was committing adultery. Any man who married a woman who had been divorced was committing adultery.

The disciples questioned Jesus. They asked if it was better for a man to not ever get married? Jesus said that not all men can remain unmarried. He said that the strength to remain celebrate is given to some men; that strength is not given to all men. A eunuch is a man who is unable to have intercourse with a woman. Some men are unable to have relations with a woman because they were born that way. There are some men who are eunuchs because other men have cut their bodies so that they cannot have intercourse. There are other men who have decided not to have intercourse with a woman so that they can better serve the kingdom of God. If a man is able to live life as a eunuch for God's sake, then let that man make that decision for himself. As far as we know all of the disciples had wives except the apostle Paul. Jesus did not mean that marriage was sinful. He meant that each man should do what he thought God wanted him to do.

What we do know from this passage is that Jesus did not ever compromise the will of God the Father. He said there was a difference between the commandments of God and the laws made by men. In our modern age we are surrounded by many temptations to divorce. Our society condones divorce. Our churches give us excuses for divorce; the parties are not equally yoked as Christians. Half of the marriages around us end in divorce. Marriage must withstand great stress—financially and culturally. The fact remains that God says that divorce is a sin unless the guilty party has committed adultery. God wills that no marriage be destroyed. Divorce is a sin. Killing another person is a sin. Being jealous of another's possessions is a sin. Telling a lie is a sin. Worshiping power and money instead of worshiping God is a sin. We are not capable of living perfect, sinless lives. God has provided forgiveness through Jesus. That does not make it okay to deliberately sin against God and go against his will.

JESUS TEACHES ABOUT ADMITTANCE INTO HEAVEN AND REWARDS

Then were there brought unto him little children that he should put his hands on them, and pray: and the disciples rebuked them.

But Jesus said, Suffer little children, and forbid them not, to come unto me: for of such is the kingdom of heaven.

And he laid his hands on them, and departed thence.

And, behold, one came and said unto him, Good Master, what good thing shall I do, that I may have eternal life?

And he said unto him, Why callest thou me good (perfect)? There is none good but one, that is, God: but if thou wilt enter into life, keep the commandments.

He saith unto him, Which? Jesus said, THOU SHALT DO NO MURDER, THOU SHALT NOT COMMIT

ADULTERY, THOU SHALT NOT STEAL, THOU SHAL NOT BEAR FALSE WITNESS.

HONOR THY FATHER AND THY MOTHER, AND THOU SHALT LOVE THY NEIGHBOR AS THYSELF.

The young man saith unto him, All these things have I kept from my youth up: what lack I yet?

Jesus said unto him, "If thou wilt be perfect, go and sell that thou hast, and give to the poor, and thou shalt have treasure in heaven: and come and follow me."

But when the young man heard that saying, he went away sorrowful: for he had great possessions.

Then said Jesus unto his disciples, Verily I say unto you, That a rich man shall hardly enter into the kingdom of heaven.

And again I say unto you, It is easier for a camel to go through the eye of a needle, than for a rich man to enter into the kingdom of God.

When his disciples heard it, they were exceedingly amazed, saying, Who then can be saved?

But Jesus beheld them, and said unto them, with men this is impossible; but with God all things are possible.

Then answered Peter and said unto him, Behold, we have forsaken all, and followed thee; what shall we have therefore?

And Jesus said unto them, Verily I say unto you, That ye which have followed me, in the regeneration when the Son of man shall sit in the throne of his glory, ye also shall sit upon twelve thrones, judging the twelve tribes of Israel.

And every one that hath forsaken houses, or brethren, or sisters, or father, or mother, or wife, or children, or lands, for my name's sake, shall receive a hundredfold, and shall inherit everlasting life.

But many that are first shall be last; and the last shall be first.

Matthew 19:13–30 (KJV)

SOME OF THE people in the crowd brought little children to Jesus so that he could lay his hands on them and pray. The disciples told them to step back. But Jesus said to let the little children come to him. He told the disciples not to keep the children away from him because the Kingdom of Heaven is full of those who are like little children. Jesus laid His hands on the little children, and the children went away.

A young man came to speak with Jesus. He addressed Jesus as "Good Master" and asked Jesus a question. The young man asked what was the good thing that he must do so that he could have eternal life.

First, Jesus asked the young man why he called Jesus, "Good Master" (Good could be translated as perfect.) Jesus said that no one was perfect but God. Then Jesus told him that he must keep (follow) all of God's commandments. The young man asked which ones. Jesus quoted the Old Testament. "Thou shalt do no murder, thou shalt not commit adultery, thou shalt not steal, thou shalt not bear false witness. Honour thy father and thy mother, and thou shalt love thy neighbor as thyself" (Matthew 19:18–19, KJV).

> Honour thy father and thy mother: that thy days may be long upon the land which the Lord thy God giveth thee.
> Thou shalt not kill.
> Thou shalt not commit adultery.
> Thou shalt not steal,
> Thou shalt not bear false witness against thy neighbor.
> Thou shalt not covet thy neighbour's wife, nor his manservant, nor his maidservant, nor his ox, nor his ass, nor any thing that is thy neighbour's.
>
> Exodus 20:12–17 (KJV)

The young man responded that he had done all of those things since he was very young. He asked what else he must do. The young man still thought that he could earn his way into heaven by himself.

Jesus told him that if he wanted to be perfect, he must go and sell everything that he had and give the money to the poor. If he did that he would have treasure in heaven. The last command was that the young man must come and follow Jesus. He must be willing to do everything that Jesus did and would do. Jesus was showing the young man that he could not be perfect enough to pay for his own sins. Jesus was going to sacrifice His physical life to atone for our sins.

The young man turned and went away sadly; he was a very wealthy man. He could not bring himself to sacrifice (give up) all that he possessed (owned). Jesus told his disciples that truly it is almost impossible for a rich man to enter into heaven. He also told then that it is easier for a camel to enter into the eye of a needle than for a rich man to enter into the kingdom of heaven. Jesus meant that no matter how wealthy a person was it was still impossible for a person to pay for his own sins so that he could enter into God's kingdom.

The disciples heard what he said and were very surprised. If a wealthy man could not pay enough alms and buy enough offerings to please God, then who could enter heaven? Jesus answered them saying that with men it was impossible to enter, but with God all things are possible. A person cannot buy his way into heaven. God would pay the price of their admittance into heaven with Jesus's life.

Peter asked Jesus another question. He said that the disciples had given up their own lives (activities and possessions) and had followed Jesus. What would they receive? Jesus responded that truly when all the world was reborn (created anew) and the Son of man (Jesus) was sitting on His throne of glory, the disciples would be seated on twelve thrones judging the twelve tribes of Israel (God's people). Not only would the disciples be honored, but everyone who had given up (sacrificed) their home, or brothers, or sisters, or father, or mother, or wife, or children, or property for the sake of the name of Jesus would receive 100 times as much as they had sacrificed. Whatever a Christian has to turn his back on and sacrifice in his earthly life will be replaced by God with 100 times as much. That person who has given up his family and possessions to prove his loyalty and obedience to Jesus will also receive eternal life with Jesus. But Jesus warned (cautioned) them that in heaven (the kingdom of God) the first (most important people judged by earthly standards) would be last (least important) in heaven. Those who are least important in their earthly life (the poor, the powerless, the humble) would be most important in God's kingdom. He was saying that the people who are allowed by God to have great wealth, power, and importance in the earthly kingdoms would have less in the kingdom of God.

JESUS COMPARES THE KINGDOM OF HEAVEN TO EMPLOYMENT

For the kingdom of heaven is like unto a man that is an householder, which went out early in the morning to hire labourers into his vineyard.

And when he had agreed with the labourers for a penny a day, he sent them into his vineyard.

And he went out about the third hour, and saw others standing idle in the marketplace,

And he said unto them; Go ye also into the vineyard, and whatsoever is right I will give you. And they went their way.

Again he went out about the sixth and ninth hour, and did likewise.

And about the eleventh hour he went out, and found others standing idle, and saith unto them, Why stand ye here all the day idle?

They say unto him, Because no man hath hired us. He saith unto them, Go ye also into the vineyard; and whatsoever is right, that shall ye receive.

So when even was come, the lord of the vineyard saith unto his steward, Call the labourers, and give them their hire, beginning from the last unto the first.

And when they came that were hired about the eleventh hour, they received every man a penny.

But when the first came, they supposed that they should have received more; and they likewise received every man a penny.

And when they had received it, they murmured against the goodman of the house,

Saying These last have wrought but one hour, and thou hast made them equal unto us, which have borne the burden and heat of the day.

But he answered one of them, and said, Friend, I do thee no wrong: didst not thou agree with me for a penny?

Take that thine is, and go thy way: I will give unto this last, even as unto thee.

Is it not lawful for me to do what I will with mine own? Is thine eye evil, because I am good?

So the last shall be first, and the first last: for may be called, but few are chosen.

Matthew 20:1–16 (KJV)

JESUS TAUGHT THEM another parable. He said that the kingdom of heaven is like a farmer (land owner) who went out to the marketplace early in the morning to hire men to pick his grapes. He offered the workers a penny a day for picking grapes in his vineyard. The workers agreed to work all day for a penny ($32).

The farmer went out again to the marketplace at about 9:00 a.m. He saw other workers standing there who had not been

314

hired. He told those workers to go into his vineyard and pick grapes, and he would give them a wage that was fair.

At noon and about 3:00 p.m., the farmer went out to the marketplace again. He hired the workers who were standing there to pick grapes, and sent them into his vineyard.

Finally at about 5:00 p.m., the farmer went out to the marketplace and found more workers who had not been hired for the day. He told those workers to go into his vineyard and pick grapes. He told these new workers that he would pay them the wages that were fair.

So when it was evening and time to quit picking, the farmer told his foreman to pay the workers beginning with the men who had come the last to the field. When the men who were hired at 5:00 PM came for their pay, they received $32.00.

When the men who were hired early in the morning came to be paid, they thought that they would receive more pay because they had worked longer. After they received only $32.00, they complained among themselves. They went to the farmer and told him that he had paid the men who only worked one hour the same wages as they received. They had worked all day, even in the heat of the day.

The farmer answered them. He addressed them as friends. He had not cheated them in any way. They had agreed to work all day for $32.00. He told them to go on home and be satisfied; he would give the workers who only worked one hour the same wages that he gave the men who began to work in the morning. It wasn't against the law for the farmer to give his own money to whomever he wanted to receive it. Were the first workers trying to say that he was evil (unfair) because he did something which was good (kind)?

Jesus told them again that the first would be last and the last would be first. We know that Jesus had told that to the disciples before. At that time he was talking about who was most important in the kingdom of God. There is second meaning included in those words. It is God who calls us to be his chosen children. He reveals himself to those who will accept God's will and believe in Jesus so that they may receive salvation. Some people are born into Christian families and grow up being taught the commandments of God. Those people receive the call to be followers of Jesus early in their lives. Other people are led to the knowledge of Jesus Christ's sacrifice for sin after they become adults. Still other people live most of their lives without being given the opportunity to know Jesus and to receive salvation through him. They are called by God to be his children in the last days of their earthly lives. The people who were Christians from childhood will not be the greatest in the kingdom of God. God sees our hearts and judges us as he sees fit. Being a Christian for many years does not make us greater in God's kingdom.

There is a third meaning for this parable. God made a covenant with Abraham that Abraham's descendants would be God's chosen people. Through thousands of years in the words of many prophets, God promised to send a Messiah to the children of Israel to free them from sin and death. Jesus came first to the Jewish people with his message of love from God the Father. But many of the Jewish people refused to accept God's message and his plan for their salvation. So the Gentiles were given the opportunity to become Christians. Still until this day many Jewish people have not received God's promise given to Abraham. The first (the Israelites) were called, and they became last to enter the kingdom of God. The Gentiles were the last to be called, but many of them were the first to be admitted into the kingdom of God.

JESUS SPEAKS ABOUT HIS ROLE AS SAVIOR AND SERVANT

And Jesus going up to Jerusalem took the twelve disciples apart in the way, and said unto them,

Behold, we go up to Jerusalem; and the Son of man shall be betrayed unto the chief priests and unto the scribes, and they shall condemn him to death,

And shall deliver him to the Gentiles to mock, and to scourge, and to crucify him: and the third day he shall rise again.

Then came to him the mother of Zebedee's children with her sons, worshipping him, and desiring a certain thing of him.

And he said unto her, What wilt thou? She saith unto him, Grant that these my two sons may sit, the one on thy right hand, and the other on the left, in thy kingdom.

But Jesus answered and said, Ye know not what ye ask. Are ye able to drink of the cup that I shall drink of, and to be baptized with the baptism that I am baptized with? They say unto him, We are able.

And he saith unto them, Ye shall drink indeed of my cup, and be baptized with the baptism that I am baptized with: but to sit on my right hand, and on my left, is not mine to give, but it shall be given to them for whom it is prepared of my Father.

And when the ten heard it, they were moved with indignation against the two brethren.

But Jesus called them unto him, and said, Ye know that the princes of the Gentiles exercise dominion over them, and they that are great exercise authority upon them.

But it shall not be so among you: but whosoever will be great among you, let him be your servant:

Even as the Son of man came not to be ministered unto, but to minister, and to give his life a ransom for many.

Matthew 20:17–28 (KJV)

AT THAT TIME Jesus started to travel toward Jerusalem; he took his twelve disciples with him. On the way to Jerusalem, Jesus took the twelve apart to speak to them. At that time he told them exactly what would happen to him when they reached Jerusalem. He was preparing them so that their faith in him would not be diminished. Later they would be able to remember that he had told them what would happen; He knew where he was going, and he knew what would happen. Jesus went to fulfill the will of God the Father even though he knew what was going to happen.

Jesus told the disciples that someone would betray him (deliver him for punishment) to the chief priests and the scribes. The chief priests and scribes (religious teachers) would condemn Jesus and sentence him to be killed. The priests and scribes would give him to the Gentiles (Romans) to ridicule and beat him. The Gentiles would crucify him, but he would rise up from death on the third day. Remember that Judas is among the twelve. Judas had been told what would happen to Jesus before he betrayed Jesus. The disciples had been warned about what would happen when they reached Jerusalem, but they were still shocked when it happened.

Jesus had told the twelve that they would sit on thrones in heaven to judge the twelve tribes of Israel. James and John's mother wanted them to have even more reward. The mother of those two disciples came to Jesus with her two sons. She fell down and worshiped Jesus. She asked him if he would do a certain thing for her and the sons. Jesus always knew what was in people's hearts, but he asked her what she wanted him to do. The mother asked Jesus if her two sons, James and John, could sit on thrones on either side of Jesus when they reached heaven. Jesus answered her saying that she didn't understand what she was asking to receive.

Jesus asked James and John if they wanted to share what would happen to him when they reached Jerusalem. They had already been told how Jesus would be abused and killed in Jerusalem. The two disciples replied that they were able to share his suffering. Jesus told them that they would share what he would suffer, but God the Father had prepared a place beside Him for the person that God the Father had chosen. The two brothers did in fact share the suffering of Jesus. John was the only one of the disciples whose love for Jesus overcame John's fear. John stood beside the cross with Mary as Jesus was being crucified. James was the first of the disciples to be killed because of his testimony and belief in Jesus.

When the other ten disciples heard what James and John's mother had asked Jesus to give them, they were very offended (indignant). Each of them thought that he had an equal right to sit beside Jesus. Jesus knew that the disciples were arguing about who should be given the honor of sitting beside Jesus. We can see that even though the disciples had been with Jesus for over two years, they were still human. They still wanted to be recognized as being superior in God's eyes. They still wanted to have power and authority in God's kingdom. Jesus spoke to the twelve disciples. He told them that the Gentiles (people who were not a part of God's people, the Jews) had kings and princes who ruled over the people with great authority. It should not be that way with God's people. If a follower of Jesus wanted to be great in God's kingdom, that person must follow Jesus's example and be a servant to everyone else. Jesus reminded them that Jesus did not come to be taken care of by men (people); Jesus came to be the servant, one who ministers, for all of God's people. Jesus came to give his own life (the ultimate sacrifice) to serve the needs of all people to be cleansed of their sins.

JESUS GIVES SIGHT TO THE BLIND

And as they departed from Jericho, a great multitude followed him.

And behold, two blind men sitting by the way side, when they heard that Jesus passed by, cried out, saying, have mercy on us, O Lord, thou son of David.

And the multitude rebuked them, because they should hold their peace: but they cried the more, saying, Have mercy on us, O Lord, thou son of David.

And Jesus stood still, and called them, and said, What will ye that I shall do unto you?

They say unto him, Lord, that our eyes may be opened.

So Jesus had compassion on them, and touched their eyes: and immediately their eyes received sight, and they followed him.

Matthew 20:29–34 (KJV)

WHEN JESUS AND the disciples left Jericho, a great crowd of people was following Jesus. There were two blind men sitting by the side of the road. When they heard that Jesus was passing by them, they began to yell at Jesus saying "Have mercy on us, O Lord, thou son of David."

Jesus was on His way to Jerusalem to perform a horrendous task. He was still in the public eye. He had no privacy to prepare for what was coming. When He passed by the two blind men, they heard the other people talking about who was passing by them. They began to yell at Jesus begging for Him to show them mercy.

The men identified Jesus as the son of David. They knew that he was the Messiah.

The large crowd tried to stop them from yelling. The crowd thought that they were too insignificant to bother Jesus. The blind men continued to plead with Jesus because they knew that Jesus was God's representative. They believed that he could help them. They were begging for mercy (help). Jesus was traveling to Jerusalem to deliver God's mercy (forgiveness) to all mankind. Jesus knew that God the Father willed that he show mercy to all people. Jesus stopped on the road and called out to the blind men asking them what they wanted from him. They answered that they wanted him to open their eyes. Jesus felt compassion for the men. He touched their eyes, and they could see. Jesus was sent from God the Father so that all men could see God and understand how much God loves us. When Jesus touched their eyes, they could see, and they followed Him. When Jesus opens our eyes spiritually so that we can see God the Father and understand how much God the Father and Jesus love us, we should follow Jesus.

JESUS FULFILLS PROPHECY AS HE ENTERS JERUSALEM

And when they drew nigh unto Jerusalem, and were come to Bethphage, unto the Mount of Olives, then sent Jesus two disciples,

Saying unto them, Go into the village over against you, and straightway ye shall find an ass tied, and a colt with her: loose them, and bring them unto me.

And if any man say ought unto you, ye shall say, The Lord hath need of them; and straightway he will send them.

All this was done that it might be fulfilled which was spoken by the prophet saying

TELL YE THE DAUGHTER OF SION, BEHOLD, THY KING COMETH UNTO THEE, MEEK, AND SITTING UPON AN ASS, AND A COLT THE FOAL OF AN ASS.

And the disciples went, and did as Jesus commanded them,

And brought the ass, and the colt, and put on them their clothes, and they set him thereon.

And a very great multitude spread their garments in the way; others cut down branches from the trees, and strawed them in the way.

And the multitudes that went before, and that followed, cried, saying, Hosanna to the son of David: BLESSSED IS HE THAT COMETH IN THE NAME OF THE Lord; Hosanna in the highest.

Matthew 21:1–9 (KJV)

Then they hasted, and took every man his garment, and put it under him on the top of the stairs, and blew with trumpets, saying Jehu is king.

2 Kings 9:13 (KJV)

Blessed be he that cometh in the name of the Lord: we have blessed you out of the house of the Lord.

Psalms 118:26 (KJV)

Behold, the Lord hath proclaimed unto the end of the world, Say ye to the daughter of Zion, Behold, thy salvation cometh; behold, his reward is with him, and his work before him.

Isaiah 62:11 (KJV)

Rejoice greatly, O daughter of Zion; shout, O daughter of Jerusalem: behold, thy King cometh unto thee: he is just, and having salvation; lowly, and riding upon an ass, and upon a colt the foal of an ass.

Zechariah 9:9 (KJV)

WHEN JESUS AND the disciples had come close to Jerusalem, they came to the village of Bethphage. Bethphage is on the Mount of Olives. Jesus sent two of his disciples into the village. Those two disciples were instructed by Jesus to go into the village of Bethphage. They would see an ass and her colt. They were to untie the ass and colt and take them to Jesus. If anyone said anything to them about taking the animals, the disciples were told to tell him that the Lord needed them. Jesus told the disciples that the man would send the animals to Jesus.

Jesus did this to fulfill the prophecy given by Zechariah (9:9). The disciples did what they were instructed to do, and they put their garments on the ass like a saddle. Then they lifted Jesus up and set Him on the ass.

A great crowd of people spread out their cloaks on the road for Jesus to ride over. Many other people cut down branches from the trees and spread them over the road too. The great crowd of people walked in front of Jesus shouting "Blessed is He who comes in the name of God; Hosanna (praise) in the highest." The cloaks were spread in front of Jesus because the custom was to show respect and allegiance for the king by spreading out garments for the king to walk over (2nd Kings 9:13). The chant that the people used to welcome Jesus in making a triumphant entry into Jerusalem was a scripture found in Psalms 118:26. Jesus's entry into Jerusalem bringing salvation for the people was prophesized in Zechariah 9:9. It was also prophesized in Zechariah that the king bringing salvation would be seated upon an ass. If a king entered a city riding upon a powerful war horse, the people would know that the king intended to make war and conquer the city. A king entering a city seated on an ass showed that the king was coming with meekness, and that the king did not intend to bring war. The people were praising God and declaring that Jesus was the son of David. The Messiah was to be a descendant of David.

JESUS THROWS THE MONEY CHANGERS OUT OF THE TEMPLE

And when he was come into Jerusalem, all the city was moved, saying, Who is this?

And the multitude said, This is Jesus the prophet of Nazareth of Galilee.

And Jesus went into the temple of God, and cast out all them that sold and bought in the temple, and overthrew the tables of the money changers, and the seats of them that sold doves,

And said unto them, It is written, MY HOUSE SHALL BE CALLED THE HOUSE OF PRAYER; but ye have made it a DEN OF THIEVES.

And the blind and the lame came to him in the temple; and he healed them.

And when the chief priests and scribes saw the wonderful things that he did, and the children crying in the temple, and saying, Hosanna to the son of David; they were sore displeased,

And said unto him, Hearest thou what these say? And Jesus saith unto them, Yea; have ye never read, OUT OF THE MOUTH OF BABES AND SUCKLINGS THOU HAST PERFECTED PRAISE?

Matthew 21:10–16 (KJV)

AFTER JESUS ENTERED Jerusalem, all of the people in Jerusalem were very curious because the large crowd with Jesus was praising him and honoring him. The people from Jerusalem began to ask the people in the crowd who Jesus was. The crowd of people who had entered the city with Jesus told them that Jesus was a prophet who came from Nazareth in Galilee. By designating that Jesus was a prophet, they were proclaiming that Jesus spoke for God.

And the Jews' Passover was at hand, and Jesus went up to Jerusalem,

And found in the temple those that sold oxen and sheep and doves, and the changers of money sitting:

And when he had made a scourge of small cords, he drove them all out of the temple, and the sheep, and the oxen; and poured out the changers' money, and overthrew the tables;

And said unto them that sold doves, Take these things hence; make not my Father's house an house of merchandise.

And his disciples remembered that it was written, THE ZEAL OF THINE HOUSE HATH EATEN ME UP.

John 2:13–17 (KJV)

Jesus went into the Temple of God. He had come to Jerusalem to declare a new Passover. Those who are covered by the Blood of God's Lamb, Jesus Christ, will never die.

And Solomon stood before the altar of the Lord in the presence of all the congregation of Israel, and spread forth his hands towrd heaven:

And he said Lord God of Israel, there is no God like thee, in heaven above, or on earth beneath, who keepest covenant and mercy with thy servants that walk before thee with all their heart:

Who hast kept with thy servant David my father that thou promisedst him: thou spakest also with thy mouth, and hast fulfilled it with thine hand, as it is this day.

Therefore now, Lord God of Israel, keep with thy servant David my father that thou promisedst him, saying, There shall not fail thee a man in my sight to sit on the throne of Israel; so that thy children take heed to their way, that they walk before me as thou hast walked before me.

And now, O God of Israel, let thy word, I pray thee, be verified, which thou spakest unto thy servant David my father.

But will God indeed dwell on the earth? behold, the heaven and heaven of heavens cannot contain thee; how much less this house that I have builded?

Yet have thou respect unto the prayer of thy servant, and to his supplication, O Lord my God, to hearken unto the cry and to the prayer, which thy servant prayeth before thee to day:

That thine eyes may be open toward this house night and day, even toward the place of which thou hast said, My name shall be there: that thou mayest hearken unto the prayer which thy servant shall make toward this place.

And hearken thou to the supplication of thy servant, and of thy people Israel, when they shall pray toward this place: and when thou hearest, forgive.

1st Kings 8: 22—30 (kjv)

Even them will I bring to my holy mountain, and make them joyful in my house of prayer: their burnt offerings and their sacrifices shall be accepted upon mine altar; for mine house shall be called an house of prayer for all people.

Isaiah 56:7 (KJV)

From the time of Solomon, the Temple in Jerusalem had been according to God's covenant (agreement) with the people of Israel (Jews) the one place that God had chosen to be worshiped by his people. It was a sacred place where God had made his covenant with his people. It was the place where blood sacrifices were made to atone for sin. Another translation says that the agreement was a covenant of God's love. The promise was given with God's own word. Jesus went to the Temple, the place chosen by God to establish the first covenant of love. Jesus went to Jerusalem to establish God's new covenant of love through Jesus.

"But the Lord is the true God, he is the living God, and an everlasting king: at his wrath the earth shall tremble, and nations shall not be able to abide his indignation" (Jeremiah 10:10, KJV). Jesus drove the moneychangers and those who sold oxen and sheep out of the Temple of God with wrath (zeal). He said that they had made the holy place dedicated to God a place of commerce, a market. The Temple was a place of prayer.

We know that God hates iniquity. Literally *iniquity* means *unequal*. The wealthy and well to do could buy oxen and sheep to sacrifice to cover their sins. Therefore a wealthy man could purchase God's greater favor. When Jesus spoke to those in the Temple, he addressed the men who sold doves. They were the ones who served the poor. They were following the leadership of the wealthy and powerful men; Jesus told them not to sell merchandize in the Temple. The Temple should be reserved for worshiping God. "The disciples remembered that it was written the Zeal of Thine house hath eaten me up" (John 2:17, KJV).

When the blind and lame came to Jesus in the temple, Jesus healed them. Remember that Jesus had not told the people to spread word of his healings earlier. Now he was healing and preaching quite openly. The chief priests and the scribes (teachers of scripture) saw the miracles that Jesus was performing. They heard the children crying out in the temple. The children were praising God and praising the son of David, Jesus. The priests and the scribes were very displeased. Up until this time they had controlled what happened in the temple. They had allowed the people to set up a market in the temple. They had taught what they said that the word of God commanded. They stood between God and the people.

Now they were no longer in control. Jesus was healing in the temple without their approval. Jesus had thrown the people who ran the temple market out of the temple. Jesus was teaching the meaning of the scriptures. The miracles proved that he was God's spokesman. So the priests and the scribes condemned Jesus and rebuked him because the children were praising him as the son of David. They were saying that it was blasphemous for the children to praise Jesus.

Again Jesus answered them with scripture (God's own words). "O Lord our lord, how excellent is thy name in all the earth! Who hast set thy glory above the heavens. Out of the mouth of babes and sucklings hast thou ordained strength because of thine enemies, that thou mightest still the enemy and the avenger." (Psalm 8:1–2, KJV).

JESUS SPEAKS AND THE FIG TREE OBEYS

And he left them, and went out of the city into Bethany; and he lodged there.

Now in the morning as he returned into the city, he hungered.

And when he saw a fig tree in the way, he came to it, and found nothing thereon, but leaves only, and said unto it, Let no fruit grow on thee henceforward forever. And presently the fig tree withered away!

And when the disciples saw it, they marveled, saying, How soon is the fig tree withered away!

Jesus answered and said unto them, Verily I say unto you, If ye have faith, and doubt not, ye shall not only do this which is done to the fig tree, but also if ye shall say unto this mountain, Be thou removed, and be thou cast into the sea; it shall be done.

And all things, whatsoever ye shall ask in prayer, believing, ye shall receive.

Matthew 21:17–22 (KJV)

JESUS LEFT THE chief priests and the scribes in the temple, and he went out of Jerusalem to Bethany where he stayed overnight. In the morning while he was walking back to Jerusalem, Jesus was hungry. He saw a fig tree growing by the roadside and went to the tree to pick fruit. The tree had leaves, but it did not have fruit. Jesus spoke to the tree saying that the tree would never have fruit again. After a time had passed the tree died. When the disciples saw that the fig tree had dried up and died, they were amazed.

Jesus used the fig tree to again impress upon the disciples the importance of believing God's promises when they prayed. Jesus told them that in truth (God's truth) if they would only believe God's promises they could do greater things than cause the tree to die. If they believed God, they could speak to a mountain, and it would be thrown into the sea. It was necessary that they believe God's word when they prayed (asked God for something). They would receive what they asked God to give them or to do if they would only believe God's words. The original sin of Adam and Eve was that they did not believe God when he said they would die if they ate the fruit of the Tree of Good and Evil. They believed the devil when he told them that they would be gods. The scripture says that without faith, it is impossible to please God. We must not look at the circumstances we see in the physical world. We must depend (believe) upon the words and promises of God. "But without faith it is impossible to please him: for he that cometh to God must believe that he is, and that he is a rewarder of them that diligently seek him" (Hebrews 11: 6, KJV).

> Now faith is the substance of things hoped for, the evidence of things not seen.
>
> For by it the elders obtained a good report.
>
> Through faith we understand that the worlds were framed by the word of God, so that things which are seen were not made of things which do appear.
>
> Hebrews 11:1–3 (KJV)

THE CHIEF PRIESTS QUESTION JESUS'S AUTHORITY

And when he was come into the temple, the chief priests and the elders of the people came unto him as he was teaching, and said, By what authority doest thou these things? And who gave thee this authority?

And Jesus answered and said unto them, I also will ask you one thing, which if ye tell me, I in like wise will tell you by what authority I do these things.

The baptism of John, whence was it? From heaven, or of men? And they reasoned with themselves, saying, If we shall say, From heaven; he will say unto us, Why did ye not then believe him?

But if we shall say, Of men; we fear the people; for all hold John as a prophet.

And they answered Jesus, and said, We cannot tell. And he said unto them, Neither tell I you by what authority I do these things.

But what think ye? A certain man had two sons; and he came to the first, and said, Son, go work to day in my vineyard.

He answered and said, I will not: but afterward he repented, and went.

And he came to the second, and said likewise. And he answered and said, I go, sir: and went not.

Whether of them twain did the will of his father? They say unto him, The first. Jesus saith unto them, Verily I say unto you, That the publicans and the harlots go into the kingdom of God before you.

For John came unto you in the way of righteousness, and ye believed him not: but the publicans and the harlots believed him: and ye, when ye had seen it, repented not afterward, that ye might believe him.

Hear another parable: There was a certain householder, which planted a vineyard, and hedged it round about, and digged a winepress in it, and built a tower, and let it out to husbandmen, and went into a far country:

And when the time of the fruit drew near, he sent his servants to the husbandmen, that they might receive the fruits of it.

And the husbandmen took his servants, and beat one, and killed another, and stoned another.

Again, he sent other servants more than the first: and they did unto them likewise.

But last of all he sent unto them his son, saying, They will reverence my son.

But when the husbandmen saw the son, they said among themselves, This is the heir, come, let us kill him, and let us seize on his inheritance.

And they caught him, and cast him out of the vineyard, and slew him.

When the lord therefore of the vineyard cometh, what will he do unto those husbandmen?

They say unto him, He will miserably destroy those wicked men, and will let out his vineyard unto other husbandmen, which shall render him the fruits in their season.

Jesus saith unto them, Did ye never read in the scriptures, THE STONE WHICH THE BUILDERS REJECTED, THE SAME IS BECOME THE HEAD OF THE CORNER; THIS IS THE LORD'S DOING, AND IT IS MARVELOUS IN OUR EYES?

Therefore say I unto you, The kingdom of God shall be taken from you, and given to a nation bringing forth the fruits thereof.

And whosoever shall fall on this stone shall be broken: but on whomsoever it shall fall, it will grind him to powder.

And when the chief priests and Pharisees had heard his parables, they perceived that he spake of them.

But when they sought to lay hands on him, they feared the multitude, because they took him for a prophet.

Matthew 21:23–46 (KJV)

AFTER JESUS HAD come into the temple, the chief priests and the elders of the Jewish people came while He was teaching to test Jesus again. The priests and the elders asked Jesus who gave him the authority to do the things He did and preach as He did. Jesus answered the priests and elders by telling them that he would answer their question if they would answer one question for him. Jesus asked them if John the Baptist's baptism (when John called the people to repent of their sins) was authorized by God in heaven, or was John's baptism authorized by men.

The priests and elders discussed the answer to Jesus's question among themselves. If they said that John's baptism was authorized by God in heaven, then Jesus would ask them why they didn't believe John. If they said that John was only authorized by men, then the people would rise up against them because the people believed that John was God's prophet. They answered Jesus saying that they could not tell which it was. Jesus told them that if they would not answer His question about John's authority, He would not answer their question about Jesus's authority.

Then Jesus asked them if they could answer his question about the parable (story) that he told them. A man had two sons. The man went to the first son and told the son to go work in the man's vineyard that day. The first son said that he would not go work in the vineyard. After the father left, the first son was sorry about what he had said to his father, and he went and worked in the vineyard that day. The man went to the second son and told the second son to go work in the man's vineyard that day. The second son said that he would go work in the vineyard, but the second son did not go work in the vineyard. Jesus asked the priests and elders which of the two sons did their father's will (wishes).

The priests and the elders answered that the first son did the father's will. Jesus told them that the publicans (tax collectors) and the harlots (prostitutes) would be accepted in God's kingdom (heaven) before the Jewish leaders would be allowed into heaven. He meant that the sinners among the Jews would be accepted in heaven because they followed God's commandments and did God's will. The priests and the elders talked about following God's commandments and doing God's will, but the Jewish leaders did not obey God's commandments and do God's will (wishes).

Jesus reasoned that John the Baptist came to the Jewish leaders preaching righteousness and repentance, but the priests and the elders did not believe John. The tax collectors and the prostitutes believed John, and repented of their sins. The Jewish leaders heard John's message about repentance, but they did not believe that John's teachings and the message of repentance were for them.

Jesus told another parable (story). There was a certain landowner. The landowner planted a vineyard and fenced it in with a hedge. He dug a wine press to use in the harvest, and he built a tower to watch for thieves. He rented the vineyard to some farmers, and he went to a far away land. When it was time to harvest the grapes, the landowner sent his servants to collect his share of the harvest. The farmers beat one of his servants; they killed another of his servants; and they stoned another of the man's servants. The landowner sent a larger group of servants the second time to collect his part of the harvest. The farmers beat and killed those servants like they had beaten and killed the first group of servants.

Finally the landowner sent his own son to collect his part of the harvest because he thought that surely the farmers would show respect for the landowner's son. When the farmers saw the son, they talked among themselves. They reasoned among themselves that the son would inherit the vineyard from his father. They decided to kill the son and seize possession of the vineyard. Jesus asked the Jewish leaders what the landowner would do to the farmers when he came to the vineyard himself. The priests and elders said that the landowner would destroy (kill, punish) the farmers when he came. Then the landowner would rent the vineyard to other farmers who would give him his share of the grape harvest.

Again Jesus quoted scripture from the Old Testament to the priests and the elders. "I will praise thee; for thou hast heard me, and art become my salvation. The stone which the builders refused is become the head stone of the corner. This is the Lord's doing, it is marvelous in our eyes" (Psalm 118:21–23, KJV).

Jesus said that the kingdom of God would be taken from the Jewish leaders and given to another nation which produced the fruits of the kingdom. The fruits of the kingdom are the fruits of the spirit listed in Galatians 5:22. He could have been speaking about the Gentiles, or he could have been speaking about the Jewish people who would break away from the leadership of the high priests and teachers of the Pharisees. In quoting the scripture from Psalm 118, Jesus was telling the Jewish leaders that if they stumbled over the corner stone (the chosen Messiah from God) and rejected Jesus, they would be broken. Those who refused to accept Jesus would be ground into powder.

The chief priests and the Pharisees understood what Jesus was teaching in his parables. They knew he was talking about them. In the story of the man who rented his vineyard to the farmers, God was the landowner, and the farmers were the priests and the Pharisees. The Jewish leadership had refused the messages that God had sent through the prophets (the man's servants). John the Baptist had been killed because he taught about repentance and obedience to God. So God the Father had sent his own son, Jesus, to the Jewish leaders. The Jewish leaders, the farmers, had refused to obey God and give up their authority over God's people. The priests and the Pharisees wanted to kill Jesus so that they could retain authority and power over God's people.

Jesus was the cornerstone chosen by God upon which to build God's kingdom. The Jewish leaders had rejected Jesus, and now they would be destroyed because they would not accept God's Messiah.

The Jewish leaders tried to capture Jesus, but they were afraid to attack Jesus physically because the people believed that Jesus was God's messenger, a prophet.

JESUS TEACHES WITH A WEDDING PARABLE

And Jesus answered and spake unto them again by parables, and said,

The kingdom of heaven is like unto a certain king, which made a marriage for his son,

And sent forth his servants to call them that were bidden to the wedding: and they would not come.

Again, he sent forth other servants, saying, Tell them which are bidden, Behold, I have prepared my dinner: my oxen and my fatlings are killed, and all things are ready: come unto the marriage.

But they made light of it, and went their ways, one to his farm, another to his merchandise:

And the remnant took his servants, and entreated them spitefully, and slew them.

But when the king heard thereof, he was wroth: and he sent forth his armies, and destroyed those murderers, and burned up their city.

Then saith he to his servants, The wedding is ready, but they which were bidden were not worthy.

Go ye therefore into the highways, and as many as ye shall find, bid to the marriage.

So those servants went out into the highways, and gathered together all as many as they found, both bad and good: and the wedding was furnished with guests.

And when the king came in to see the guests, he saw there a man which had not on a wedding garment.

And he saith unto him, Friend, how camest thou in hither not having a wedding garment? And he was speechless.

Then said the king to the servants, Bind him hand and foot, and take him away, and cast him into outer darkness, there shall be weeping and gnashing of teeth.

For many are called, but few are chosen.

Matthew 22:1–14 (KJV)

JESUS SPOKE TO the high priests and Pharisees again telling another parable.

He said that the Kingdom of Heaven was like a marriage feast that a king prepared for his son. The king sent out servants to notify the people who were invited to the son's wedding. The people who received invitations would not come.

So the king sent out other servants to tell the people chosen to attend the wedding that the king had butchered the oxen and fattened animals. The king had prepared the complete feast. The king again invited the people to the wedding. The people who received invitations ridiculed the invitations from the king and went about their own ways. One man went to his farm, and another man went to his shop where he sold merchandize. The other guests seized the king's servants and mockingly abused them and killed them. When the king learned what the invited guests had done to his servants, he was very angry. He sent out his army to kill the men who had killed his servants, and he had his army burn their cities.

Then the king said to his servants that the wedding feast was ready, and the guests who were invited to come were not worthy (deserving) of an invitation to attend. He told the servants to go out on the highway and bring to the feast as many people as they could find. They were to bring people who were good and people who were bad. So the banquet place was filled with guests.

When the king came into the feast to see the guests, he saw that one man had come to the wedding feast without clothing which was appropriate to wear to a wedding. The king asked the man why he came to the wedding wearing clothing that was not fit to wear to a wedding. The man had no answer to give to the king. Then the king said to his servants that they were to tie up the man hand and foot. They were to throw the man into outer darkness. The king said that there would be great crying and grinding of teeth. Jesus finished by saying that many are called, but few people are chosen.

The priests and the Pharisees understood that this last parable was about them too. The king in the story was God. The wedding feast was the coming of God's Messiah to claim God's people to live in heaven. God had prepared a Kingdom of Heaven where the people would have eternal life with Jesus. The servants, God's prophets, were sent to command God's people to repent of their sins and to make themselves ready to live in God's kingdom. Some of God's people ignored God's messages sent through the prophets and went about their normal lives trying to store up earthly wealth. Other Jewish people responded to the prophets by seizing the messengers and killing them. The king, God, was very displeased with the actions of the Jewish people. He had his army destroy the cities of the Jewish people and kill the people who had killed the prophets.

Then the king, God, gave orders that everyone, even the Gentiles, could come to the wedding feast, which was salvation and eternal life with Jesus. All people were invited to come to God's kingdom, heaven. When the king came to judge the guests, he singled out the man who had not cleansed himself and prepared himself to live in God's kingdom. He was not clothed in the righteousness of Jesus Christ. So the man was thrown out of heaven for eternity. Jesus meant that many people would be invited to accept Jesus as their savior, but few of those people would prepare themselves by following God's commandments and repenting of their sins so that they could be cleansed of sin through Jesus's blood. Many are called to accept God's offer of eternal life with Jesus, but few of those who are invited prepare themselves to be judged worthy of entering God's kingdom.

JESUS IS QUESTIONED ABOUT PAYING TRIBUTE AND ETERNAL MARRIAGE

Then went the Pharisees, and took counsel how they might entangle him in his talk.

And they sent out unto him their disciples with the Herodians, saying Master, we know that thou art true, and teachest the way of God in truth, neither carest thou for any man: for thou regardest not the person of men.

Tell us therefore, What thinkest thou? Is it lawful to give tribute unto Caesar, or not?

But Jesus perceived their wickedness, and said, Why tempt ye me, ye hypocrites?

Shew me the tribute money. *A*nd they brought unto him a penny.

And he saith unto them, Whose is this image and superscription?

They say unto him, Caesar's. Then saith he unto them, Render therefore unto Caesar the things which are Caesar's; and unto God the things that are God's.

When they had heard these words, they marveled, and left him, and went their way.

The same day came to him the Sadducees, which say that there is no resurrection, and asked him,

Saying, Master, Moses said, If a man die, having no children, his brother shall marry his wife, and raise up seed unto his brother.

Now there were with us seven brethren: and the first, when he had married a wife, deceased, and having no issue, left his wife unto his brother:

Likewise the second also, and the third, unto the seventh.

And last of all the woman died also.

Therefore in the resurrection whose wife shall she be of the seven for they all had her.

Jesus answered and said unto them, Ye do err, not knowing the scriptures, nor the power of God.

For in the resurrection they neither marry, not are given in marriage, but are as the angels of God in heaven.

But as touching the resurrection of the dead, have ye not read that which was spoken unto you by God, saying,

I AM THE GOD OF ABRAHAM, AND THE GOD OF ISAAC, AND THE GOD OF JACOB? God is not the God of the dead, but of the living.

And when the multitude heard this, they were astonished at his doctrine.

Matthew 22:15–33 (KJV)

THE PHARISEES GATHERED together in a group and discussed how they could trick Jesus into saying something wrong while he taught. They sent their students with the Herodians (a political group that supported King Herod) back to Jesus. The Pharisees' students addressed Jesus as Master and said that they knew that he was God's messenger and that he taught the truth. The Pharisees' students said that Jesus did not respect the opinion of any man; he did not follow the instructions of any person but listened only to God. The men sent by the Pharisees asked Jesus if it was lawful for Jews to pay tribute to Caesar. They knew that Jesus taught that only God had authority over the Jewish people.

Jesus recognized that they were sent to trick him. He said that they were hypocrites because they pretended to be his followers but were really there to bring shame upon him. Jesus told the men to show him the tribute coin. Then Jesus asked them whose picture and name were on the coin. They answered that the picture on the coin was Caesar's. Jesus told them to give Caesar what was his (the coins) and to give God what was God's. When the Pharisee students heard the answer that Jesus gave to them, they were surprised and impressed, and they left the place where Jesus was teaching.

On that same day, the Sadducees, who did not believe that there is a resurrection, came to ask Jesus a question. They also addressed him as Master. They told him that they knew that Moses had taught that if a married man died without having any children, his brother could marry the first man's wife and conceive children with the wife in the dead brother's name. They said that in their group was a family with seven brothers. The first brother married and then died. The second brother married the dead brother's wife, but she still did not bear a child. Progressively every one of the seven brothers married the woman after her present husband died so that she could have a baby who would carry on the blood line of the past husband. Finally after all of the brothers were dead, the woman died. The Sadducees asked Jesus whose wife the woman would be in the resurrection of the dead. Jesus told the Sadducees that they were making a mistake because they did not know what the scriptures in the Old Testament said or how powerful God is. He explained that when God's people are resurrected from the dead, God's people would not marry. The people who would be resurrected would be like the angels of God. He went on to tell them that in regard to the question of whether there would be a resurrection, Did they not know that God had said that there would be a resurrection when God said, "I am the God of Abraham, and the God of Isaac, and the God of Jacob." God is not the God of the dead so Abraham, Isaac, and Jacob would be alive.

When the large group of people who were listening heard Jesus, they were astonished at the truths of God that he taught.

JESUS SPEAKS TO THE PHARISEES ABOUT GOD'S LAW AND THE MESSIAH

But when the Pharisees had heard that he had put the Sadducees to silence, they were gathered together.

Then one of them, which was a lawyer, asked him a question, tempting him, and saying,

Master, which is the great commandment in the law?

Jesus said unto him, THOU SHALT LOVE THE LORD THY GOD WITH ALL THY HEART, AND WITH ALL THY SOUL, AND WITH ALL THY MIND.

This is the first and great commandment.

And the second is like unto it, THOU SHALT LOVE THY NEIGHBOR AS THYSELF.

On these two commandments hang all the law and the prophets.

While the Pharisees were gathered together, Jesus asked them,

Saying, What think ye of Christ? Whose son is he? They say unto him, The son of David.

He saith unto them, How then doth David in spirit call him Lord, saying,

THE LORD SAID UNTO MY LORD SIT THOU ON MY RIGHT HAND, TILL I MAKE THINE ENEMIES THY FOOTSTOOL?

If David then call him Lord; how is he his son?

And no man was able to answer him a word, neither durst any man from that day forth ask him any more questions.

Matthew 22:34–46 (KJV)

WHEN THE PHARISEES heard that Jesus had silenced the Sadducees, they were gathered together in a group. One man, who was a lawyer, asked Jesus a question to try and prove Jesus wrong. Addressing Jesus as Master, the lawyer asked Jesus what was the greatest of God's commandments. Jesus quoted scripture from the Old Testament saying, "Thou shalt love the Lord thy God with all thy heart, and with all thy soul, and with all thy mind." He said that it was the first and greatest commandment given to men. Jesus said that the second greatest commandment is very much like the first commandment. The second commandment is "Thou shalt love thy neighbour as thyself." Jesus said that all of God's commandments are related to those two commandments. Everything that God has commanded in the Jewish Law and all of the prophets' words relate back to those two great commandments.

While the Pharisees were gathered together, Jesus asked them a question. What did they think about God's Christ? Whose son was the Christ? The Pharisees said that the Christ was the son of King David. Jesus asked them if the Christ was the son of David, then why did David when he was speaking under the influence of the Holy Spirit call the Messiah, Lord. Jesus again quoted scripture from the Old Testament. If King David called the Messiah, Lord, then how could the Messiah be King David's son? No one had the answer to Jesus's question; from that day on, no one tried to debate with Jesus. They knew they would not win an argument with Jesus.

JESUS SPEAKS ABOUT THE CONDUCT OF A FOLLOWER OF JESUS

Then spake Jesus to the multitude, and to his disciples.

Saying, The scribes and the Pharisees sit in Moses' seat:

All therefore whatsoever they bid you observe, that observe and do; but do not ye after their works: for they say, and do not.

For they bind heavy burdens and grievous to be borne, and lay them on men's shoulders; but they themselves will not move them with one of their fingers.

But all their works they do for to be seen of men: they make broad their phylacteries, and enlarge the borders of their garments,

And love the uppermost rooms at feasts, and the chief seats in the synagogues,

And greetings in the markets, and to be called of men, Rabbi, Rabbi.

But be not ye called Rabbi: for one is your Master, even Christ; and all ye are brethren.

And call no man your father upon the earth: for one is your Father, which is in heaven.

Neither be ye called masters: for one is your Master, even Christ.

But he that is greatest among you shall be your servant.

And whosoever shall exalt himself shall be abased; and he that shall humble himself shall be exalted.

Matthew 23:1–12 (KJV)

JESUS THEN SPOKE to the great crowd and to His disciples. He said that the scribes (teachers of the Mosaic Law) and the Pharisees were recognized to have the authority of Moses. Therefore they had the authority of Moses to interpret the Laws of God given to the Jews by Moses. Whatever they told the Jews to do, they must do. Beware; the Jews must not do what they did. They made laws, but they did not follow those laws themselves. They created laws which were very difficult to keep, and they commanded other Jewish people to keep those rules, but they would not even try to obey their own rules.

Jesus said everything they did was done to draw attention to themselves. They made their phylacteries big. Phylacteries were little leather boxes holding scriptures which were worn on the left arm and forehead to fulfill the laws given in Deuteronomy.

And these words, which I command thee this day, shall be in thine heart:

And thou shalt teach them diligently unto thy children, and shalt talk of them when thou sittest in thine house, and when thou walkest by the way, and when thou liest down, and when thou risest up.

And thou shalt bind them for a sign upon thine hand, and they shall be as frontlets between thine eyes.

Deuteronomy 6:6–8 (KJV)

> Therefore shall you lay up these my words in your heart and in your soul, and bind them for a sign upon your hand, that they may be as frontlets between your eyes.
>
> And ye shall teach them your children, speaking of them when thou sittest in thine house, and when thou walkest by the way, when thou liest down, and when thou risest up.
>
> Deuteronomy 11:18–19 (KJV)

The scribes and the Pharisees lengthened the tassels on their prayer clothes. Jewish men wore tassels on the four corners of their garments.

> Speak unto the children of Israel, and bid them that they make them fringes in the borders of their garments throughout their generations, and that they put upon the fringe of the borders a ribband of blue.
>
> And it shall be unto you for a fringe, that ye may look upon it, and remember all the commandments of the Lord, and do them; and that ye seek not after your own heart and your own eyes, after which ye use to go a whoring:
>
> That ye may remember, and do all my commandments, and be holy unto your God.
>
> Numbers 15:38–40 (KJV)

> Thou shalt make thee fringes upon the four quarters of thy vesture, wherewith thou coverest thyself.
>
> Deuteronomy 22:12 (KJV)

Jesus was saying that the scribes and Pharisees had all the outward appearances of following God's commandments, but they did not follow the commandments they symbolized. He said that they wanted to be seated in the places of honor at feasts. People were seated at feasts with the most important ones sitting at the head of the table and the least important ones sitting at the end of the table further away from the host. They wanted to have the most important seats in the synagogues (churches). They wanted to be recognized as being special when they walked through the selling stalls in the marketplace. They wanted to be addressed as "Rabbi, Rabbi" (Teacher). They wanted to be treated with the respect and honor that belongs to God.

Jesus told them that they should not want to be called Rabbi because there is only one Master; Christ is our Master, and all of God's children are brothers. God does not want some to be elevated. We are all brothers; we are all God's much loved children. Then Jesus said no one should be addressed as "Father'. We all have one Father; God is our Father in heaven. No one should be our Master but Christ. The person who is greatest among the followers of Jesus Christ should be the servant of everyone.

Anyone who exalts himself (raises himself above others) will be shamed. The person who humbles himself will be raised up by God. God wills that all of us be humble; He does not want us to be full of pride.

JESUS DECLARES WOE UNTO THE SCRIBES AND PHARISEES

But woe unto you scribes and Pharisees, hypocrites! For ye shut up the kingdom of heaven against men: for ye neither go in yourselves, neither suffer ye them that are entering to go in.

Woe unto you, scribes and Pharisees, hypocrites! For ye devour widows' houses, and for a pretence make long prayer: therefore ye shall receive the greater damnation.

Woe unto you, scribes and Pharisees, hypocrites! For ye compass sea and land to make one proselyte, and when he is made, ye make him twofold more the child of hell than yourselves.

Woe unto you, ye blind guides, which say, Whosoever shall swear by the temple, it is nothing' but whosoever shall swear by the gold of the temple, he is a debtor!

Ye fools and blind: for whether is greater, the gold, or the temple that sanctifieth the gold?

And, Whosoever shall swear by the altar, it is nothing; but whosoever sweareth by the gift that is upon it, he is guilty.

Ye fools and blind: for whether is greater, the gift, or the altar that sanctifieth the gift?

Whoso therefore shall swear by the altar, sweareth by it, and by all things thereon.

And whoso shall swear by the temple, sweareth by it, and by him that dwelleth therein.

And he that shall swear by heaven, sweareth by the throne of God, and by him that sitteth thereon.

Woe unto you, scribes and Pharisees, hypocrites! For ye pay tithe of mint and anise and cumin, and have omitted the weightier matters of the law, judgment, mercy, and faith: these ought ye to have done, and not to leave the other undone.

Ye blind guides, which strain at a gnat, and swallow a camel.

Woe unto you, scribes and Pharisees, hypocrites! For ye make clean the outside of the cup and of the platter, but within they are full of extortion and excess.

Thou blind Pharisee, cleanse first that which is within the cup and platter, that the outside of them may be clean also.

Woe unto you, scribes and Pharisees, hypocrites! For ye are like unto whited sepulchers, which indeed appear beautiful outward, but are within full of dead men's bones, and of all uncleanness.

Even so ye also outwardly appear righteous unto men, but within ye are full of hypocrisy and iniquity.

Woe unto you, scribes and Pharisees, hypocrites! Because ye build the tombs of the prophets, and garnish the sepulchers of the righteous,

And say, If we had been in the days of our fathers, we would not have been partakers with them in the blood of the prophets.

Wherefore ye be witnesses unto yourselves, that ye are the children of them which killed the prophets.

Fill ye up then the measure of your fathers.

Ye serpents, ye generation of vipers, how can ye escape the damnation of hell?

Wherefore, behold, I send unto you prophets, and wise men, and scribes: and some of them ye shall kill and crucify; and some of them shall ye scourge in your synagogues, and persecute them from city to city:

That upon you may come all the righteous blood shed upon the earth, from the blood of righteous Abel unto the blood of Zacharias son of Barachias, whom ye slew between the temple and the altar.

Verily I say unto you, All these things shall come upon this generation.

O Jerusalem, Jerusalem, Thou that killest the prophets, and stonest them which are sent unto thee, how often would I have gathered thy children together, even as a hen gathereth her chickens under her wings, and ye would not!

Behold, your house is left unto you desolate.

For I say unto you, Ye shall not see me henceforth, till ye shall say, BLESSED IS HE THAT COMETH IN THE NAME OF THE LORD.

Matthew 23:13–39 (KJV)

JESUS BEGAN TO speak directly to the scribes (teachers of the Mosaic Law) and the Pharisees (a group of Jewish leaders who made laws for all the Jews). It was the scribes and Pharisees who were plotting to kill Jesus. As the leaders of the Jewish people they did not want to recognize that Jesus was sent from God because they would not be God's representatives any longer and would not hold power over all Jews. Jesus frequently called the Pharisees "hypocrites". He meant that they were not the righteous, holy men that they pretended to be. They made a public pretense of following God's commandments, but they did not obey God or do God's will.

In verse thirteen, Jesus said that the scribes and the Pharisees shut up heaven. He meant that they made so many strict rules for the Jews that the people could not obey them all. Since they acted as God's representatives, the scribes (teachers of the Old Testament scriptures) and the Pharisees made it impossible for the Jewish people to enter into God's heaven by obeying God's commandments. Not only did they block the way so that others could not go into God's kingdom, but they refused to follow God's commandments so that they themselves could go into God's kingdom. It is very significant that the people of God were blocked from entrance into God's kingdom of heaven. Jesus became our High Priest when he died on the cross. As our priest he takes us into heaven with him.

> If therefore perfection were by the Levitical priesthood, (for under it the people received the law,) what further need was there that another priest should rise after the order of Melchisedec, and not be called after the order of Aaron?
>
> For the priesthood being changed, there is made of necessity a change also of the law.
>
> For he of whom these things are spoken pertaineth (belong) to another tribe, of which no man gave (served) attendance at the altar.
>
> For it is evident that our Lord sprang out of Juda; of which tribe Moses spake nothing concerning priesthood.
>
> And it is yet far more evident: for that after the similitude (likeness) of Melchisedec there ariseth another priest,
>
> Who is made, not after the law of a carnal commandment, but after the power of an endless life.
>
> For he testifieth, THOU ART A PRIEST FOR EVER AFTER THE ORDER OF MELCHISEDE.
>
> For there is verily a disannulling of the commandment going before for the weakness and unprofitableness thereof.
>
> For the law made nothing perfect, but the bringing in of a better hope did; by the which we draw nigh unto God.

And inasmuch as not without an oath (vow) he was made priest:

For those priests were made without an oath; but this with an oath by him that said unto him, THE LORD SWARE AND WILL NOT REPENT, THOU ART A PRIEST FOREVER AFTER THE ORDER OF MELCHISEDEC.

By so much was Jesus made a surety of a better testament.

And they truly were many priests, because they were not suffered to continue by reason of death:

But this man, because he continueth ever, hath an unchangeable priesthood.

Wherefore he is able also to save them to the uttermost that come unto God by him, seeing he ever liveth to make intercession for them.

For such an high priest became us, who is holy, harmless, undefiled, separate from sinners, and made higher than the heavens;

Who neeedeth not daily, as those high priests, to offer up sacrifice, first for his own sins, and then for the people's: for this he did once, when he offered up himself.

For the law maketh men high priests which have infirmity; but the word of the oath, which was since the law, maketh the Son, who is consecrated for evermore.

Hebrews 7:11–28 (KJV)

The passage above is an explanation by Paul of the fact that the old order of priests in the Old Testament under the Mosaic Law was replaced by a new order of eternal priests when Jesus became our High Priest to take us into God the Father's presence. Paul shows that this was always God's intent because the sentences in the passage from Hebrews are written in all capital letters. That is an indication that they are quotes from the Old Testament. It was always God's plan that Jesus would become our eternal High Priest.

Note that Jesus was openly confronting the scribes and the Pharisees with accusations that they had failed to fulfill their assignments from God to be the authorities over the Jewish people (God's chosen people). The fact that He was accusing them in a very public manner is an indication that God the Father chose the time and place where Jesus would give up his life on the cross. Jesus was following God the Father's directions.

Again Jesus accused the scribes and Pharisees of acting against the will of God. God was very specific that God himself took the widows and the orphans as his responsibility to provide for them and to protect them. The scribes and Pharisees were making rules that enabled them to take away the homes of the widows who were powerless to help themselves. At the same time the scribes and Pharisees were praying long prayers to God in public pretending to be serving God. "Ye shall not afflict any widow or fatherless child. If thou afflict them in any wise, and they cry at all unto me, I will surely hear their cry: And my wrath shall wax hot, and I will kill you with the sword; and your wives shall be widows, and your chidren fatherless" (Exodus 22:22–24, KJV).

> A father of the fatherless, and a judge of the widows, is God in his holy habitation.
>
> Psalm 68:5 (KJV)

> Leave thy fatherless children, I will preserve them alive; and let thy widows trust in me.
>
> Jeremiah 49:11 (KJV)

> And I will come near to you to judgment; and I will be a swift witness against the sorcerers, and against the adulterers, and against false swearers, and against those that oppress the hireling in his wages, the widow, and the fatherless, and that turn aside the stranger from his right, and fear not me, saith the Lord of hosts.
>
> Malachi 3:5 (KJV)

Jesus said that because the scribes and the Pharisees oppressed the widows (caused them harm) in direct disregard for God's instructions and then made a pretense of serving God in public that they would receive greater damnation.

Again Jesus declared the scribes and the Pharisees would be woeful; they were hypocrites because they pretended to serve God but did not follow God's commandments. He said that they traveled over the ocean and land to make one convert to the Jewish faith, and when that person became a Jew, they made him twice as much a child of hell as they were themselves. They were like blind guides who could not see for themselves the truth so that they could lead others into the ways that God wanted them to walk.

He said if a person swears by the gold of the temple, that person is a debtor. He said that they were blind fools because they did not understand that the temple (the building designated as God's place) was greater than the gold (money) that was sanctified because it was in the temple.

Jesus told them that they could not see that the altar where holy sacrifice was offered to God was greater than the gift that is sanctified because it is on the altar. Whoever swears by the altar swears by it and all the things upon it. And whoever swears by the temple swears by the temple and the God who lives there. A person who swears by heaven swears by the throne of God and by God who is seated there. The scribes and Pharisees thought that the gold and sacrifices that they brought were greater than the temple and the altar made sacred by God.

Again Jesus said woe to the scribes and Pharisees because they thought and taught that the tithes of mint and anise and cumin were more important than obeying God. They valued their own sacrifices and ignored God's law, God's judgment, God's mercy, and faith in God. They were blind guides (leaders) who choked on a gnat (a small sin against their own rules) and swallowed a camel (much greater offense toward God).

The scribes and the Pharisees should have listened to the warnings about woe because they were cleaning the outside of the cup (outward appearance) while the inside of the cup was filthy (secret acts of extortion and excess). Extortion is to obtain money from a person by using force or illegal power to cause them to give up what is rightfully theirs. The scribes and Pharisees were like sepulchers (burial tombs) which were painted white to show purity. But those sepulchers were filled with uncleanliness (sin) and death (spiritual death). They appeared to be righteous and holy men, but they were full of hypocrisy and iniquity. Hypocrisy is pretending to be what someone is not. Literally iniquity means unequal. God regards unequal treatment of his children as iniquity (great evil).

Jesus said that there was woe to come to the scribes and Pharisees because they built the tombs where the prophets sent by God were buried. They decorated the sepulchers of the righteous messengers from God. They said that if they had been alive when the prophets came, they would never have killed them as their parents had done. By saying that their fathers killed the prophets, they spoke as witnesses that they were the descendants of the people who killed God's prophets. They would repeat the actions of their parents. They were a generation of vipers (snakes). They dealt in trickery and lies just as Satan had done in the Garden of Eden when Satan convinced Eve to eat of the Tree of the Knowledge of Good and Evil. How would they escape punishment in hell?

There is a double meaning for the word *generation*. We think of the word as a designation for all the people who were born at approximately the same time. There is a second meaning to the word *generation*. We can look at the meaning of the word when we say that a fire generates heat. We are the generation of Jesus Christ because our eternal life is generated through him. God the Father does not have grandchildren. As Christians we are all the children of God generated through the salvation and eternal life we receive through sharing the life of Jesus. We are all a part of the generation born through Jesus even if some of us were born in AD 100 and some of us were born in 1990 AD.

When Jesus spoke of a generation of vipers who cannot escape the place that is hell, he was talking about those people whose lives are generated by their association with Satan. Satan took the form of a snake (viper) in the Garden of Eden. His lies convinced Adam and Eve to disobey God and accept the Devil's lies instead of God's truth. The generation of vipers is made up of all those who choose to serve Satan instead of God. Their lives are generated (influenced, shaped) by their acceptance of Satan as their God. Their acceptance of evil has made them subject to spiritual death.

Jesus said that He would send prophets and wise men and scribes (teachers) to teach them the meaning of God's words. Some of those messengers would be killed and crucified by the Jewish scribes and Pharisees. Some of them would be beaten in the synagogues. And some of Jesus's messengers would be driven from city to city by the Jewish scribes and Pharisees. That would happen so that they would be held accountable for all the righteous blood that had been shed upon the earth. He meant the innocent blood shed since Cain killed his brother Abel up to the blood of Zacharias whom they had killed between the temple and the altar of God. The punishments for all of that bloodshed would be laid upon the leaders of the Jews who fought to kill Jesus.

He addressed the city of Jerusalem as the city that killed the prophets sent to them by God. It was the city of the people who stoned the messengers sent by God. Jesus had wanted to gather the people of Jerusalem, God's chosen people, to himself many times. He wanted to protect those descendants of Abraham. He told them to observe (look) and see that their house was becoming empty. They had been chosen by God to receive God's promises and to receive the Messiah. But they would not listen to

God and follow His commandments. They would not welcome the Messiah God sent to them. So the privilege of receiving the Messiah and the eternal life he brought would be given to others. Their house was empty of God's blessings. God's presence would no longer be found in their temple. And so Jesus said to these descendants of Abraham, the chosen people of Israel, that they (their descendants) would not see Jesus again until they would welcome Jesus. They must welcome Him saying, " Blessed is he that cometh in the name of the Lord." They (the Jewish people) must welcome Him as their Messiah and declare that He comes in the name of their God and is God's own son. Jesus will not return to Jerusalem until the Jewish people accept Him.

JESUS TELLS THE DISCIPLES WHAT WILL HAPPEN AFTER THE CRUCIFIXION

And Jesus went out, and departed from the temple: and his disciples came to him for to shew him the buildings of the temple.

And Jesus said unto them, See ye not all these things? Verily I say unto you, There shall not be left here one stone upon another, that shall not be thrown down.

And as he sat upon the Mount of Olives, the disciples came unto him privately, saying, Tell us, when shall these things be? And what shall be the sign of thy coming, and of the end of the world?

And Jesus answered and said unto them, Take heed that no man deceive you.

For many shall come in my name, saying, I am Christ; and shall deceive many.

And ye shall hear of wars and rumours of wars: see that ye be not troubled: for all these things must come to pass, but the end is not yet.

For nation shall rise against nation, and kingdom against kingdom: and there shall be famines, and pestilences, and earthquakes, in divers (various) places.

All these are the beginning of sorrows.

Then shall they deliver you up to be afflicted, and shall kill you: and ye shall be hated of all nations for my name's sake.

And then shall many be offended (stumble), and shall betray one another, and shall hate one another.

And many false prophets shall rise, and shall deceive many.

And because iniquity (sin)shall abound, the love of many shall wax cold.

But he that shall endure unto the end, the same shall be saved.

And this gospel of the kingdom shall be preached in all the world for a witness unto all nations, and then shall the end come.

When ye therefore shall see the ABOMINATION OF DESOLATION, spoken of by Daniel the prophet, stand in the holy place, (whoso readeth, let him understand:)

Then let them which be in Judaea flee into the mountains:

Let him which is on the housetop not come down to take anything out of his house:

Neither let him which is in the field return back to take his clothes.

And woe unto them that are with child, and to them that give suck in those day!

But pray ye that your flight be not in the winter, neither on the Sabbath day:

For then shall be great tribulation, such as was not since the beginning of the world to this time, no, nor ever shall be.

And except those days should be shortened, there should no flesh be saved: but for the elect's sake those days shall be shortened.

Then if any man shall say unto you, Lo, here is Christ, or there, believe it not.

For there shall arise false Christs, and false prophets, and shall shew great signs and wonders; insomuch that, if it were possible, they shall deceive the very elect.

Behold, I have told you before.

Wherefore if they shall say unto you, Behold, he is in the desert: go not forth: behold, he is in the secret chambers: believe it not.

For as the lightning cometh out of the east, and shineth even unto the west; so shall also the coming of the Son of man be.

For wheresoever the carcase is, there will the eagles be gathered together.

Immediately after the tribulation (trouble) of those days shall the sun, be darkened, and the moon shall not give her light, and the stars shall fall from heaven, and the powers of the heavens shall be shaken.

Matthew 24:1–29 (KJV)

AS JESUS LEFT the temple, his disciples came to him and called His attention to the magnificent buildings that composed the temple devoted to the worship of God. Jesus responded telling them that all of the temple at Jerusalem would be destroyed. It would be completely wiped away so that no stone walls were left standing. They did not understand that Jesus was speaking not only about the physical temple; He was also telling them about the spiritual building. The leadership of the Jewish people (the scribes and the Pharisees) would be totally destroyed; they would no longer stand as God's spokesmen to his people.

When Jesus had walked to the Mount of Olives and seated Himself there, his disciples came and asked him questions privately. They asked him to tell them when all of those things would happen. They wanted to know what sign would show them that Jesus was returning to earth. The disciples wanted to know when the end of the earth would happen.

Jesus speaking to only his disciples began to give them a specific description of what would happen after he returned to heaven. Jesus warned them not to let any man deceive (trick) them. He said that many men would come to the Christians claiming to be Christ. Those deceivers (impersonators) would fool many people.

The Christians would hear about many wars and stories about wars that would start. He did not want the disciples to be troubled (distressed, worried) about the wars because all of those things had to happen before the end of the world came. Nations (countries) would make war on other countries. There would be periods of starvation and disease (plagues). There would be great storms and earthquakes over all the earth. But those signs were just the warnings of the sorrowful time that would come next.

Then the Christians would be captured and tortured. The Christians would be killed for their faith in Jesus. Every nation (country, culture) on the earth would hate them because they belonged to Jesus. Then many of the Christians would fall away from their faith and devotion to Jesus. Some of the Christians would deny that they were Christians and turn their fellow Christians over to be tortured. Christians would hate other Christians. Many false prophets (preachers claiming to speak for God) would appear. Those false prophets would convince many of the Christians and lead them away from Jesus and His truth.

There will be great evil and injustice all over the world. Many who claim to be Christians will turn away from (give up) their Christian beliefs. The evil in the world will influence the beliefs and actions of some Christians. But the believers who hold firm in the beliefs and refuse to be pulled away from Jesus Christ will be saved (given eternal life).

The good news about salvation through belief in Jesus Christ and about the kingdom of heaven will be preached to all people all over the earth. That universal preaching of God's word will stand as a witness that all people had the opportunity to be saved from their sins. Then the end of the world will come.

So when you see the Abomination of Desolation spoken about by Daniel the prophet has come, stand firm in the holy place. Christians who are the living temple of God made holy because Jesus Christ lives in us will stand firm in their faith and in their belief in the promises of their God.

> And he shall confirm the covenant with many for one week: and in the midst of the week he shall cause the sacrifice and the oblation to cease, and for the overspreading of abominations he shall make it desolate, even until the consummation, and that determined shall be poured upon the desolate.
>
> Daniel 9:27 (KJV)

> And arms shall stand on his part, and they shall pollute the sanctuary of [strength], and shall take away the daily sacrifice, and they shall place the abomination that maketh desolate (causes ruin).
>
> And such as do wickedly against the covenant shall be corrupt by flatteries: but the people that do know their God shall be strong, and do exploits.
>
> And they that understand among the people shall instruct many: yet they shall fall by the sword, and by flame, by captivity, and by spoil, many days.
>
> Daniel 11: 31–33 (KJV)

> And from the time that the daily sacrifice shall be taken away, and the abomination that maketh desolate set up, there shall be a thousand two hundred and ninety days.

Blessed is he that waiteth, and cometh to the thousand three hundred and five and thirty days.

Daniel 12: 11–12 (KJV)

We very often do not understand the prophesies of the Old Testament. Only God can interpret them accurately. Frequently things that happen in the physical realm in the Old Testament are a fore shadowing of what will happen spiritually in the New Testament. Some think that Jesus was talking about the destruction of the temple in AD 70. It may be that Jesus was speaking about events that will happen in the future before the end of the world.

We do know that Jesus was warning Christians through the disciples that no matter what happens, even if false gods are set up by the rulers all over the earth, Christians are to stand firm in their beliefs.

When that rebellion against God and the blasphemy which will occur happens, Christians should be ready to leave all that they have and follow the leadership of the Holy Spirit instantaneously. God will protect us, but we must respond without question. We must abandon all that we hold valuable in the physical world and go wherever he tells us to go.

The destruction that happens at that time will be colossal. We are warned not to go back to take anything with us. Jesus said that it would be very difficult for pregnant women or women carrying babies to move fast enough to escape. We should pray that it will not happen in the winter or on the Sabbath day when Jews were not supposed to move about or travel.

There will be great suffering at that time when men deny the sovereignty of God over all creation and set up false gods or declare themselves to be equal to God.

There will be greater suffering and destruction at that time than at any other time before or after upon the earth. If God did not shorten that time, there would be no life left upon the earth.

But God out of his love for his Christian children will shorten the days of destruction.

After that occurs if anyone tells you that Christ is at any place, do not believe them. Many men will claim to be Christ or a prophet; those false Christs will perform miracles. They will show so much power that the chosen people of God would be fooled if it was possible.

Be aware that Jesus has told you these things about what will happen as a warning to you. So at that time if you are told that Christ is on the desert or in a secret room, do not believe them. When Jesus Christ returns, there will be no question about when or where He comes. His glory will shine from the east to the west; He will be revealed to all life. Jesus said to remember that the eagles go to the place where they find food (the carcase, dead animal). So will all the Christians be drawn to the place where Jesus, who provides us with the eternal life that He shares with us, will be located.

Immediately after the tribulation (the great suffering and destruction) has stopped, there will be other signs that the world is coming to an end. The sun will be darkened; there will be no light. The moon will not give us any light. The stars will fall from the sky. All of the planets and stars in the heaven will be shaken.

WHEN JESUS WILL RETURN TO THE EARTH

And then shall appear the sign of the Son of man in heaven: and then shall all the tribes of the earth mourn, and they shall see the Son of man coming in the clouds of heaven with power and great glory.

And he shall send his angels with a great sound of a trumpet, and they shall gather together his elect from the four winds, from one end of heaven to the other.

Now learn a parable of the fig tree; When his branch is yet tender and puttieth forth leaves, ye know that summer is nigh:

So likewise ye, when ye shall see all these things, know that it is near, even at the doors.

Verily I say unto you, This generation shall not pass, till all these things be fulfilled.

Heaven and earth shall pass away, but my words shall not pass away.

But of that day and hour knoweth no man, no, not the angels of heaven, but my Father only.

But as the days of Noe were so shall also the coming of the Son of man be.

For as in the days that were before the flood they were eating and drinking, marrying and giving in marriage, until the day that Noe entered into the ark,

And knew not until the flood came, and took them all away; so shall also the coming of the Son of man be.

Then shall two be in the field, the one shall be taken, and the other left.

Two women shall be grinding at the mill; the one shall be taken and the other left.

Watch therefore: for ye know not what hour your Lord doth come,

But know this, that if the goodman of the house had known in what watch the thief would come, he would have watched, and would not have suffered his house to be broken up.

Therefore be ye also ready for in such an hour as ye think not the Son of man cometh.

Who then is a faithful and wise servant, whom his lord hath made ruler over his household, to give them meat in due season?

Blessed is the servant, whom his lord when he cometh shall find so doing.

Verily I say unto you, That he shall make him ruler over all his goods.

But and if the evil servant shall say in his heart, My lord delayeth his coming;

And shall begin to smite his fellowservants, and to eat and drink with the drunken;

The lord of that servant shall come in a day when he looketh not for him, and in an hour that he is not aware of,

And shall cut him asunder, and appoint him his portion with the hypocrites: there shall be weeping and gnashing of teeth.

Matthew 24:30–51 (KJV)

MOST OF THE preceding passage beginning with Matthew 24:4 and including all of Matthew 24:30–51 are exclusively the words of Jesus. All of the words were given to the disciples when they were sitting away from the crowds that usually followed Jesus. Therefore please remember that all of these words are the words given to the disciples before the crucifixion of Jesus.

After the sun and the moon have stopped giving light and the stars have fallen from the heaven, the sign of the Son of man will be seen in heaven. Then all of the people on the earth will be filled with great sadness and mourning. All the people on the earth will see the Son of man coming in the clouds of heaven. They will see that Jesus comes with power and great glory.

Jesus will send His angels with a great sound of trumpets blowing. The angels will gather together the people chosen by God from over all the earth. This is contrary to the popular belief that the people left behind will not know when God's elect are taken; it would be impossible for anyone to not know when the sun and moon no longer give light or when the stars fall from heaven. Everyone will know when Jesus returns and sends his angels to gather the people chosen by God.

Jesus told the disciples to learn from the fig tree. When the fig tree turns green and puts on new leaves, everyone knows that summer is coming. Just so when you observe that the sun and moon no longer shine, that the time has come for Jesus to come back to the earth. Jesus said that in truth he was telling them that the generation of Christians would not cease to be on the earth until all of the prophecies that He was giving them would happen. He said that the heaven and the earth would be destroyed, but the words of Jesus would always be true forever.

No man knows what day and what hour Jesus will come back. The angels do not know either. Only God the Father knows the time. When God told Noah to build the ark, no one knew when the flood would come. That is the way it will be when Jesus returns. Before God sent the flood, people were eating, drinking, and getting married. They lived their lives as they always did right up to the day that God told Noah to enter the ark. The people did not know that they were all about to be destroyed until the flood came. The coming of Jesus will be the same. At that time two people will be working in a field, and one will be taken by the angels of Jesus and the other will be left in the field. Two women will be grinding flour; one will be taken by the angels, and one will be left. Be alert and watch because you will not know when Jesus is coming. Remember that if the owner of a house knew when the thief was coming, he would have watched for the thief so that his house would not have been broken into. You should always be alert and ready for the coming of Jesus because you will not know before he comes suddenly.

Who has God decided is a faithful and wise servant so that God has put that servant in charge of his whole house full of servants. The servant who is always working to care for the owner of the house's property will be blessed; that good servant will be doing his appointed work when the owner of the house comes suddenly. Jesus said that truly that servant will be made the ruler over all of the owner's goods and possessions.

But if there is an evil servant, he will say to himself, "My boss isn't coming soon." That servant will begin to beat the other servants, and he will eat and drink to excess with people who are always drunk. Then the owner of the house will come when he is not expected to come. The owner will remove the evil servant from his position, and he will send him to live with the hypocrites (people who pretend to be good servants but are not good servants). Then the evil servant and the hypocrites will weep and grind their teeth.

JESUS DESCRIBES THE PEOPLE ADMITTED INTO HEAVEN

Then shall the kingdom of heaven be likened unto ten virgins, which took their lamps, and went forth to meet the bridegroom.

And five of them were wise, and five were foolish.

They that were foolish took their lamps, and took no oil with them.

But the wise took oil in their vessels with their lamps.

While the bridegroom tarried, they all slumbered and slept.

And at midnight there was a cry made, Behold, the bridegroom cometh; go ye out to meet him.

Then all those virgins arose, and trimmed their lamps.

And the foolish said unto the wise, Give us of your oil; for our lamps are gone out.

But the wise answered, saying, Not so; lest there be not enough for us and you: but go ye rather to them that sell, and buy for yourselves.

And while they went to buy, the bridegroom came; and they that were ready went in with him to the marriage: and the door was shut.

Afterward came also the other virgins, saying, Lord, Lord, open to us.

But he answered and said, Verily I say unto you, I know you not.

Watch therefore, for ye know neither the day nor the hour wherein the Son of man cometh.

For the kingdom of heaven is as a man travelling into a far country, who called his own servants, and delivered unto them his goods.

And unto one he gave five talents, to another two, and to another one; to every man according to his several ability; and straightway took his journey.

Then he that had received the five talents went and traded with the same, and made them other five talents.

And likewise he that had received two, he also gained other two.

But he that had received one went and digged in the earth, and hid his lord's money.

After a long time the lord of those servants cometh, and reckoneth with them.

And so he that had received five talents came and brought other five talents, saying, Lord, thou deliveredst unto me five talents: behold, I have gained beside them five talents more.

His lord said unto him, Well done, thou good and faithful servant: thou hast been faithful over a few things, I will make thee ruler over many things: enter thou into the joy of thy lord.

He also that had received two talents came and said, Lord, thou deliveredst unto me two talents: behold, I have gained two other talents beside them.

His lord said unto him, Well done, good and faithful servant; thou hast been faithful over a few things, I will make thee ruler over many things: enter thou into the joy of thy lord.

Then he which had received the one talent came and said, Lord, I knew thee that thou art an hard man, reaping where thou hast not sown, and gathering where thou hast not strawed:

And I was afraid, and went and hid thy talent in the earth: lo, there thou hast that is thine.

His lord answered and said unto him, Thou wicked and slothful servant, thou knewest that I reap where I sowed not, and gather where I have not strawed:

Thou oughtest therefore to have put my money to the exchangers, and then at my coming I should have received mine own with usury.

Take therefore the talent from him, and give it unto him which hath ten talents.

For unto every one that hath shall be given, and he shall have abundance: but from him that hath not shall be taken away even that which he hath.

And cast ye the unprofitable servant into outer darkness: there shall be weeping and gnashing of teeth.

Matthew 25:1–30 (KJV)

JESUS AGAIN USED parables to teach the disciples about the Kingdom of Heaven. Those who want to enter God's heaven are like ten virgins, who were told to wait at a location to light the way with their lamps for the bridegroom when he came to the wedding. Note that the virgins were virgins, and they had been selected to participate in the wedding. The problem was not that they were not worthy or not invited. Their problem was that they were unprepared.

Five of the virgins were wise, and five of the virgins were foolish. Five virgins took oil to use in their lamps, and five virgins took no oil. The groom did not come as soon as they thought that he would. All of the virgins got tired and went to sleep. They were awakened when someone yelled that the groom was coming. The virgins were supposed to go out and meet the groom with their lamps burning. All ten virgins fixed their lamps so that they were ready to serve the groom. It was then that five of the virgins discovered that they had run out of lamp oil.

The five foolish virgins asked the five wise virgins to share the oil that they had brought with them. The five wise virgins refused to share their oil because they would not have enough for themselves and the foolish virgins. They told the foolish (unprepared) virgins to go buy oil for themselves. While the foolish virgins were gone to buy oil, the groom came. The five wise virgins went into the marriage with the groom, and the door was locked. When the foolish virgins returned with their oil, they cried out to the groom begging to be let into the marriage. He answered then that he truly did not know them.

The virgins were the people of God. They were told to wait for the coming of Jesus and enter into the Kingdom of Heaven with Jesus. Some of the people of God were diligent and prepared for the coming of Jesus. They filled their lives with obedience to God's commandments and belief in the promises of Jesus. The people of God who were wise acted upon their faith; their lives were filled with the development of the fruits of the spirit. "But the fruit of the spirit is love, joy, peace, longsuffering, gentleness, goodness, faith, Meekness, temperance: against such there is no law. And they that are Christ's have crucified the flesh with the affections and lusts" (Galatians 5:22–24, KJV).

> Blessed are the poor in spirit: for their's is the kingdom of heaven.
> Blessed are they that mourn: for they shall be comforted.
> Blessed are the meek: for they shall inherit the earth.
> Blessed are they which do hunger and thirst after righteousness: for they shall be filled.
> Blessed are the merciful: for they shall obtain mercy.
> Blessed are the pure in heart: for they shall see God.

Blessed are the peacemakers: for they shall be called the children of God.

Blessed are they which are persecuted for righteousness' sake: for their's is the kingdom of heaven.

Blessed are ye, when men shall revile you, and persecute you, and shall say all manner of evil against you falsely, for my sake.

Rejoice, and be exceeding glad: for great is your reward in heaven: for so persecuted they the prophets which were before you.

Ye are the salt of the earth: but if the salt have lost his saviour, wherewith shall it be salted? It is thenceforth good for nothing, but to be cast out, and to be trodden under foot of men.

Ye are the light of the world. A city that is set on an hill cannot be hid.

Neither do men light a candle, and put it under a bushel, but on a candlestick; and it giveth light unto all that are in the house.

Let your light shine before men, that they may see your good works, and glorify your Father which is in heaven.

Matthew 5:3–16 (KJV)

Jesus described those things which God wants us to do to prepare for his coming. he also taught about how those who believe in him should provide light for the world so that all people can see their way to him. The foolish virgins (followers of Jesus) did not prepare for his coming. Their lives were not filled with light.

When the groom (Jesus) came to take the virgins (followers of Jesus) into heaven, the foolish virgins (followers) were not ready, and they did not have time to prepare themselves (get oil). They were left outside the wedding (heaven), and the groom did not recognize them; their lives and actions did not identify them as God's people.

Jesus also told a parable about a man who traveled to a far country after he had given instructions to his servants. Jesus was the man who went away to the Kingdom of Heaven after leaving instructions with his servants (the followers of Jesus).

Before the man in the parable went away he gave one of his servants five talents to be responsible for keeping. (A talent was a weight equal to three thousand shekels – or about six thousand pounds of gold.) Another servant was given two talents; and a third servant was given one talent. The man gave out the talents in relation to the abilities of the three servants. The man gave out the talents in relation to the servants' abilities so he already knew what the abilities of each servant were.

The man who was given five talents invested the gold so well that he had ten talents when the master returned. The man who was given two talents invested the gold so well that he had four talents when the master returned. Note that the master did not expect the man with two talents to earn the same amount as the man who was given five talents. The master commended both of the men and made them both rulers (supervisors) over many things. He told them both to enter into the joy of their lord.

When the servant who was given one talent was called to report to the master, he gave excuses for his negligence. He had buried the one talent in the dirt. The servant told the master that he, the servant, knew how hard it was to please his master. The servant knew that the master used every opportunity to gain more money. The master harvested grain from areas where he had not planted seeds so that any opportunity to gain more grain would be used. That doesn't mean that the master stole other farmers' grain; he just harvested not only what he planted, but he harvested what grew on ground where no one had planted. The servant reasoned that since the master expected so much, it would be safer to bury the money so that he could return all of it to the master.

The master rebuked the servant because the servant knew that the master never wasted an opportunity to gain more grain, but the servant did not try to gain from the investment of the one talent. The master told the servant that the least he could have done with the money was to have invested the money with the money lenders (bankers) so that the master could have collected interest with the original amount when the master returned. The master ordered that the original talent was to be taken from the negligent servant. It was to be given to the man who used the five talents to earn five talents more. Then the negligent servant was thrown into outer darkness where there is weeping and grinding of teeth.

Jesus was talking about His second coming to the earth. Each Christian is given talents (It is interesting that Jesus used the word talents for the gold that was given. He was not talking about money given to His followers.) He was talking about talents (skills, aptitudes) which are given to believers. All believers are not given the same talents, and all believers do not receive the same amount of talent. But all believers are expected to use those talents to bring more believers into the kingdom of God.

Those talents may be the physical talents that we are given. They might include speaking, singing, organizing, explaining scriptures, preaching, evangelizing, leading, giving, or listening in sympathy. But there are spiritual gifts that are given to the body of Christ, and which are manifested in different ways and amounts (strengths).

> Now concerning spiritual gifts, brethren, I would not have you ignorant.
>
> Ye know that ye were Gentiles, carried away unto these dumb idols, even as ye were led.
>
> Wherefore I give you to understand, that no man speaking by the Spirit of God calleth Jesus accursed: and that no man can say that Jesus is the Lord, but by the Holy Ghost.
>
> Now there are diversities of gifts, but the same Spirit.
>
> And there are differences of administrations, but the same Lord.

And there are diversities of operations, but it is the same God which worketh all in all.

But the manifestation of the Spirit is given to every man to profit withal.

For to one is given by the Spirit the word of wisdom; to another the word of knowledge by the same Spirit;

To another faith by the same Spirit; to another the gifts of healing by the same Spirit;

To another the working of miracles; to another prophecy; to another discerning of spirits; to another divers kinds of tongues; to another the interpretation of tongues:

But all these worketh that one and the selfsame Spirit, dividing to every man severally as he will.

For as the body is one, and hath many members, and all the members of that one body, being many, are one body: so also in Christ.

For by one Spirit are we all baptized into one body, whether we be Jews or Gentiles, whether we be bond or free; and have been all made to drink into one Spirit.

For the body is not one member, but many.

If the foot shall say, Because I am not the hand, I am not of the body; is it therefore not of the body?

And if the ear shall say, Because I am not the eye, I am not of the body; is it therefore not of the body?

If the body were an eye, where were the hearing? If the whole were hearing, where were the smelling?

But now hath God set the members every one of them in the body, as it hath pleased him.

And if they were all one member, where were the body?

But now are they many members, yet but one body.

And the eye cannot say unto the hand, I have no need of thee: nor again the head to the feet, I have no need of you.

Nay, much more those members of the body, which seem to be more feeble, are necessary.

And those members of the body, which we think to be less honourable, upon these we bestow more abundant honour; and our uncomely parts have more abundant comeliness.

For our comely parts have no need: but God hath tempered the body together, having given more abundant honour to that part which lacked:

That there should be no schism in the body; but that the members should have the same care one for another.

And whether one member suffer, all the members suffer with it; or one member be honoured, all the members rejoice with it.

Now ye are the body of Christ, and members in particular.

And God hath set some in the church, first apostles, secondarily prophets, thirdly teachers, after that miracles, then gifts of healing, helps, governments, diversities of tongues.

Are all apostles? Are all prophets? Are all teachers? Are all workers of miracles?

Have all the gifts of healing? Do all speak with tongues? Do all interpret?

1st Corinthians 12:1–30 (KJV)

For as we have many members in one body, and all members have not the same office:

So we have many members in one body, and all members have not the same office:

So we, being many, are one body in Christ, and every one members one of another.

Having then gifts differing according to the grace that is given to us, whether prophecy, let us prophesy according to the proportion of faith;

Or ministry let us wait on our ministering: or he that teacheth, on teaching;

Or he that exhorteth, on exhortation: he that giveth, let him do it with simplicity; he that ruleth, with diligence; he that sheweth mercy, with cheerfulness.

Romans 12:4–8 (KJV)

In the parable of the talents, Jesus admonished each one of us to use whatever talents (abilities) we have been given to further the kingdom of heaven here on earth. Talents, abilities, and spiritual gifts have been given to each Christian to help the body of Christ to draw more believers toward Jesus so that they may pass into the kingdom of heaven.

WHAT WILL HAPPEN WHEN JESUS COMES IN HIS GLORY?

When the Son of man shall come in his glory, and all the holy angels with him, then shall he sit upon the throne of his glory:

And before him shall be gathered all nations: and he shall separate them one from another, as a shepherd divideth his sheep from the goats:

And he shall set the sheep on his right hand, but the goats on the left.

Then shall the King say unto them on his right hand, Come, ye blessed of my Father, inherit the kingdom prepared for you from the foundation of the world:

For I was an hungred, and ye gave me meat: I was thirsty, and ye gave me drink: I was a stranger, and ye took me in:

Naked, and ye clothed me: I was sick, and ye visited me: I was in prison, and ye came unto me.

Then shall the righteous answer him, saying, Lord, when saw we thee an hungred, and fed thee? Or thirsty, and gave thee drink?

When saw we thee a stranger, and took thee in? or naked, and clothed thee?

Or when saw we thee sick, or in prison, and came unto thee?

And the King shall answer and say unto them, Verily I say unto you, Inasmuch as ye have done it unto one of the least of these my brethren, ye have done it unto me.

Then shall he say also unto them on the left hand, Depart from me, ye cursed, into everlasting fire, prepared for the devil and his angels.

For I was an hungred, and ye gave me no meat: I was thirsty, and ye gave me no drink:

I was a stranger, and ye took me not in: naked, and ye clothed me not: sick, and in prison, and ye visited me not.

Then shall they also answer him, saying, Lord, when saw we thee an hungred, or a thirst, or a stranger, or naked, or sick, or in prison, and did not minister unto thee?

Then shall he answer them, saying, Verily I say unto you, Inasmuch as ye did it not to one of the least of these, ye did it not to me.

And these shall go away into everlasting punishment: but the righteous into life eternal.

Matthew 25:31–46 (KJV)

WHEN JESUS THE Christ comes in his glory, all the angels will come with him. Jesus will sit upon the throne of his glory. All the countries (nations) and people of the earth will be gathered in front of Him. Jesus will separate every one of them into one of two groups. he will divide them like a shepherd divides his sheep and his goats. The sheep will be put on his right side, and the goats will be put on his left side.

Then King Jesus will say to the people on his right side, "Come ye blessed of my Father." Come, those of you who are blessed by my Father. You have inherited the Kingdom of God that was prepared for you by God when God created the universe.

Jesus will say to those blessed by his Father that they saw him when he was hungry, and they gave him food. They saw him when he was thirsty, and they gave him something to drink. They saw him when he was a stranger, and they invited him into their homes. They saw him when he was naked, and they gave him clothing. When he was sick, they visited him. When he was in prison, they came to him. Then those righteous people who are blessed by God will say that they never saw him when he was hungry or thirsty or naked. They will ask when they saw him when he was a stranger or sick or in prison and ministered to him. Then King Jesus will answer them saying that truly when they saw others in need, and they ministered to others who were the least important of all his spiritual brothers, they ministered to him.

Then King Jesus will address those who stand on his left side. He will tell them that they are cursed. he will send them into the everlasting fire that was created by God for the devil and the angels who followed the devil. Jesus will tell those people that they saw him when he was hungry, and they did not feed him. They saw him when he was thirsty, and they did not give him something to drink. They saw him when he was a stranger, and they would not give him shelter. They saw him when he was naked, and they did not give him clothing. They knew that he was in prison, and they did not visit him. The people who are cursed will ask him when they saw him hungry, thirsty, or naked. They will ask when saw they him as a stranger, in sickness, or in prison, and they did not minister to him. Then Jesus will answer them that when they refused to minister to the least of his spiritual brothers they did not minister to him. Jesus has made it possible for all of us to become God the Father's children and the brothers and sisters of Jesus. If we refuse to minister to the least important of those who have accepted Jesus as their savior and who believe (faith) in him then we have refused to serve (minister to) Jesus himself.

So then those who refuse to serve other Christians as they would serve Jesus will be cursed and sent into eternal punishment. Those who serve other Christians will be welcomed into eternal life with Jesus.

> For the poor shall never cease out of the land: therefore I command thee, saying, Thou shalt open thine hand wide unto thy brother, to thy poor, and to thy needy, in thy land.
> And if thy brother, an Hebrew man, or an Hebrew woman, be sold unto thee, and serve thee six years; then in the seventh year thou shalt let him go free from thee.
> And when thou sendest him out free from thee, thou shalt not let him go away empty:
> Thou shalt furnish him liberally out of thy flock, and of thy floor, and out of thy winepress: of that wherewith the Lord thy God hath blessed thee thou shalt give unto him.
>
> Deuteronomy 15:11–14 (KJV)

This concept of serving or providing for the poor or those in need was not a new commandment from God. It was a part of the Mosaic Law found in Deuteronomy. Jesus was drawing from commandments that the Jewish people already knew. They already knew that they were responsible for providing for their own people, those who were also Jews. They were to regard other Jews as brothers just as we are to regard other Christians as brothers.

> Then said he also to him that bade him, When thou makest a dinner or a supper, call not thy friends, nor thy brethren, neither thy kinsmen, nor thy rich neighbours; lest they also bid thee again, and a recompence be made thee.
> But when thou makest a feast, call the poor, the maimed, the lame, the blind:

And thou shalt be blessed; for they cannot recompense thee: for thou shalt be recompensed at the resurrection of the just.

Luke 14:12–14 (KJV)

Jesus addressed the responsibility of his followers to provide for those less fortunate than themselves in a passage found in the fourteenth chapter of Luke. He admonished his disciples to minister to the poor, the crippled, and the blind. We are to minister to brothers in the faith as we would minister to members of our physical families.

THE CHIEF PRIESTS AND THE SCRIBES CONSPIRE TO KILL JESUS

And it came to pass, when Jesus had finished all these sayings, he said unto his disciples,

Ye know that after two days is the feast of the Passover, and the Son of man is betrayed to be crucified.

Then assembled together the chief priests, and the scribes, and the elders of the people, unto the palace of the high priest, who was called Caiaphas.

And consulted that they might take Jesus by subtility, and kill him.

But they said, Not on the feast day, lest there be an uproar among the people.

Now when Jesus was in Bethany, in the house of Simon the leper,

There came unto him a woman having an alabaster box of very precious ointment, and poured it on his head, as he sat at meat.

But when his disciples saw it, they had indignation, saying, To what purpose is this waste?

For this ointment might have been sold for much, and given to the poor.

When Jesus understood it, he said unto them, Why trouble ye the woman? For she hath wrought a good work upon me.

For ye have the poor always with you; but me ye have not always.

For in that she hath poured this ointment on my body, she did it for my burial.

Verily I say unto you, Wheresoever this gospel shall be preached in the whole world, there shall also this, that this woman hath done be told for a memorial of her.

Then one of the twelve, called Judas Iscariot, went unto the chief priests.

And said unto them, What will ye give me, and I will deliver him unto you? And they covenanted with him for thirty pieces of silver.

And from that time he sought opportunity to betray him.

Matthew 26:1–16 (KJV)

WHEN JESUS HAD finished His teachings for the disciples, he again warned them that he would be crucified during the Passover. He specified that he would be betrayed by one of his own followers.

At that time the chief priests (those who were to stand between God and the Hebrew people to provide sacrifices to God for the forgiveness of sin), the scribes (those who taught and explained the Mosaic Law to the people), and the elders of the people (those who led the people) all met at the palace of the high priest whose name was Caiaphas. They all met to discuss how they could seize Jesus using trickery so that they could kill him. They determined that they would not kill him on the feast day, the Passover, because they were afraid of what the people would do.

Jesus had been invited to eat at the home of Simon, who had been a leper, in Bethany near the Mount of Olives. A woman came into the room while the men were eating. While Jesus was seated (reclining) at the table, the woman came and poured precious (expensive) ointment from an alabaster box over Jesus's head. The disciples were offended (disturbed, put out) because she had wasted the ointment. They were indignant because they thought the ointment should have been sold so the money could have been given to the poor. Jesus understood what they were discussing. He told them not to rebuke the woman. Jesus told them that the woman had used the ointment to prepare him for burial. Again he had warned them that he would die. He said that for as long as the good news of salvation through Jesus was preached all over the world, the actions of the woman would be remembered as a memorial to her. The woman had believed what Jesus had told the disciples about his death.

Judas Iscariot, one of the twelve disciples, was the one who kept the money for Jesus's band of disciples. After Judas had heard Jesus say again that he would die and had seen the woman use the ointment without letting Judas have access to the money, Judas went to the chief priest. We know from a passage in the book of Luke that Satan entered Judas at that time. Was it Judas' love of money (a false god) that made him a willing participant with Satan?

> Then entered Satan into Judas surnamed Iscariot, being of the number of the twelve.
>
> And he went his way, and communed with the chief priests and captains, how he might betray him unto them.
>
> And they were glad, and covenanted to give him money.
>
> And he promised, and sought opportunity to betray him unto them in the absence of the multitude.
>
> Luke 22:3–6 (KJV)

Judas met with the high (chief) priest and asked how much he would be paid if he helped the priests and scribes capture Jesus. Note that the scripture says that Judas formed a covenant with the priests. The priests and Jewish leaders were already bound by a covenant with God to obey God and worship God alone. They formed a new covenant with Judas to capture and kill God's son. Their covenant with Judas to capture and kill God's Son cancelled out their covenant with God.

> And I took my staff, even Beauty, and cut it asunder, that I might break my covenant which I had made with all the people.
> And it was broken in that day: and so the poor of the flock that waited upon me knew that it was the word of the Lord.
> And I said unto them, If ye think good, give me my price; and if not, forbear. So they weighed for my price thirty pieces of silver.
>
> Zechariah 11:10–12 (KJV)

The passage from Zechariah prophesied that the Jew's covenant with God would be broken and purchased for thirty pieces of silver. After Judas made the covenant with the High Priest, Judas began to look for an opportunity to betray Jesus when the people would not be present to protest.

JESUS CELEBRATES THE LAST SUPPER WITH THE DISCIPLES

Now the first day of the feast of unleavened bread the disciples came to Jesus, saying unto him, Where wilt thou that we prepare for thee to eat the Passover?

And he said, Go into the city to such a man, and say unto him, The Master saith, My time is at hand; I will keep the Passover at thy house with my disciples.

And the disciples did as Jesus had appointed them; and they made ready the Passover.

Now when the even was come, he sat down with the twelve.

And as they did eat, he said, Verily I say unto you, that one of you shall betray me.

And they were exceeding sorrowful, and began every one of them to say unto him, Lord, is it I?

And he answered and said, He that dippeth his hand with me in the dish, the same shall betray me.

The Son of man goeth as it is written of him: but woe unto that man by whom the Son of man is betrayed! It had been good for that man if he had not been born.

Then Judas, which betrayed him, answered and said, Master, is it I? He said unto him, Thou hast said.

And as they were eating, Jesus took bread, and blessed it, and brake it, and gave it to the disciples, and said, Take, eat; this is my body.

And he took the cup, and gave thanks, and gave it to them, saying, Drink ye all of it:

For this is my blood of the New Testament, which is shed for many for the remission of sins.

But I say unto you, I will not drink henceforth of this fruit of the vine, until that day when I drink it new with you in my Father's kingdom.

And when they had sung an hymn, they went out into the mount of Olives.

Then saith Jesus unto them, All ye shall be offended because of me this night: for it is written, I WILL SMITE THE SHEPHERD, AND THE SHEEP OF THE FLOCK SHALL BE SCATTERED ABROAD.

But after I am risen again, I will go before you into Galilee.

Peter answered and said unto him, Though all men shall be offended because of thee, yet will I never be offended (confused).

Jesus said unto him, Verily I say unto thee, That this night, before the cock crow, thou shalt deny me thrice.

Peter said unto him, Though I should die with thee, yet will I not deny thee. Likewise also said all the disciples.

Matthew 26:17–35 (KJV)

ON THE FIRST day when the Jews celebrated the feast of unleavened bread, the disciples came to Jesus and asked him where he wanted them to prepare for Jesus to eat the Passover. He told them to go into the city and speak to a man (He named the specific person.) The disciples were to tell the man that Jesus had sent him a message. Jesus said that his time had come. He would eat the Passover meal at the man's house with his disciples. The message indicates that Jesus had spoken to the man before about the Passover meal. Jesus was announcing to the man that the time they had spoken about before was happening.

The disciples did as Jesus instructed them to do. They helped to prepare for the Passover meal. Please note that Jesus had chosen what was to be served at this last supper that he would eat with the disciples and where he would eat it.

> And the Lord spake unto Moses and Aaron in the land of Egypt, saying,
>
> This month shall be unto you the beginning of months: it shall be the first month of the year to you.
>
> Speak ye unto all the congregation of Israel, saying, In the tenth day of this month they shall take to them every man a lamb, according to the house of their fathers, a lamb for an house:
>
> And if the household be too little for the lamb, let him and his neighbor next unto his house take it according to the number of the souls; every man according to his eating shall make your count for the lamb.
>
> Your lamb shall be without blemish, a male of the first year: ye shall take it out from the sheep, or from the goats:
>
> And ye shall keep it up until the fourteenth day of the same month: and the whole assembly of the congregation of Israel shall kill it in the evening.
>
> And they shall take of the blood, and strike it on the two side posts and on the upper door post of the houses, wherein they shall eat it.
>
> And they shall eat the flesh in that night, roast with fire, and unleavened bread; and with bitter herbs they shall eat it.

Eat not of it raw, nor sodden at all with water, but roast with fire; his head with his legs, and with the purtenance thereof.

Ye shall let nothing of it remain until the morning; and that which remaineth of it until the morning ye shall burn with fire.

And thus shall ye eat it; with your loins girded, your shoes on your feet, and your staff in your hand; and ye shall eat it in haste; it is the Lord's Passover.

For I will pass through the land of Egypt this night, and will smite all the firstborn in the land of Egypt, both man and beast; and against all the gods of Egypt I will execute judgment: I am the Lord.

And the blood shall be to you for a token upon the houses where ye are: and when I see the blood, I will pass over you, and the plague shall not be upon you to destroy you, when I smite the land of Egypt.

This day shall be unto you for a memorial; and ye shall keep it a feast to the Lord throughout your generations; ye shall keep it a feast by an ordinance for ever.

Exodus 12:1–14 (KJV)

We should recognize the extreme importance of the instructions given by God to Moses when God established the Feast of the Passover. This happened before God brought the children of Israel out of slavery in Egypt. The descendants of Abraham, Isaac, and Jacob went down to Egypt because there was a famine in the land where they lived. The Passover and the things that happened before and after it are full of symbolism. Mankind was forced to go into the earthly kingdom of Satan because they (Adam and Eve) chose death over obedience to God. God told Adam and Eve that they would die on the same day that they ate fruit from the Tree of the Knowledge of Good and Evil. They chose to believe and obey Satan thus bringing about their spiritual death. They became slaves to Satan (living and serving him in the earthly kingdom where they would always be subject to death). The Hebrew nation had chosen to go to Egypt, the kingdom where they became slaves. God was in the process of freeing them from slavery when God instructed the Hebrews to celebrate the Passover.

God told Moses that for all time the Passover would be the beginning of the year. The Passover would be of primary (greatest) importance for them for ever. It would be celebrated as the first day on their calendar year. Jesus's sacrifice and atonement for our sin is the beginning of our new spiritual life.

The Hebrews knew that God had established the Passover for them to celebrate in a physical manner. God was actually establishing the spiritual rebirth of mankind. God gave instructions that every member of the Hebrew nation without exception was to participate in the Passover. If a family was too small or if one person lived alone, they were all to be included with a neighbor so that every person was represented by a lamb (blood sacrifice). God intends that every person will be sanctified and cleansed of sin by the sacrifice of Jesus's blood. The animal to be sacrificed could be a lamb or a young goat, but the animal had to be without blemish (perfect). Jesus who became our sacrifice was perfect (without sin). All of the animals used for the sacrifice were to be killed at the same time. Jesus represented all of mankind as a blood sacrifice so the death of Jesus was the single and only sacrifice. The Hebrews were to take the blood of the lamb and strike the side posts and the top of the doorway of the house thus showing the sign of the cross on which Jesus would die.

They were to eat the roasted flesh during the night with unleavened bread and bitter herbs. The animal was to be roasted whole without removing the legs or organs and intestines of the lamb. The lamb had to be eaten at night to symbolize that mankind lived in darkness separated from the light and life of God before the death of Jesus. The animal had to be kept whole just as Jesus was crucified in a complete form without breaking any bone. None of the sacrificed animal could be eaten the next day. When

Jesus gave His life on the cross, He said that it was finished. He died once to atone completely for all our sins. God experienced great bitterness that Jesus had to suffer death to redeem mankind. "When Jesus therefore had received the vinegar, he said, It is finished: and he bowed his head, and gave up the ghost" (John 19:30, KJV).

The Hebrews were to eat dressed in their traveling clothes with their shoes on their feet. They were to have their staff already in their hand, and they were to eat quickly. The children of Israel were to be dressed for traveling immediately and to quickly eat the unleavened bread because there was no time to bake leavened bread. When Jesus has rescued us from slavery to sin, we must believe that he will take us out of slavery to our physical existence immediately taking us into the spiritual kingdom of God.

God passed through the kingdom of Egypt that night and killed the first born son of every family. The first born sons of the Hebrews were not killed. God gave his own first born son, Jesus, to be killed on the cross so that we (God's chosen people) would be saved from eternal death.

Please note that from the very day that Adam and Eve first sinned, God had already made a plan to save mankind from eternal death. "And I will put enmity between thee and the woman, and between thy seed and her seed; it shall bruise thy head, and thou shalt bruise his heel" (Genesis 3:15, KJV).

God always intended to rescue mankind through the seed of the woman, Jesus.

Even before God brought the children of Israel out of bondage in Egypt, God was establishing the Passover which represented the process he would use to save mankind. It was not that God did not have the ability to explain about spiritual rebirth to men. All the way through the Old Testament, God was explaining to man how he, God, would save mankind. It was the men who were unable to understand and accept spiritual rebirth. In order for a man or woman to be spiritually reborn, he or she must believe God's word (faith) and accept God as his or her Spiritual Father by an act of the human's individual free will.

When the evening had come, Jesus sat down to eat that last Passover meal with His twelve disciples. He told his disciples that one of the twelve would betray Him. All of them but Judas were shocked. They began to ask Jesus which one of them would betray Him. They were very sad to think that one of them would betray Him. These were the men whom Jesus had chosen to be his closest circle of followers. They had seen great miracles. He had given them power from God to perform miracles. They had lived with Jesus as a closely knit family. They were taught spiritual truths that no one else was given. It was inconceivable to them that one of the twelve disciples would try to help kill Jesus. When they asked Jesus who would betray Him, he indicated that the person who dipped his hand into the same dish with Jesus would betray Him. Jesus had told them what would happen to Him repeatedly so that when those things did happen, their faith in him would not be destroyed. While Judas was still with them at the Passover Feast, Jesus warned Judas about what would happen to Judas if he betrayed Jesus. Jesus knew that he was going to be crucified, but he wanted to warn Judas that he could still save himself from eternal damnation. He said that it would have been better for Judas if he had never been born.

Judas still thought that maybe Jesus didn't know what Judas was about to do. Judas asked Jesus if the betrayer was Judas. Jesus replied that Judas had said that it was true. Judas was making the decision to betray Jesus himself. After Judas had left, Jesus took bread from the table and spoke a blessing from God over it. He broke the bread into pieces and passed it around to the disciples. Jesus had told his followers at an earlier time that they must eat his flesh and drink his blood. Some of his followers were so upset when he told them they must do that, that they left Jesus and stopped following him. He was showing the disciples now that the bread and the wine were to be used as symbols for his flesh and blood. Then he picked up the wine cup and gave thanks to God the Father for the blood that it represented. He told them all to drink from the cup.

With the wine Jesus was declaring the covenant between God and man that would be brought about by the sacrifice of his flesh and blood. He told them that they must be redeemed by his death so that their sins could be forgiven. Then Jesus told the disciples that he would not share wine with them again until he shared it with them in God the Father's kingdom. To end the ceremonial feast, they all sang a song together. Jesus led the disciples toward the Mount of Olives.

As they were walking Jesus told them that during that night they would all be greatly disturbed (confused) because of what would happen to Jesus. Again He recited scripture from the Old Testament to explain that He had to fulfill all that God had told them would happen.

> Awake, O sword, against my shepherd, and against the man that is my fellow, saith the Lord of hosts: smite the shepherd, and the sheep shall be scattered: and I will turn mine hand upon the little ones.
>
> And it shall come to pass, that in all the land, saith the Lord, two parts therein shall be cut off and die; but the third shall be left therein.
>
> And I will bring the third part through the fire, and will refine them as silver is refined, and will try them as gold is tried: they shall call on my name, and I will hear them: I will say, It is my people; and they shall say, The Lord is my God.
>
> Zechariah 13:7–9 (KJV)

Again Jesus was trying to prepare the disciples for what was going to happen. He told them that after he was risen from the dead, he would meet them in Galilee. He would be in Galilee before they arrived there.

Peter answered Jesus telling Him that even if every man was disturbed and frightened because of Jesus, Peter would never deny and abandon Jesus. Jesus spoke to Peter telling him that truly that very night before the rooster crowed, Peter would deny that he knew Jesus three times. Peter declared that even if he had to die with Jesus, he would never deny that he knew Jesus. All the other disciples also declared that nothing could make them deny and abandon Jesus.

JESUS PRAYS IN GETHSEMANE AND IS CAPTURED THERE

Then cometh Jesus with them unto a place called Gethsemane, and saith unto the disciples, Sit ye here, while I go and pray yonder.

And he took with him Peter and the two sons of Zebedee, and began to be sorrowful and very heavy (troubled, anguished, distressed).

Then saith he unto them, My soul is exceeding sorrowful, even unto death: tarry ye here, and watch with me.(Stay here, and be alert.) (My heart is overwhelmed with grieve.)

And he went a little farther, and fell on his face, and prayed, saying, O my Father, if it be possible, let this cup pass from me: nevertheless not as I will, but as thou wilt.

And he cometh unto the disciples, and findeth them asleep, and saith unto Peter, What could ye not watch with me one hour?

Watch and pray, that ye enter not into temptation: the spirit indeed is willing, but the flesh is weak.

And he came and found them asleep again: for their eyes were heavy.

And he left them, and went away again, and prayed the third time, saying the same words.

Then cometh he to his disciples, and saith unto them, Sleep on now, and take your rest: behold, the hour is at hand, and the Son of man is betrayed into the hands of sinners.

Rise, let us be going; behold, he is at hand that doth betray me.

And while he yet spake, lo, Judas, one of the twelve, came, and with him a great multitude with swords and staves, from the chief priests and elders of the people.

Now he that betrayed him gave them a sign, saying, Whomsoever I shall kiss, that same is he: hold him fast (firmly).

And forthwith he came to Jesus, and said, Hail, master; and kissed him.

And Jesus said unto him, Friend, wherefore art thou come?

Then came they, and laid hands on Jesus, and took him.

And, behold, one of them which were with Jesus stretched out his hand, and drew his sword, and struck a servant of the high priest's, and smote off his ear.

Then said Jesus unto him, Put up again thy sword into his place; for all they that take the sword shall perish with the sword.

Thinkest thou that I cannot now pray to my Father, and he shall presently give me more than twelve legions of angels?

But how then shall the scriptures be fulfilled, that thus it must be?

In that same hour said Jesus to the multitudes, Are ye come out as against a thief with swords and staves (clubs) for to take me? I sat daily with you teaching in the temple, and ye laid no hold on me.

But all this was done, that the scriptures of the prophets might be fulfilled. Then all the disciples forsook him, and fled.

Matthew 26:36–56 (KJV)

JESUS LED THE disciples to a garden called Gethsemane. He told the disciples to sit at a certain spot in the garden while he went to another location to pray. He took Peter, James, and John to the other location with him. Jesus became very sorrowful (sad) and troubled (anguished, distressed). He told the three disciples that his soul was overwhelmed with grief. He said for them to stay there awake, and be alert (watchful) with him.

Jesus walked a little further away by himself. He fell on his face and prayed addressing his Father God. Jesus begged God to take away the assignment that he had been given by God. But he ended his prayer with his willingness to do what Father God willed for him to do, not what Jesus wanted to do.

Jesus knew what he was going to be required to do and what would be done to him by others. He had told the disciples frequently what would happen. He was more aware than anyone of what he would endure. When we think about what Jesus knew that he would experience during the crucifixion, we are amazed by the terrible pain and disgrace that Jesus endured in obedience to God the Father.

What we do not think about was the spiritual anguish that Jesus endured at the crucifixion. Jesus is God. He and God the Father had always been One. Jesus had to become our blood sacrifice to atone for our sins. When Jesus died willingly upon the cross, he was married to all the children of God, the bride of Christ, the church. When a man married a woman he took responsibility for all of her debts. He assumed responsibility to provide for all her needs as long as they both lived. Jesus, who had never sinned, took our debts, sins, as his own debt. He assumed responsibility to provide for all our needs eternally. He knew that God the Father hated sin; after the crucifixion, Jesus would be constantly cleansing us from our new sins. The greatest anguish that Jesus was going to endure was the change in his relationship to God the Father. Their perfect union would never be the same again. When he rose from the dead, Jesus would be one with us; he would also be one with God the Father. For that time when Jesus took on our sins and experienced death for us, he would be separated from God the Father spiritually.

Jesus was always more interested in spiritual truth instead of physical truth. He knew that physically he was going to suffer greatly. He also knew that he was going to suffer spiritually much more.

Jesus was also concerned for the spiritual safety of the disciples. He knew that their faith was about to be greatly tested. He didn't want them to lose salvation. He knew that the mob was coming for him. He wanted the disciples to be alert and able to make good decisions. He wanted them to be strengthened by their prayers to God the Father. When Jesus asked Peter if he couldn't stay awake with Jesus for one hour, they were sharing a condition. Peter was being tempted and would be tempted to sin because his flesh (physical body) was not as strong as his soul. Jesus was also being tested physically; He had prayed to be relieved of His future assignment by God the Father because the physical part of his nature was weaker than his Spirit too.

Jesus begged God the Father to change God the Father's directions concerning the crucifixion three times. Then he accepted God the Father's will over his own will (desires). We remember that Matthew's primary goal in writing the Book of Matthew was to show that Jesus fulfilled all of the prophesies about the Messiah proving that he was the Son of God. Jesus had to die just as he did to fulfill the prophesies God had given to mankind.

Jesus knew what all the prophesies and words spoken by God to mankind were because he is the Word of God. Jesus knows all of God's words because He is the one who delivered them to mankind.

> In the beginning was the Word, and the Word was with God, and the Word was God.
> The same was in the beginning with God.
> All things were made by him; and without him was not any thing made that was made.
>
> John 1:1–3 (KJV)

> And the Word was made flesh, and dwelt among us, (and we beheld his glory, the glory as of the only begotten of the Father,) full of grace and truth.
>
> John 1:14 (KJV)

> No man has seen God at any time; the only begotten Son, which is in the bosom of the Father, he hath declared him.
>
> John 1:18 (KJV)

The third time that Jesus returned to the disciples, they were sleeping again. He told them to go ahead and rest; He had accepted the will of the Father. He knew that the mob was almost there.

The chief priests and the elders had sent with Judas a huge group of people armed with swords and clubs to capture Jesus. Judas had told them to identify Jesus by watching which man Judas kissed. It was dark in the garden. There were no pictures of Jesus. Judas stepped up to Jesus, greeted Jesus, and kissed him. Jesus asked Judas why Judas had come. Judas did not answer Jesus. Jesus was seized immediately. Judas had warned the men to grab Jesus quickly. Several times before the Pharisees and the priests had tried to catch Jesus; he always slipped away.

Jesus therefore, knowing all things that should come upon him, went forth, and said unto them, Whom seek ye?

They answered him, Jesus of Nazareth. Jesus saith unto them, I am he. And Judas also, which betrayed him, stood with them.

As soon then as he had said unto them, I am he, they went backward and fell to the ground.

Then asked he them again, Whom seek ye? And they said, Jesus of Nazareth.

Jesus answered, I have told you that I am he; if therefore ye seek me, let these go their way:

That the saying might be fulfilled, which he spake, Of them which thou gavest me have I lost none.

Then Simon Peter having a sword drew it, and smote the high priest's servant, and cut off his right ear. The servant's name was Malchus.

Then Jesus said unto Peter, Put up thy sword into the sheath: the cup which my Father hath given me, shall I not drink it?

And the band and the captain and officers of the Jews took Jesus, and bound him.

John 18:4–12 (KJV)

We can gain additional insight into what occurred in the garden when the mob came to capture Jesus by reading about the same occasion in the Book of John.

Jesus knew what was going to happen and whom they had come to capture. He asked them for whom they were looking for specific reasons. The question led to his identification as God. Only God was allowed to identify himself as I Am. It was an indication that God is eternal. Jesus identified himself twice as I Am He. It was necessary that the group that came to take Jesus to be killed knew that he was God or God's representative. They knew that they were attacking God. Judas was standing with them; he certainly knew that Jesus was God. The first time that Jesus identified Himself as God, all of those who had come to seize Jesus fell over backward. The combination of the spiritual presence of Jesus and the Holy Spirit was so strong that the men were overwhelmed by the force of their power. The people who came to take Jesus to the High Priest certainly knew that Jesus had the power of God.

The second time that Jesus asked them to identify for whom they were looking, he wanted them to state that they had come to seek only him. He was protecting the disciples.

Jesus reminded the mob that he had been teaching every day in the temple. They had not tried to seize him there. Now they were coming by night to capture him with violence.

Peter had been sure that he would never abandon or deny Jesus. He thought that his faith in Jesus was great enough so that he would die with Jesus if it became necessary. Peter was a strong, aggressive man. He was a fisherman by trade so he was muscular. He met all the problems and challenges in his life with physical action. He assumed that he could fight for Jesus. Peter drew his sword, and with one swift blow he cut off the ear of the High Priest's servant. Jesus rebuked him for temping Jesus to disobey the will of God the Father. Jesus told Peter to put his sword away; and Jesus healed the man's ear. Jesus reminded Peter that if he willed to do so he could ask God the Father for legions of angels to fight for him. Jesus gave up his own life on the cross. He could have overpowered the men who came to capture him at any time. He was the one in total control of what happened. After Jesus left the garden with the mob, the disciples all ran away in dismay and confusion fulfilling the prophecy that Jesus had said to them.

JESUS APPEARS
BEFORE THE HIGH PRIEST

And they that had laid hold on Jesus led him away to Caiaphas the high priest, where the scribes and the elders were assembled.

But Peter followed him afar off unto the high priest's palace, and went in, and sat with the servants, to see the end.

Now the chief priests, and elders, and all the council, sought false witness against Jesus, to put him to death;

But found none: yea, though many false witnesses came, yet found they none. At the last came two false witnesses,

And said, This fellow said, I am able to destroy the temple of God, and to build it in three days.

And the high priest arose, and said unto him, Answerest thou nothing? What is it which these witness against thee?

But Jesus held his peace. And the high priest answered and said unto him, I adjure thee by the living God, that thou tell us whether thou be the Christ, the Son of God.

Jesus saith unto him, Thou hast said: nevertheless I say unto you, Hereafter shall ye see the Son of man sitting on the right hand of power, and coming in the clouds of heaven.

Then the high priest rent his clothes, saying, He hath spoken blasphemy; what further need have we of witnesses? Behold, now ye have heard his blasphemy.

What think ye? They answered and said, He is guilty of death.

Then did they spit in his face, and buffeted him; and others smote him with the palms of their hands.

Saying, Prophesy unto us, thou Christ, Who is he that smote thee?

Now Peter sat without in the palace: and a damsel came unto him, saying, Thou also wast with Jesus of Galilee.

But he denied before them all, saying, I know not what thou sayest.

And when he was gone out into the porch, another maid saw him, and said unto them that were there, This fellow was also with Jesus of Nazareth.

And again he denied with an oath, I do not know the man.

And after a while came unto him they that stood by, and said to Peter, Surely thou also art one of them; for thy speech betrayeth thee.

Then began he to curse and to swear, saying, I know not the man. And immediately the cock crew.

And Peter remembered the word of Jesus, which said unto him, Before the cock crow, thou shalt deny me thrice. And he went out, and wept bitterly.

Matthew 26:57–75 (KJV)

THE MEN WHO were holding Jesus took Jesus to Caiaphas, the high priest. The scribes (those who taught what the scriptures meant) and the Jewish elders were all gathered together with Caiaphas.

Peter followed Jesus staying way back in the crowd as they entered the high priest's palace. Peter went in and sat down with the high priest's servants so that he would know what they were going to do to Jesus.

The chief priests, and the Jewish elders, and everyone who was a member of the Jewish council tried to find false witnesses to bring evidence accusing Jesus so that they would have a reason to kill Jesus. They heard many witnesses, but they could not find one that would enable them to charge Jesus. At last two witnesses came who said to the elders, the scribes, and the priests that Jesus had said that he, Jesus, was able to destroy the great temple in Jerusalem which was dedicated to God. They said that Jesus had also claimed that he could rebuild the temple in three days.

> Deliver me not over unto the will of mine enemies: for false witnesses are risen up against me, and such as breathe out cruelty.
>
> I had fainted, unless I had believed to see the goodness of the Lord in the land of the living.
>
> Wait on the Lord: be of good courage, and he shall strengthen thine heart: wait, I say, on the Lord.
>
> Psalm 27:12–14 (KJV)

The high priest rose up out of his chair, and he asked Jesus if Jesus had nothing to say for himself? He asked if what those two witnesses said was true. Jesus ignored the high priest and did not answer him. Then the high priest said to Jesus that he commanded Jesus in God's name to tell those gathered there if Jesus was the Messiah, the Christ, the Son of God.

Jesus said that the high priest had just identified him as the Christ, the Son of God. As high priest Caiaphas was the highest Jewish authority. Jesus went on to tell Caiaphas that Caiaphas would at some time see the Son of man, Jesus, sitting at God's right hand. He declared that it was God who held all power (not Caiaphas). Jesus also said that Caiaphas would see Jesus coming to earth from the clouds of heaven, God's kingdom. Caiaphas knew that Jesus had performed many miracles with the power of God. In his heart Caiaphas knew that he was challenging God. Because of his position as high priest Caiaphas thought he had God's authority and the power of God to reign over the Jewish people.

Making a public show of his great distress that anyone would claim to be God's Son, Caiaphas tore his own clothing shouting that Jesus had spoken blasphemy. There was no reason to continue looking for witnesses to convict Jesus; now they were all witnesses that Jesus had claimed to be God.

So Caiaphas asked the large group of priests, scribes, and Jewish leaders what they thought should be done. He wanted them to share responsibility for the decision to kill Jesus. They all agreed. Jesus was guilty. He should be killed.

Then everyone there began to spit on Jesus's face as a sign of disrespect. They hit him, pushed him, and slapped him in the face. They told him to go ahead and prophesy again (speak for God) if he was the Christ, God's Messiah. Could he tell them which one of them had hit him?

Peter was still sitting outside the chamber where Caiaphas and the Jewish leaders were meeting. A girl among the high priest's servants came to Peter and accused him of being one of the men who was with Jesus. Peter denied her claim in front of all of the servants saying that he didn't know what she was talking about. Peter went out to wait on the porch area with some more of the servants. Another girl saw him there, and she began to say that Peter was one of the men with Jesus of Nazareth. Again Peter said it was not true swearing that he did not know Jesus. In a little while some of the people who were standing there came to Peter and accused him again saying that they could tell from the way he pronounced his words that he was from Galilee. Again

Peter began to curse and swear declaring that he, Peter, did not know Jesus. Immediately as Peter began to deny Jesus for the third time, a rooster began to crow. Then Peter remembered that he had told Jesus that he would follow Him into any danger, and Jesus had told Peter that Peter would deny knowing Jesus three times before a rooster crowed. Peter was devastated that he had not been brave enough to stand with Jesus when threatened with death. Peter went out of that place and cried bitterly because he had forsaken and denied Jesus.

THE CHIEF PRIESTS AND ELDERS PAY JUDAS FOR BETRAYING JESUS

When the morning was come, all the chief priests and elders of the people took counsel against Jesus to put him to death.

And when they had bound him, they led him away, and delivered him to Pontius Pilate the governor.

Then Judas, which had betrayed him, when he saw that he was condemned, repented himself, and brought again the thirty pieces of silver to the chief priests and elders.

Saying, I have sinned in that I have betrayed the innocent blood, And they said, What is that to us? See thou to that.

And he cast down the pieces of silver in the temple, and departed, and went and hanged himself.

And the chief priests took the silver pieces, and said, It is not lawful for to put them into the treasury, because it is the price of blood.

And they took counsel, and bought with them the potter's field, to bury strangers in.

Wherefore that field was called, The field of Blood, unto this day.

Then was fulfilled that which was spoken by Jeremy the prophet, saying, AND THEY TOOK THE THIRTY PIECES OF SILVER, THE PRICE OF HIM THAT WAS VALUED, whom they of the children of Israel did value; AND GAVE THEM FOR THE POTTER'S FIELD, AS THE LORD APPOINTED ME.

Matthew 27:1–10 (KJV)

"THE KINGS OF the earth set themselves, and the rulers take counsel together, against the Lord, and against his anointed, saying" (Psalm 2:2, KJV). On the morning after Jesus was seized in the garden, all of the chief priests and Jewish elders met together to discuss how they could kill Jesus. That is to say that all the leaders of the Jewish nation who had authority over the people discussed how they could legally kill Jesus, God's only son. This was prophesized in the second Psalm of the Old Testament.

After they had tied his hands, they took Jesus to Pontius Pilate, the governor appointed by the Romans.

When Judas, the disciple who betrayed Jesus, saw what was going to happen, he was sorry that he had helped them to seize Jesus. Judas took the thirty pieces of silver to the chief priests and elders. He tried to return the money and change his accusations against Jesus telling the priests and elders that he had sinned; he said that Jesus was innocent of any charges. Even though the priests had encouraged Judas to lie about Jesus and lead them to his location, the priests, the spiritual leaders of the Jewish people, were not interested in helping Judas. They told Judas that his spiritual condition was not their problem. He could try to find a solution for himself so that his sin could be forgiven. Judas threw down the silver coins at the feet of the priests and left them. Then he went out and hanged himself dieing without having his sin forgiven.

Then the chief priests decided that they could not legally return the silver to the synagogue's treasury because it was blood money. After they discussed the problem, they bought the potter's field (a field that belonged to a potter). They determined that strangers (people who were not Jews) could be buried there. That field was still called the field of blood (because it was paid for with Jesus's blood) when Matthew wrote his gospel.

Matthew continued to prove that Jesus was the chosen Messiah by quoting the scripture from the Old Testament that prophesized that the thirty pieces which was the value that the Jews placed upon Jesus's life would buy the potter's field. "And the Lord said unto me, Cast it unto the potter: a goodly price that I was prised (valued at) at of them. And I took the thirty pieces of silver, and cast them to the potter in the house of the Lord" (Zechariah 11:13, KJV).

JESUS APPEARS BEFORE PILATE

And Jesus stood before the governor: and the governor asked him, saying, Art thou the King of the Jews? And Jesus said unto him, Thou sayest.

And when he was accused of the chief priests and elders, he answered nothing.

Then said Pilate unto him, Hearest thou not how many things they witness against thee?

And he answered him to never a word; insomuch that the governor marveled greatly.

Now at that feast the governor was wont to release unto the people a prisoner, whom they would.

And they had then a notable prisoner, called Barabbas.

Therefore when they were gathered together, Pilate said unto them, Whom will ye that I release unto you? Barabbas, or Jesus which is called Christ?

For he knew that for envy they had delivered him.

When he was set down on the judgment seat, his wife sent unto him, saying,

Have thou nothing to do with that just man: for I have suffered many things this day in a dream because of him.

But the chief priests and elders persuaded the multitude that they should ask Barabbas, and destroy Jesus.

The governor answered and said unto them, Whether of the twain will ye that I release unto you? They said Barabbas.

Pilate saith unto them, What shall I do then with Jesus which is called Christ? They all say unto him, Let him be crucified.

And the governor said, Why, what evil hath he done? But they cried out the more, saying, Let him be crucified.

When Pilate saw that he could prevail nothing, but that rather a tumult was made, he took water, and washed his hands before the multitude, saying, I am innocent of the blood of this just person: see ye to it.

Then answered all the people, and said, His blood be on us, and on our children.

Then released he Barabbas unto them: and when he had scourged Jesus, he delivered him to be crucified.

Then the soldiers of the governor took Jesus into the common hall, and gathered unto him the whole band of soldiers.

And they stripped him, and put on him a scarlet robe.

And when they had platted a crown of thorns, they put it upon his head, and a reed in his right hand: and they bowed the knee before him, and mocked him, saying, Hail, King of the Jews!

And they spit upon him, and took the reed, and smote him on the head.

Matthew 27:11–30 (KJV)

JESUS STOOD BEFORE the governor, Pilate, and Pilate asked Jesus if he was the King of the Jews. Jesus replied that Pilate had said so. While Jesus was being accused by the chief priests and the Jewish elders, he was silent. Pilate spoke to Jesus again asking him if he did not hear all the things that the priests and elders were accusing him of doing.

> Jesus answered, My kingdom is not of this world: if my kingdom were of this world then would my servants fight, that I should not be delivered to the Jews: but now is my kingdom not from hence.
>
> Pilate therefore said unto him, Art thou a king then? Jesus answered, Thou sayest that I am a king. To this end was I born, and for this cause came I into the world, that I should bear witness unto the truth. Everyone that is of the truth heareth my voice.
>
> John 18:36–37 (KJV)

> Then saith Pilate unto him, Speakest thou not unto me?
>
> Knowest thou not that I have power to crucify thee, and have power to release thee?
>
> Jesus answered, Thou couldest have no power at all against me, except it were given thee from above: therefore he that delivered me unto thee hath the greater sin.
>
> John 19:10–11 (KJV)

Pilate was greatly surprised that Jesus made no move to defend himself. The passages from John give us further insight into the conversation that Jesus had with Pilate. Jesus told Pilate that his kingdom was not of this world, therefore hi s servants would not fight for him. Jesus said that he was born to be the King of the Jews. He said that he came into the world to bear witness to the truth. Every one that was of the truth would hear and understand him. In the nineteenth chapter of John, Pilate asked Jesus if he did not know that Pilate had the power to crucify Jesus or release him. Jesus replied that Pilate would not have any power unless God had given that power to him. Since that power to make the decision about Jesus's death was given to Pilate from God himself, those who brought Jesus to Pilate to judge had a greater sin.

Jesus told Pilate that he had no wish or plan to set up a kingdom on the earth. That was why his servants (angels) were not fighting for his release. Jesus said that God caused Jesus to be born and take human form so that he could save the Jews as their king. He was sent to the earth in human form to explain, teach, reveal to mankind the truth about who God is. He came to deliver God's message to mankind that God loved men and had provided a way for them to be forgiven and to have eternal life.

At the Feast of the Passover, Pilate always let the people decide which prisoner would be released from prison. Because there was a large group of Jews gathered in the place, Pilate asked the crowd whom they wanted him to release. Did they want Barabbas, a famous murderer and robber, or Jesus, who was called Christ (the Messiah)? The priests had been working among the crowd encouraging them to choose Barabbas. The Jewish people were accustomed to obeying the priests.

Pilate knew that the high priests and the Jewish elders had brought Jesus to him because they were jealous of Jesus's popularity, miracles, and teaching. When Pilate sat down in the seat where he acted as judge, his wife sent him a message. She told him not to do anything to Jesus because he was an innocent man. She had experienced a very bad dream about Jesus. Remember that in this time people placed a great deal of importance on what they dreamed. God frequently spoke through angels to people in dreams. Pilate knew that the priests were telling lies about Jesus. He was afraid of the dream that his wife reported. Pilate really did not want to crucify Jesus.

The Jewish people, encouraged by the priests, were shouting that they wanted Jesus to be crucified. Pilate asked them why they wanted to crucify Jesus. What should he do with this Jesus who was called Christ (Messiah)? Pilate did not want to deal with a riot. Finally Pilate realized that he could not change the demands of the people. Pilate called for water and washed his hands in front of the crowd. As he washed his hands, he declared to the people that he would take no responsibility for killing an innocent person. If they wanted Jesus crucified, then they would have to take care of it. The crowd shouted to Pilate that they wanted Jesus's blood (death) to be on them and their children (descendants). The Jewish people declared that they would accept responsibility for killing God's son and that curse should be on their descendants. The blood of Jesus did in fact become the sacrifice that atoned for all of mankind's sins.

The people had chosen to believe the priests and chose a murderer and robber just as Adam and Eve had chosen to believe Satan who is a murder and a robber instead of believing God. Pilate had his soldiers release Barabbas, and he ordered the soldiers to scourge (whip) Jesus before they crucified him.

Then the soldiers took Jesus into the headquarters of the palace. About five hundred soldiers stood around Jesus. They stripped Jesus's clothing off, and they put a scarlet (royal) robe on him.

> I gave my back to the smiters, and my cheeks to them that plucked off the hair: I hid not my face from shame and spitting.
>
> For the Lord God will help me; therefore shall I not be confounded: therefore have I set my face like a flint, and I know that I shall not be ashamed.
>
> He is near that justifieth me; who will contend with me? Let us stand together: who is mine adversary? Let him come near to me.
>
> Isaiah 50:6–8 (KJV)

The passage from Isaiah is obviously a prophesy about Jesus. He turned his back to be flogged without fighting back. He did not hide his face from the spitting and the slapping of the soldiers. He accepted the shame he carried for us. He set his face like flint; he did not cringe. But Jesus was not alone. The one that justified him, God the Father, was with him. And the Holy Spirit who was with him without limits while he lived in human form was with Jesus.

The soldiers braided a crown of thorns (large, sharp stickers) and put it on Jesus's head. They put a reed (stick) in his right hand as a scepter and they mocked him because he was the King of the Jews. They spit on Jesus and beat him with the reed. After they had mocked (ridiculed) him, they took away the robe. They dressed him in his own clothing and took him out to be crucified.

> And unto Adam he said, Because thou hast hearkened unto the voice of thy wife, and hast eaten of the tree, of which I commanded thee, saying, Thou shalt not eat of it: cursed is the ground for thy sake; in sorrow shalt thou eat of it all the days of thy life;
>
> Thorns also and thistles shall it bring forth to thee; and thou shalt eat the herb of the field;
>
> In the sweat of thy face shalt thou eat bread, till thou return unto the ground; for out of it wast thou taken: for dust thou art, and unto dust shalt thou return.
>
> Genesis 3:17–19 (KJV)

In the Garden of Eden after Adam and Eve had not believed God and had disobeyed God, God spoke to them. Jesus is the Word of God. He was with God in the beginning, and it was the Word of God, Jesus, who spoke to Adam. God had warned Adam and Eve that if they ate fruit from the Tree of the Knowledge of Good and Evil they would die spiritually. They did die spiritually just as God had warned them. Then the Word of God, Jesus, spoke to them and told them what would happen to them because they no longer shared spiritual life with God.

God loved Adam and Eve so even then after they had disobeyed God, he was preparing a way for them to be reborn spiritually. He told Adam that the earth would no longer serve Adam as it had before. The earth had become the kingdom of Satan. Man would live in sorrow all of his life because man would know that his physical life would end, and man would become a part of the earth again after he died. The earth would give thorns to man, and man would have to work hard to survive. This condition of sorrow, endless labor, pain, and death had been forced upon man because Adam and Eve sinned against God and died spiritually.

As Jesus prepared to give his life to atone for our sins, he who was God himself took upon himself our condition of sorrow, pain, and death. Jesus became the King of the Jews; he became the king who represented all of God's chosen people. The crown of thorns was a symbol foretold in the Garden of Eden of man's pain and death.

JESUS IS CRUCIFIED AND GIVES HIS LIFE

And as they came out, they found a man of Cyrene, Simon by name: him they compelled to bear his cross.

And when they were come unto a place called Golgotha, that is to say, a place of a skull.

They gave him vinegar to drink mingled with gall: and when he had tasted thereof, he would not drink.

And they crucified him, and parted his garments, casting lots: that it might be fulfilled which was spoken by the prophet, THEY PARTED MY GARMENTS AMONG THEM, AND UPON MY VESTURE DID THEY CAST LOTS.

And sitting down they watched him there;

And set up over his head the accusation written, THIS IS JESUS THE KING OF THE JEWS.

Then were there two thieves crucified with him, one on the right hand, and another on the left.

And they that passed by reviled him, wagging their heads,

And saying, Thou that destroyest the temple, and buildest it in three days, save thyself. If thou be the Son of God, come down from the cross.

Likewise also the chief priests mocking him, with the scribes and elders, said,

He saved others; himself he cannot save. If he be the King of Israel, let him now come down from the cross, and we will believe him.

He trusted in God; let him deliver him now, if he will have him: for he said, I am the Son of God.

The thieves also, which were crucified with him, cast the same in his teeth.

Now from the sixth hour there was darkness over all the land unto the ninth hour.

And about the ninth hour Jesus cried with a loud voice, saying, Eli, lamasabachthani? That is to say, MY GOD, MY GOD, WHY HAST THOU FORSAKEN ME?

Some of them that stood there, when they heard that, said, This man calleth for Elias.

And straightway one of them ran, and took a spunge, and filled it with vinegar, and put it on a reed, and gave him to drink.

The rest said, Let be, let us see whether Elias will come to save him.

Jesus when he had cried again with a loud voice, yielded up the ghost.

Matthew 27:32–50 (KJV)

AS THEY WERE bringing Jesus out of the city, the soldiers found a man named Simon who was from Cyrene. They forced him to carry Jesus's cross. John said in the Book of John that Jesus carried his own cross. We can assume that after Jesus had carried his cross part of the way to Calvary, the soldiers thought that he would need help, and they forced Simon to help him. When Jesus and the soldiers reached Golgotha, a location named the place of the skull, the soldiers gave him vinegar to drink that was mixed with gall. After Jesus had tasted the vinegar, he refused to drink it.

> Speak unto the children of Israel, and say unto them, When either man or woman shall separate themselves to vow a vow of a Nazarite, to separate themselves unto the Lord:
> He shall separate himself from wine and strong drink, and shall drink no vinegar of wine, or vinegar of strong drink, neither shall he drink any liquor of grapes, nor eat moist grapes, or dried.
>
> Numbers 6:2–3 (KJV)

> For this is my blood of the New Testament, which is shed for many for the remission of sins.
> But I say unto you, I will not drink henceforth of this fruit of the vine, until that day when I drink it new with you in my Father's kingdom.
>
> Matthew 26:28–29 (KJV)

> Thou hast known my reproach, and my shame, and my dishonor: mine adversaries are all before thee.
> Reproach hath broken my heart; and I am full of heaviness: and I looked for some to take pity, but there was none; and for comforters, but I found none.
> They gave me also gall for my meat; and in my thirst they gave me vinegar to drink.
>
> Psalm 69:19–21 (KJV)

There is a significance to the vinegar that Jesus was offered. If we refer back to Numbers 6:2–3 in the Mosaic Law, we learn that when a man dedicated himself to God for a period of time, he could not drink wine or vinegar during the period of time that he was dedicated as a Nazarite. A Nazarite separated (dedicated

) himself unto God to perform something that he had vowed to do. When we combine this law given by God to the Jews with the words that Jesus spoke to the disciples during their last Passover feast, we see a different meaning to Jesus's refusal to accept the vinegar as he hung on the cross. When Jesus told the disciples that he would not drink of the wine until he drank it with them in the Father's kingdom, he was taking a vow as a Nazarite that he would not drink with them until he had completed his death and resurrection. This vow that he took as a Nazarite, explains why he refused the vinegar.

If we look at Matthew 27:34, "They gave him vinegar to drink mingled with gall: and when he had tasted thereof, he would not drink." We can see that Jesus was also fulfilling the prophecy given in Psalm 59:21. Jesus was offered vinegar and gall.

"For the dogs have compassed me: the assembly of the wicked have enclosed me: they pierced my hands and my feet. I may tell all my bones: they look and stare upon me. They part my garments among them, and cast lots upon my vesture" (Psalm 22:16–18, KJV). When the soldiers cast lots for the clothing of Jesus, they fulfilled another prophecy from the Old Testament.

The soldiers had put a sign above Jesus's head which said that he was the King of the Jews.

> And Pilate wrote a title, and put it on the cross. And the writing was, JESUS OF NAZARETH THE KING OF THE JEWS.
>
> This title then read many of the Jews: for the place where Jesus was crucified was nigh to the city: and it was written in Hebrew, and Greek, and Latin
>
> Then said the chief priests of the Jews to Pilate, Write not, The King of the Jews; but that he said, I am King of the Jews.
>
> Pilate answered, What I have written I have written.
>
> John 19:19–22 (KJV)

The chief priests who forced Pilate to crucify Jesus because the priests were jealous of Jesus demanded that the sign be changed so that it accused Jesus of blasphemy. Pilate allowed them to crucify Jesus even though Pilate believed that Jesus was innocent. The priests had stirred up the people so that Pilate was afraid the people would riot. Pilate did not allow the priests to change the sign; he left the words (written in three languages so that everyone understood) proclaiming that Jesus was the King of the Jews.

Jesus was crucified hanging between two thieves, This also fulfilled prophecy from the Old Testament.

> Yet it pleased the Lord to bruise him; he hath put him to grief: when thou shalt make his soul an offering for sin, he shall see his seed, he shall prolong his days, and the pleasure of the Lord shall prosper in his hand.
>
> He shall see of the travail of his soul, and shall be satisfied: by his knowledge shall my righteous servant justify many; for he shall bear their iniquities.
>
> Therefore will I divide him a portion with the great, and he shall divide the spoil with the strong; because he hath poured out his soul unto death: and he was numbered with the transgressors; and he bare the sin of many, and made intercession for the transgressors.
>
> Isaiah 53:10–12 (KJV)

> And when they had crucified him, they parted his garments, casting lots upon them, what everyman should take. And it was the third hour, and they crucified him.
>
> And the superscription of his accusation was written over, THE KING OF THE JEWS.
>
> And with him they crucify two thieves; the one on his right hand and the other on is left.
>
> And the scripture was fulfilled, which saith, and he was numbered with the transgressors.
>
> Mark 15:24–28 (KJV)

The passage from Isaiah 53:10–12 prophesied that Jesus would pray for the transgressors. That prophecy was fulfilled in the twenty-third chapter of Luke. "Then said Jesus, Father, forgive them; for they know not what they do. And they parted his raiment, and cast lots" (Luke 23:34, KJV).

The same Jewish leaders, the scribes, the Pharisees, the chief priests, and the Jewish elders (leaders) who had told lies about Jesus and who had brought about his crucifixion, followed Jesus to the place of the skull. They were not content to have brought about his death. They mocked and slandered him as he hung on the cross. They knew that he had said he would rebuild the temple in three days. They challenged Jesus to come down from the cross. They mocked him because he had healed so many and raised others from death. They said that he should save himself. They taunted him saying that if he was really God's son, God would deliver him now. Even their taunting had been prophesied. "All they that see me laugh me to scorn: they shoot out the lip, they shake the head, saying, He trusted on the Lord that he would deliver him: let him deliver him, seeing he delighted in him" (Psalm 22: 7–8, KJV).

At noon the sky became dark. The darkness covered over all the earth until three o'clock. Even this darkness had been prophesied in the Old Testament. "And it shall come to pass in that day, saith the Lord God, that I will cause the sun to go down at noon, and I will darken the earth in the clear day" (Amos 8:9, KJV).

About three o'clock Jesus cried out with a loud voice. He was quoting from the Old Testament again. "My God, my God, why hast thou forsaken me, and from the words of my roaring?" (Psalm 22:1, KJV).

Some of the people who stood around the cross thought that he was calling for Elijah. One man ran to give him some vinegar to drink from a sponge on a stick. But all the other people wanted him to stop; they wanted to see if Elijah would come. When Jesus had cried out with a loud voice again, he gave up his life.

We need to remember that no one took Jesus's life. No one had the power to take his life. He gave his life freely so that our sins would be atoned (forgiven, paid for by sacrifice).

> After this, Jesus knowing that all things were now accomplished that the scripture might be fulfilled, saith, I thirst.
>
> Now there was set a vessel full of vinegar: and they filled a spunge with vinegar, and put it upon hyssop, and put it to his mouth.
>
> When Jesus therefore had received the vinegar, he said, It is finished: and he bowed his head, and gave up the ghost.
>
> John 19:28–30 (kjv)

Jesus knew that all the prophecies about his death had been fulfilled. He knew that he had fulfilled the Father's will. He knew that he had fulfilled his Nazerite vow to die as a sacrifice for man's sin. That was why he would drink the vinegar at the end. He had finished everything that he was born to accomplish. So Jesus gave up his own life. It was not taken from him.

JESUS DEFEATS DEATH AND HIS BODY IS BURIED

And behold the veil of the temple was rent in twain from the top to the bottom; and the earth did quake, and rocks rent;

And the graves were opened; and many bodies of the saints which slept arose.

And came out of the graves after his resurrection, and went into the holy city, and appeared unto many.

Now when the centurion, and they that were with him, watching Jesus, saw the earthquake, and those things that were done, they feared greatly, saying, Truly this was the Son of God.

And many women were there beholding afar off, which followed Jesus from Galilee, ministering unto him:

Among which was Mary Magalene, and Mary the mother of James and Joses, and the mother of Zebedee's children.

When the even was come, there came a rich man of Arimathaea, named Joseph, who also himself was Jesus's disciple.

He went to Pilate, and begged the body of Jesus. Then Pilate commanded the body to be delivered.

And when Joseph had taken the body, he wrapped it in a clean linen cloth.

And laid it in his own new tomb, which he had hewn out in the rock: and he rolled a great stone to the door of the sepulcher, and departed.

And there was Mary Magdalene, and the other Mary, sitting over against the sepulcher. Now the next day, that followed the day of the preparation, the chief priests and Pharisees came together unto Pilate.

Saying, Sir, we remember that that deceiver said, while he was yet alive, After three days I will rise again.

Command therefore that the sepulcher be made sure until the third day, lest his disciples come by night, and steal him away, and say unto the people, he is risen from the dead: so the last error shall be worse than the first.

Pilate said unto them, Ye have a watch: go your way, make it as sure as ye can.

So they went, and made the sepulcher sure, sealing the stone and setting a watch.

Matthew 27:51–66 (KJV)

AT THE TIME when Jesus laid down his life, the veil of the temple that was between the people and the Most Holy Place was split without human hands from the top to the bottom dividing the veil into two pieces. "And the priests brought in the ark of the covenant of the Lord unto his place, to the oracle of the house, into the most holy place, even under the wings of the cherubims" (2nd Chronicles 5:7, KJV).

It came even to pass, as the trumpeters and singers were as one, to make one sound to be heard in praising and thanking the Lord, and when they lifted up their voice with the trumpets and cymbals and instruments of musick, and praised the Lord, saying, For he is good; for his mercy endureth for ever: that then the house was filled with a cloud, even the house of the Lord.

So that the priests could not stand to minister by reason of the cloud: for the glory of the Lord had filled the house of God.

2 Chronicles 5:13–14 (KJV)

The priests had to have known that God's presence had left the Most Holy Place. In the temple devoted to God in Jerusalem, there was a place, the Most Holy Place. It was also called the Tabernacle. There was a veil in front of the Most Holy Place dividing God from the Jewish people. Only the priests were allowed to approach God without fear of death by standing in God's presence. The priests were interceding for the people. When Jesus died, the veil starting from the top was torn into two pieces. Jesus had become the High Priest of all God's children. God's children had access through Jesus Christ to approach God for themselves.

There was a great earthquake, and the rocks split. After Jesus's resurrection, the graves of God's righteous people who had already died were opened. The people of God rose from the dead and went into the holy city of Jerusalem. Jesus had defeated death.

When the centurion officer and his soldiers who were watching Jesus saw the earthquake begin at the moment that Jesus died, they were very afraid. When they saw all of the miraculous things that were happening, they declared that Jesus truly was God's Son.

There were many women standing some distance from Jesus's cross. They were the women who had traveled with Jesus and his followers ministering to the needs of the men. Among that group were Mary Magdalene, Mary the mother of James and Joseph, and Mary, the wife of Zebedee, the mother of the disciples James and John.

When it was evening, Joseph, a rich man from Arimathaea, went to Pilate and asked if he could have the body of Jesus. Joseph was one of Jesus's followers. After Pilate ordered that Jesus's body should be given to Joseph, Joseph took the body and wrapped it in clean linen cloth. Joseph had a new tomb (cave) that he had cut from the rock; he had prepared the tomb for his own grave. Joseph placed the body of Jesus in the new tomb. Then Joseph rolled a great stone in front of the burial cave (sepulcher), and he left. Mary Magdalene and one of the other Marys were sitting close to the tomb.

The next day, the chief priests and the Pharisees went to see Pilate. They were feeling quite proud and successful because they had overcome Pilate's wishes and had Jesus crucified. They had come to demand that Pilate do what they wished for him to do. The Jewish priests and leaders told Pilate that Jesus had said that he would rise from the dead in three days. They wanted Pilate to order a guard of soldiers around the tomb of Jesus. The leaders and priests were afraid that the followers of Jesus would steal his body so that they could say that he had risen from the dead. If that happened, his fame would become even greater, and the people would believe his words instead of their own.

JESUS RISES FROM DEATH AND APPEARS TO HIS FOLLOWERS

In the end of the Sabbath, as it began to dawn toward the first day of the week, came Mary Magdalene and the other Mary to see the sepulcher.

And behold, there was a great earthquake: for the angel of the Lord descended from heaven, and came and rolled back the stone from the door, and sat upon it.

His countenance was like lightning and his raiment white as snow:

And for fear of him the keepers did shake, and became as dead men.

And the angel answered and said unto the women, Fear not ye: for I know that ye seek Jesus, which was crucified.

He is not here: for he is risen, and he said. Come, see the place where the Lord lay.

And go quickly, and tell his disciples that he is risen from the dead; and, behold, he goeth before you into Galilee, there shall ye see him: lo, I have told you.

And they departed quickly from the sepulcher with fear and great joy; and did run to bring his disciples word.

And as they went to tell his disciples, behold, Jesus met them, saying, All hail. And they came and held him by the feet, and worshipped him.

Then said Jesus unto them, Be not afraid: go tell my brethren that they go into Galilee, and there shall they see me.

Now when they were going, behold, some of the watch came into the city, and shewed unto the chief priests all the things that were done.

And when they were assembled with the elders, and had taken counsel, they gave large money unto the soldiers,

Saying, Say ye, His disciples came by night, and stole him away while we slept.

And if this come to the governor's ears, we will persuade him, and secure (protect) you.

So they took the money, and did as they were taught: and this saying is commonly reported among the Jews until this day.

Then the eleven disciples went away into Galilee, into a mountain where Jesus had appointed them

And when they saw him, they worshipped him: but some doubted.

And Jesus came and spake unto them, saying, All power is given unto me in heaven and in earth.

Go ye therefore, and teach all nations, baptizing them in the name of the Father, and of the Son, and of the Holy Ghost:

Teaching them to observe all things whatsoever I have commanded you: and, lo, I am with you always, even unto the end of the world.

Amen.

Matthew 28:1–20 (KJV)

AT THE END of the Sabbath day, at dawn of the first day of the week, Mary Magdalene and the other woman named Mary went to see the sepulcher (tomb). "And the Lord spake unto Moses and Aaron in the land of Egypt, saying, This month shall be unto you the beginning of months: it shall be the first month of the year to you" (Exodus 12:1–2, KJV).

> And it shall come to pass, when your children shall say unto you, What mean ye by this service?
> That ye shall say, it is the sacrifice of the Lord's Passover, who passed over the houses of the children of Israel in Egypt, when he smote the Egyptians, and delivered our houses. And the people bowed the head and worshipped.
>
> Exodus 12:26–27 (KJV)

When God gave the children of Israel instructions for the Passover before they left captivity in Egypt, he told them that the Passover would always be the most important day and the first day of their calendar year. Please note that Matthew 28:1 has the same message for the followers of Jesus Christ. The day that Jesus arose from death eliminating the power that death and Satan had over the children of God was the first day of our new life. When Jesus rose from death, we were resurrected into new life as well.

A great earthquake was caused when God's angel came down from heaven and rolled back the huge stone away from the tomb where Jesus was buried. The angel sat down on the stone. His countenance (face expression) was as bright as lightning, and his clothing was as white as snow. The guards that the priests had left at the grave were terrified. They shook with fear and fainted (or were paralyzed).

The angel sent by God the Father did not address the guards; he spoke to the two women. The angel told them not to be afraid. He knew that they were looking for Jesus who had been crucified. The angel invited them to look at the place where Jesus had been laid. He told them that Jesus was not in the tomb; Jesus had risen from death. Jesus was going to Galilee, and he would arrive there before they did. The angel told them that they would see Jesus again in Galilee.

The women ran quickly from the tomb filled with fear (awe) and great joy. They ran to tell the disciples what they had seen and heard from the angel. As they were hurrying to reach the disciples, Jesus met them. He greeted them, and they touched his feet and worshipped him. Jesus told the women not to be afraid. They were instructed to go and tell the disciples that they were to go to Galilee. They would see Jesus when they arrived in Galilee.

As the women were rushing to tell the disciples, some of the guards from the tomb went into the city, Jerusalem. They told the chief priests about what they had seen and heard. The priests and the Jewish elders met together to discuss what they could do next. The group, which represented the highest Jewish authority, decided that they would bribe the guards. They gave the soldiers large sums of money and instructed them to lie to the Jewish people. The guards were to give false witness accusing the disciples of Jesus of coming during the night and stealing Jesus's body. If the governor was told that Jesus had risen from death and that the Jewish leaders had bribed the guards not to tell, the priests would protect the guards. The priests would say the guards had told the truth.

So the guards took the money and told the lies that the priests told them to tell to the people. At the time that Matthew wrote his book, the Jewish people still believed the false witness that the guards gave.

The eleven remaining disciples traveled up on a mountain in Galilee where Jesus had told them to go. When they saw Jesus, they bowed down and worshipped him. But some of the followers of Jesus doubted that Jesus was alive again.

Jesus spoke to the disciples telling them what they were to do after he returned to heaven. Jesus told them that all power in heaven and on the earth had been given to him. He held and still holds total authority over everything. Because he was the ruler over all of creation, they were ordered to go all over the world to every nation and group of people. They were to teach everyone about salvation through Jesus and God's gift of eternal life in union with Jesus. The disciples were to baptize in the name of the Father, the Son, and the Holy Ghost. Note that they were to baptize in the name of all three persons in the Trinity of God. They were not to baptize in the name of any human person or group or church. They were to teach everyone to obey all of the commandments of God the Father and Jesus. Jesus promised the disciples that he would always be with them even though they could not see him. He would live in union with them no matter where they went until the end of the world when he would return to earth to claim all of his people.